Balance and Control

ISBN: 1484917162

ISBN 13: 9781484917169

Library of Congress Control Number: 2013909138

CreateSpace Independent Publishing Platform

North Charleston, South Carolina

Balance and Control

A Guide to Managing Human Beings by Understanding Human Nature and Human Interactions

by

Marvin Dixon

Welcome to **Balance and Control** - *A guide to Managing Human Beings by Understanding Human Nature and Human Interactions.* This book is the parent book and the source of a 4 book series of the same name. The books in the series have been published under separate cover for the benefit of the single topic reader, and were taken from Chapters 15, 16, 17 & 19 of this book.

The books in the series include:

Balance and Control – *On the Responsibilities of the Manager*
Balance and Control – *On Personal and Professional Morality and Ethics*
Balance and Control – *On Communications and Image Projection*
Balance and Control – *On Managing Subordinates, Peers, and your Manager*

Preface:

On Learning and Knowledge Acquisition

I don't know how we learn, though Kierkegaard argued that we do so in the presents of God where we must take a "Leap of Faith" each time we acquire new knowledge. On each occasion we have to be willing to lay ourselves bare and accept whatever comes. Each time, there is a death of the person we were and a birth of the person we have become. We undergo a complete metamorphosis and can never go back to who we once were. Socrates argued that we are born with the knowledge and we don't learn anything, but only recall what we already knew; how else could we know the truth about anything unless we already knew what was true from the start? Plato argued that we learn new knowledge and recall that knowledge through the many reincarnations of the self. But I believe that you can only learn when you are able to admit to yourself that you don't already know. I hope you will find learning here.

Marvin Dixon

.

Dedication:

This book is dedicated to all the people moving through life and their careers without having the beneficial guidance of mentors. My hope is that the contents will provide you some degree of support and guidance, clarification and foreknowledge of what you should expect to encounter along the way. It is my hope that the tools I've included will be useful to you when you're called upon to lead, direct, and manage people. No one should have to embark upon this journey alone and uninformed. I hope that you find value here, and I wish you success and all the best.

I also dedicate this book to the memories of Dr. Witney Holland Rose and Fire Fighter Jarrett Aliber Dixon; both of which left us far too soon.

Marvin Dixon

Contents:

Balance and Control

A Guide to Managing Human Beings by Understanding Human Nature and Human Interactions

Introduction:

Balance and Control is a guide to managing people at many different levels of technical and psychological maturities and at different hierarchical ranks (subordinates, peers, and superiors). It takes an unvarnished look at the interface between the manager and those they manage or interacts with and helps the manager to get a better appreciation of the human dynamics that are likely at play. My intent is to help the individual reader grow as a manager and help them avoid the majority of the professional and political pitfalls that are always present when any attempt is made to manage the competitive, narcissistic, and un-contented animal that is man. I designed the book to provide the manager a window into their own basic nature in order to give them a better understanding of the nature of man. In addition, the book was designed to bring together many of the same standard operational management strategies and tools, found elsewhere, but I put them into situational context so the manager could see how their actions (or lack thereof) might be being interpreted on a psychological and emotional level by those directly affected by what they do. The book takes the reader on a *blue collar* journey through the *white collar* challenges of management. It will walk you through many of the human interactions a manager is likely to encounter while keeping you mindful of man's natural motivational drivers (his desires and fears), his pursuit of higher hierarchical status, individual recognition, pride, and personal respect. The book was constructed in a cumulative fashion, allowing each new section to build upon the last, and I chose to take a holistic approach to the information provided. Therefore, the subject matter is connected, interrelated, wide-ranging, and somewhat detailed. In addition, I have included demonstrative examples, scenarios, and actual case studies to provide the reader with added clarity and situational perspective. Lastly, I've presented man to the reader as a compartmentalized being so that each of the three separate and distinct levels of his being can be examined individually (the aspirational being, the competitive being, and the primordial being). The book was written for the sole purpose of helping the reader (the manager) become skilled at managing and leading man at all three of those levels – not just the aspirational man.

You shouldn't expect to find any gimmicks or short cuts in this book because there are none in *Human Sociology or Psychology*. Consequently, there won't be any *"Magic Formulas"* to instantly becoming a better manager, and there won't be any *"5 Simple Steps to Superior Leadership"* or a *"60 Second Solution"* to anything. What you should expect is to be able to learn the tools of human management and to be able to *take control* and become an *effective manager and leader of men*. You should also expect to develop an insight into man's nature which will allow you to avoid unintended consequences while facilitating cooperation and compliance with your leadership; your requests, recommendations, or dictates.

It is my expectation that the information contained in this book will provide you a solid foundation upon which you can start to build, or continue to build, your managerial acumen and career success.

Chapter # 1:

Setting the Stage

Many of you have read other books on management, or have taken management classes, or seminars, and found when you tried to apply what you've learned, it either didn't work or your results were less than what you expected or had hoped for. Even on those occasions when you've had some success, the success was short lived. Then, after one or two more attempts, you got discouraged and decided that what you'd learned had little-to-no application or effectiveness in your particular work environment, and you put the book and/or seminar information on your bookshelf where it is only consigned to gathering dust. If you've purchased a book that presented itself as a guide to management or attended a management class, and after which, you came away believing it was a waste of time and money then you have a very common problem. By in large, from what I've seen, there's nothing wrong with the vast majority of course materials that are available out there. The real problem might not be with the material's content but, more likely, in the ways, the situations and/or environments in which you've tried to apply your new knowledge. Most management training classes and seminars are rather good in what they offer, but students often have difficulty knowing when, and under what circumstances they should use a particular method, technique, or strategy. Students have to recognize that most management training is limited in scope and are only designed to provide you with a single-dimensional, topical view of a particular scenario and their objective is to teach you some basic skills to help you successfully navigate your way through that specific situation. They prepare you for the most commonly expected situations, but in doing so, they also make assumptions; they all assume that you will exercise common sense in using the strategies and methods. The course materials that are offered only expose you to the techniques, strategies and skills. But unfortunately the majority of the materials are silent when it comes to understanding *"the whys"* of problematic situations. And from my prospective, without understanding why things happen the way they do, and with a lack of common sense, no amount of training will help you grow as a manager. In order to become a good manager, it will require some training and an ability to make a human connection with the people you encounter, and common sense will come as you learn to connect and empathize with your staff, peers and managers. But the key to your success will ultimately be found in the knowledge you gain; your ability to understand *"the whys"* of human interactions and *"what"* drives human nature. And, because I believe *"the whys and the what's"* to be vitally important to any discussion on leadership and management, you should expect to find that I have devoted a substantial amount of time and effort in this book trying to help you understand the hidden motivators of man's nature. You'll find that management and leadership is involved and sometimes challenging, but you'll also find that it's not difficult provided you have the right tools to help guide you. Though, a criticism I would make of the available management training materials is that the majority of them are reactionary, backward-looking and focused on the resolution of problems...after the fact, and not enough emphasis is placed on problem prevention. In addition, they seem to rely heavily on your position as a manager *(position power)* to be enough to encourage your staff to follow your lead and directions. Position power is a very valuable tool and is an essential part of every manager's toolbox. But position power can never be fully relied upon, if it could, there would be no need for words like insubordination, mutiny, coup d'état, rebellion, uprising, revolution, and so on. The successful manager is one that will stay vigilant and be in-tune with their organization and learn how to *"skillfully"* head-off problematic issues before they become full blown crises. And, for the novice... you'll have to recognize that all your training and class work have only armed you with basic skills that are *no more than antiseptic quick fixes, bandages, to cover an existing problem without really getting down to the root cause of the issue or injury.* So you'll need to take care and be aware that there are differences in how you would approach one type of problem as compared to another. For example, when you're dealing with physical problems such as manufacturing defects, mechanical breakdowns, logistical issues, system or database failures, it quickly becomes clear as to what the problems are and how best to fix, or work around them; they are **tangible**, something you can pinpoint and get your hands around. These types of problems are usually easier to overcome and can usually be approached directly and fixed or patched (at least in the short term) with a bandage. But when the problems involve people, they become **intangible** and nebulous, and the *real* problems are seldom overtly apparent. If you plaster over them with a bandage, the wound could very easily fester and become a much greater problem for you in the future. These problems are far more nuanced and will require more of your time and attention. Then lastly, I would have to say that my major criticism of most management train-ing books and seminar materials, and one of the primary reasons for writing this book, is that they don't confront the **"elephant"** in the room. They ignore the baser and competitive natures of man. What they present is very good, but I find it to be incomplete and inadequate. Their focus is directed at managing the *aspirational human being*, not the primordial and competi-tive beings that are actually in control of the whole person. So in my view, they do an excellent job preparing you to be a successful manager of *"compliant and benign"* little shiny red apples, but when you get to your job-site, you'll find that the vast majority of your employees are *"reluctant, competitive, and opinionated"* oranges, bananas, and even prickly pears…at least that's been my experience. So from the very start, there's a disconnect; you've prepared to manage one type of employee but you're faced with managing another. Consider this, if in fact, you were only working with the aspirational component of our beings (our better nature), managing people would be a breeze, but you're not, and it's not. Further, truly aspirational people wouldn't need a manager; they would only need someone to tell them what needs to get done. Your job is in the *real world*, and as a consequence, you'll be working with *real people* and all three of the manifestations of the human being: the primordial being that makes up the foundation of who we are and insures our survival; the competitive being that compels us to battle for dominance and position within the human hierarchy; and the aspirational being (the weakest of them all) that allows us to conceal the other facades of our nature and project an illusion of compliance and civility. And while we might all appear to be shiny little apples, most of us are not. And many of us that are in fact apples are, more likely than not, rotten to the core. Now before I begin losing some of you, I'm not saying that we are wicked, corrupt, and combative people, though it is in our nature. I am just stating the obvious, that as a species, we are opportunistic and predatory (sometimes you just have to call a *spade* a *spade*). Therefore, I won't paint an unrealistic optimistic picture of human management and, in order to benefit the reader, I will confined my discussions to the world of the **"is"** (the way things are) and not the world of the **"ought"** (the way things ought to be). My approach will be to bring together all three of the components of the human being in such a way that the reader will have a better understanding of what might actually be happening at the interface between the manager and those they manage. Also, in putting this work together, I have made a significant effort to identify, examine and evaluate the benefits of as many management techniques and tools that I've found of value and believe would be beneficial to the attentive reader. My intent is to provide value to all readers, but the contents are primarily geared to helping those individuals looking to grow their careers and help them navigate their way through some of the professional obstacles and political pitfalls that lay along their path. However, because every management situation is different from the next and the nature of your workforce, your company, your politics and your social cultures are varied, this and other writings on the subject should never be viewed as sufficiently comprehensive or complete; the subject matter is too diverse and the human element is seldom, if ever, easy to predict with any degree of certainty. What I have provided are situations and circumstances that you're likely to encounter along with some techniques, strategies, tools and behaviors that have proven to be effective for managers of all types throughout the ages and are still valid today. Lastly, I will continually be making reference to how your actions might be being perceived by those in your immediate environment, and even when I don't point to it specifically, you have to stay mindful that you are always being observed. Just remember that all of your verbal and nonverbal communications speak volumes about you to onlookers, and they are always sizing you up and forming opinions as to who you really are.

Let's get started by agreeing that in our world, the manager is the leader (the person in charge), the one that has the final say and the person that will ultimately be held account-able in the event of failure. And, if you can agree with this simplistic characterization, then we have established a working definition of a manager and have simultaneously encapsu-lated the primary causes of managerial conflict, pushback and failure. Everyone wants to be the leader and be the person in charge, everyone has ideas and methods that they believe to be the best and should be the ones that get implemented, and everyone wants to have the final say... but no one is willing to accept responsibility when things go wrong. As a result, the position of manager was created so that there can be a single point of contact and coordina-tion; someone that's responsible and someone to blame. The basic concept of management is simple really; it's only an organized approach that focuses resources to achieve a desired (defined) outcome. But your success as a manager is a bit more complicated, your success will depend upon how well you are able to take charge of a situation, how effectively and decisively you are in identifying and implementing the best ideas and methods, and your ability to lead people in such a way that they **can follow,** and **will follow,** you and achieve the desired objectives. We should consider this to be *"The Holy Grail of Management".* When we look around, we see a handful of individuals that, from our perspective, appeared to be exceptional leaders in full command of their operations. Many of us hold them up as role models and aspire to be more like them. But we only get to see them from the outside and after the results of actions they've already taken and, to us; they appear to be successful and accomplished managers and leaders. But if we had the opportunity to get beyond their public facade, and get a glimpse of their actual scorecards, we would likely find that all of them have had their own individual failings, setbacks, and shortcomings. None of them are perfect. They all made mistakes, suffered missteps, and had bad days. Their successes (those apparent to us) were not the result of happenstance, but were the consequences of their training, planning, preparation and execution. And while we will be exploring each of these steps in much greater detail further on, for now we'll just say that they were able to evaluate a given situation, to accurately determine (both) the upside benefits and downside risk, they were able to quickly formulate the best path forward using the best information available at the time and were able to communicate that path clearly and unambiguously to their supporting staff. In addition, they had full knowledge of the abilities and limitations of their supporting staff and were confident in their staff's ability to deliver to targeted expectations. They used all their available tools, information, and tactics at their disposal to roll forward with a winning action plan. And with all that, they knew that success was not guaranteed. But by having prepared themselves (beforehand) and using the stated techniques, these leaders kept their missteps and setbacks to an absolute minimum and, hopefully, were able to avoid a major catastrophe altogether. Every manager is expected to be successful, but every manager should expect and prepare for failures as well. You will have failures in your career, the key is to keep your successes in the high 90th percentiles and keep your failures small and infrequent. Take Napoleon for instance, he was one of the greatest leaders the world had ever known; ranking with Alexander The Great, Saladin, Moses, Genghis and Kublai Khan, Martin Luther, Hannibal and the like. By any measure his strategic thinking and leadership was exceptional. But Napoleon was far from perfect, he made mistakes, as did every other one of the leaders noted here. But the difference, between him and them, was that they kept their failures and setbacks to a minimum, and as a result, their legacies still speaks to their greatness. But Napoleon went a step too far and had that thing at Waterloo that he could have and should have avoided. As a consequence, Napoleon and Waterloo have been forever linked and are synonymous with catastrophic failure.

Before we go much further, I think it is important to note that not everyone is cut out to be a manager; even though everyone might want to lead, and will lead when there are no consequences to failure. But a manager has to confront the risk of failure every day and failure is always a real possibility with every undertaking. Every manager should always keep a healthy respect for failure, but they should never be afraid to fail or afraid to try, even if their actions could result in failure. This goes to their knowledge base, their independence, and their self-confidence and worth; we will explore them all in greater detail further on. But for now, just consider how fear brings on paralysis, and paralysis leads to inaction, and failing to act when action is required leads to failure. So if you have a fear of failure and a hyper-sensitivity to the prospects of your own Waterloo, you might want to reassess exactly why it is you think you want to be a manager. Put any thoughts of your Waterloo aside, odds are, it's not in the cards for you and this is a *Boogieman* you don't need in your closet. Napoleon was a great general and a proven leader, and in our day and age, there are only a handful of positions where someone would have that amount of power and latitude to make that great-a-blunder, and if you're reading this, chances are, you're not in one of those positions. If you are to be a successful manager, you'll need to develop a sense of confidence and assurance in yourself and rely on your own intellect and ingenuity in order to survive and thrive in the position. If you become paralyzed by fear of failure…then, you have already failed.

I will be covering a variety of subject matter as we move through this book in an effort to provide a multifaceted view of the arena that is management. Some of the areas we will be covering include Human Nature, The Manager and the Boss, Style Awareness, Root Cause Analysis & Problem Solving and Decision Making, Ways to Win, Conflict Resolution, Situational Leadership, The Responsibilities of the Manager, Power, Responsibility and Authority, Supervision, Communications, Morality and Ethics, Effective Meetings and Presentations, Image and its Projections, Pride, Honor and Respect, Ego, Vanity and Humiliation, as well as a number of other smaller tangential topics that I believe will be of benefit to you. In addition, I have included some demonstrative scenarios, actual case studies, and relevant examples that should afford you a situational awareness of routine challenges to management and managerial strategies and techniques that can be used to overcome them. The book has been constructed to provide information in a cumulative fashion, where each new section builds upon the preceding section or branches into a new and relevant area. My intent is to make you a better manager and to demonstrate how everything in human management is related and interconnected. But before getting started, we should take a moment to get to learn a few things about ourselves. For example, what do you expect to get out of this work;

how do you expect to use what you learn; and, why do you think it would be relevant to you in your life and in your work? What is your current knowledge level, and what are some of your fears. And lastly, what are your career objectives; are they realistic, and what would constitute career success for you?

The following Self-assessment should help you to answer some of those questions and bench-mark where you are currently in your career. In addition, it should be instrumental in helping you determine your best path forward.

Chapter # 2:

Your Self-assessment
Individual Survey; Your own Realistic and Balance Path Forward

Before starting out on any journey it's essential to know where you want to go, how you plan to get there, and where you're starting out from. This chapter of the book is intended to help provide answers to those questions.

Take some time to write down your personal responses to the following list of questions. The questions are intended to help you become consciously aware of your current situation and career path; with that knowledge you will be able to focus on those areas that are of particular interest and value to you. In addition, it will make it easier for you to decide what corrective or forward actions you need to take in order to move your career in the desired direction. I would recommend that you make an effort to periodically return to your responses to these questions at different points along your way through the book, and again, when you've completed it; just to see, if and/or how your responses may have changed.

Individual Survey:
Try to answer the following questions as truthfully and honestly as you can. While your answers are confidential to you, they are intended to provide you a benchmark as to where you are currently in your career and help you to chart a path to where you want to be.

- Are you satisfied in your current position?

- What type of position are you in, a *Continuity* position or a *Transitional* position?

    o   A *continuity* position is a key position within the company where individuals with significant amounts of experience and institutional knowledge are posted. These people are responsible for the continuous day-to-day operations of the company. There is generally little opportunity for promotions or cross-training because their greatest value to the company is where they are. Most people in these positions are satisfied and content with that arrangement.

    o   A *transitional* position is a position the company uses as a training platform for those they are grooming for leadership and/or management positions within the organization. As a rule of thumb, these employees are rotated in and out of these positions of higher responsibility and authority about every 2-3 years.

- What career track are you on, technical or managerial? Is this where you want to be?

- Most large companies have personnel development plans, sometimes called *Succession Plans*, are you part of such a plan in your company?

- How relevant is your job to the overall success of the operation (how easy can you be replaced)?

- How are you viewed by your superiors (what's your contribution), your peers (your leadership qualities), and your reports (your managements skills)?

- What is important to you: family, career development, quality of life, financial security, etc...?

- Why do you work: to maintain or improve your quality of life, for professional recognition and career growth, to be able to contribute your considerable knowledge and expertise to the successful operation of an organization which results in a personal sense of accomplishment and satisfaction, etc...?

- What are you afraid of: loss of your job, loss of financial security, lack of recognition, career stagnation, lack of personal fulfillment, etc...?

- o   Do any of these keep you up at night?

- How easy is it for you to lie to yourself and deny reality?

- How do you feel about the quality of your work life?

  - o   Living near or away from your family

  - o   Your current working conditions

  - o   Your current reporting structure

  - o   Recognition of your contributions to the organization

- How well do you relate to others in the work place?

- What do you know about human nature?

- What do you know about power and authority?

- What does it mean to you when people reach a consensus? Do you know what a consensus is?

- What is your current management style?

- How flexible are you working with superiors, with peers, with reports?

- What do you really have control over in your job, in your life?

- In working with a team, what is more important to you, to build and strengthen relationships, or to be right about it?

- What does a win-win situation mean to you?

- What does situational leadership mean to you?

- What is your definition of ethics and morality?

- Do you understand the 3 components people use to weigh the relevance and truth in what you say verbally and how they are weighted?

  o   What you say, the tone you use and your choice of words, and your apparent body language.

- Do you know what's required to assure accuracy and clarity in communications?

  o   The transmitter, the receiver, and the feedback loop.

- Do you know how to approach people and put them at ease before trying to work with them?

- Do you know what goes in to making an effective presentation?

- Do you know what communication is, and the many ways it's done?

- Do you know how to dismiss or sidestep a person or their suggestions and questions without offending them?

- Do you know the difference between a manager and a boss?

  o   If so, what do you think it is?

- Do you think there is a difference between a manager and a leader?

  o   If so, what do you think it is?

- Do you know the true nature of people and what drives them, what they avoid, and what they are like underneath their civil façade?

- Did you know that you and those around you were operating in a modified style while projecting an ultra-ego publicly?

- Do you know how to lead and control the outcome of a meeting before you assemble the group?

- Do you know what the "6 Cs Standards of Persuasion and Innovation" are?

- Do you know what the "Three Tells" are when communicating verbally?

- Are you able to stay focused and on a task in the middle of numerous and conflicting distractions?

- What is really important to you in your life?

- Where would you really rather be at this point in your career?

- What are the competing objectives in your life?

- What would make you happy in a job?

- What in your mind would constitute realistic and attainable success?

- Who are you competing with and what are you competing for?

- Have you ever read Emerson's essay *"Self Reliance"*? (I would recommend it)

We will be addressing the lion's share of these questions and more over the course of this book, but there are some questions that can only be answered by you, and when answering them, they will require you to be as honest with yourself as you possibly can if you want to benefit from your responses.

Now, with the survey behind us, let's do the hard part. Let's find out what's really driving you and what you actually have control of. For example, what are your goals and why do you work... to put bread on the table, for a better quality of life, for professional recognition, for financial security, or for some other reason? How's that working out for you? In my case and throughout my career I gave a higher weighting to having financial security, then came quality of life objectives and finally professional objectives. My rationale was personal and relevant to me, as yours will be to you. I saw financial security as something, that with proper planning was in my power to control, and which in the long run, would afford me more control over my quality of life objectives. As for my professional objectives, they were no different than yours; both grandiose and unrealistic. But I gave them a lower weighting because nothing about my chosen career path spoke to any guarantees of a manifest destiny. While I knew that I wanted my career trajectory to be upward, I also knew that every environment, opportunity, many of the people I would encounter, as well as good and bad fortune would play a role in writing its final chapter. This book will help you to positively influence your career direction and objectives, and while it will afford you some control, your control will never be absolute; there are just simply too many variables beyond your control. The best you can hope for is to fortify yourself with the knowledge you think you'll need, and make the best decisions you can at the right times. But regardless of how you weight your goals and objectives, there will always be a tradeoff; the economists would call it *opportunity cost*. You can't have it all; if you select one you can't have the other (or as much of the other). Once you set your initial goals and priorities, and then weight them, you should stay vigilant and flexible and, you should expect to see your objectives change over time depended upon the action plans you put in place and their results over time. Also, you should expect that there will always be competing external forces and events beyond your control, so you should plan for them as well. But for now, it's your time to decide what's fundamentally important to you, and come up with an initial set of goals and objectives, along with their weightings and a realistic plan to get you where you want to be. If you don't have realistic objectives and a rational plan of how to get where you want to go, you're just wandering without a destination; and that does nothing to advance your career. The last point, and at first glance, you'll find the list of objectives rather innocuous and straightforward, but when you actually try to define what it is you want, you'll find that they get much harder to define. Just do the best you can.

Your Own Realistic and Balanced Path Forward:

What are your Life Objectives?

What is your Flexible Action Plan to get there?

What are your Critical Milestones and Timing to meet these objectives?

1.

2.

3.

What are your Professional Objectives?

What is your Flexible Action Plan to get there?

What are your Critical Milestones and Timing to meet these objectives?

    1.

    2.

    3.

What are your Financial Security Objectives?

What is your Flexible Action Plan to get there?

What are your Critical Milestones and Timing to meet these objectives?

    1.

    2.

    3.

You should look at these objectives at least twice a year and make adjustments where needed in order to keep your momentum moving in the right direction. But your prospects for success in meeting any objectives will be directly proportional to your level of personal commitment, psychological maturity, intellectual flexibility, self-confidence, and your willingness to change and adapt to changes in your environment and to mankind.

Chapter # 3 :

Change and Adaptation

I recognize that each of you are from different walks of life and are at different points in your careers. So, I am going to make the assumption that while you all came to this book for a variety of different reasons, collectively, you all hope to learn something that will make you better at managing people and to increase your prospects for long-term success in management. If that's so, then some of the first and possibly most important things you'll have to learn and accept about management are *that management is going to require you to grow as an individual, make significant changes (real changes) in the way you approach challenges and in the way you think about and interact with people.* I would love to say that this stuff is "new, new and improved" but there's nothing new here, much of what I say has already been etched in stone tablets, painted in pictographs, put down on papyrus, cataloged in ancient texts and old manuscripts and repackaged with a lot of glitz and glamour and marketed as the *"Next New Best Thing in Management Training"* by some management consulting firms. Now, that's not meant as a knock on those firms or their programs because most of them provide good and valuable training, but there's just nothing new about any of it. I have just chosen to approach the subject matter somewhat differently than the sanitized, politically correct versions that most of us are accustomed to. You've studied management for the nice people (the nice little compliant apples) that live in the nice part of town, and that's fine. You've studied management from a distance, the way management *ought* to be; and that's ok too. But in reality, if you've seen it from a distance, you haven't really seen anything at all. My intent is to take you across the tracks where good people don't go after dark. I will be taking positions on both sides of the issues by representing the position of management as well as postulating on the thoughts of the subordinates (labor). On our tour, I hope to show you the dark and seedy side of human emotions through the unvarnished underbelly of human nature in an attempt for you to discover what might really be transpiring during most human interactions. My rationale is that once you're able to recognize and learn to appreciate the intelligence and the nature of man, you will have a better understanding and clearer picture of exactly who and what you are responsible for managing. With greater insight you should be able to make the adjustments and changes that will be required to control your staff, your peers, and your manager; not just keep them at bay. And, without question, the key to managing anything is to first know what it is you are managing. And if you are managing human beings, you'll have to accept that in our quiet moments of isolation, there are precious few qualities that could be considered noble about us. We are opportunistic predators, and have always been...that's not to say that we're bad people, it's just our fundamental nature and a matter of fact. We have yet to take the next step along the evolutionary ladder that would move us closer to where we would like to be (and pretend to be) and further away from our innate baser beings. We are evolving, but for now, we are what we are and it would be to your own peril to assume otherwise. We can't change our baser nature and any changes to our interactions, *with you*, will have to come *from you*. We are all human and we know who we are down deep, including our darker thoughts and emotions. This is not something that is distant or foreign and needs to be explained to you, it's an undeniable part of our nature (and yours) and no explanation should be needed. As a manager, it is *you* that will have to adapt and change your approach to how you choose to work with us; the basic nature of man is fixed and unchanging. Reader, this is worth repeating (particularly for those of you that are starry-eyed, optimistic humanitarians), man's baser nature is unchanging and you are the one that has to change and adapt to him, mankind will not change for you. And the amount of change and adaptation that will be required to lead and manage people will be difficult for most of us, and impossible for some others. Your ability to change and adapt in order to control the primitive and competitive natures of man will be directly proportional to your success as a manager and your own sense of self-confidence, self-worth, and self-esteem. You have to learn to recognize and improve flaws in your own personality...not just the flaws you find in others; you'll have to learn to stay above the fray, above the ongoing conflicts that accompanies every human interaction; and, you'll have to learn to be unbiased, and even generous, in your assessment of others. Put simply, this will help you to build character (in other words, it's going to be painful), and it won't be an easy road for any of us. We are all flawed and will have to fight-off some of our own demons along the way. But if you want to be a success at leading and managing people, the journey will be worth it.

But then, there are those that won't be able to change and adapt, your ego will keep getting in your way. You know who you are and I've seen you self-destruct over the course of my career. You shouldn't read any further because there's nothing to be gained for you here; you lack psychological maturity, intellectual flexibility and you're unwilling to change and adapt. You already *"know it all"*. You should just put the book aside and come back at another time when you're more receptive to a different approach and to different ideas. To the rest of you, this is a necessary diatribe so please bear with me. I have provided assistance, guidance, direction and have been a mentor to people at all levels throughout my career, as have a number of my colleagues. During that time we've all found a particular personality type that simply could not be coached. They will come to you for guidance, but will never accept your recommendations. They don't like what they hear because your recommendations are contrary to their pre-determined plan of action, so they reject your guidance outright. Then, in the throes of their latest disaster, they come screaming back to you for some quick and easy solution to some massive problem of their own creation. They are always in free-fall and everything and everyone around them are in open revolt. They have refused to make any changes to their leadership or management styles and nothing and no one has been able to get through to them; no classes or seminars, no publications, or mentors. Even their long lists of failures have had no effect in getting them to change course. In time I have come away with mixed opinions about these people; on the one hand, their belief in themselves and their approach to leadership and management must have been so strong (bordering on arrogance and self-righteousness) that nothing could sway them from their chosen path. On the other, they must have been convinced that they already had all the answers, and if they had all the answers, then they were incapable of learning anything. And, if they couldn't learn, then they could neither be taught nor coached. Their egos were so inflated and so far estranged from reality that they were blind to what was happening all around them. And lastly, I did have another thought about them that was just the opposite of the first. And that was that they were so insecure in who they were, and the hole they had dug for themselves was so deep, that in order to save face and try to preserve their status, they just refused to accept any meaningful help that would have turn their situation around. They were so selfish, prideful, and protective of their image and their position within the social or professional hierarchy that they would have rather driven their department and/or company into a ditch before they would be willing to admit their error or failure. In their minds, they saw a corrective course change as an admission that their initial course had been wrong; pride and insecurity wouldn't let them acknowledge that fact. But if I, or anyone else, had a quick fix for them (a panacea) they would have quickly slipped it into place, provided it could be done quietly and wouldn't cause them any public embarrassment. If you are one of these special personalities, there's nothing of value for you here. On the one hand, you are blinded by egotism and arrogance, and on the other you are blinded by pride and insecurity. You are so locked into who you are, or who you pretend to be, that you can neither change nor adapt your behavior. And, since the ability to do both is an essential requirement for leaders and managers of people, my expectation is that you will fail.

Ok, my tirade is over.

Some of you might find the next section somewhat controversial and possibly difficult to accept and others may come away thinking that there was nothing here that you didn't already know. I'll leave it to you to decide its merits and whether it will be of any value to you going forward. But your managerial success and your ability to effectively lead people will ultimately rest on your understanding of some of the basic tenets of human nature and the drivers of the human animal.

Chapter # 4:

The Nature of Man
Confrontational Peers, Examples # 1 & 2; Reaching Perfection

There should be no question that technical skills and self-confidence are essential to the success of every manager, and they have to, in some way, be demonstrated to staff before the staff will voluntarily follow your leadership; but technical skills and self-confidence are not enough to secure your position. Throughout time, there has been a parade of very competent managers and leaders that have been upset and undone by an adversary they either couldn't or wouldn't acknowledge or fully appreciate. They failed to acknowledge and appreciate the powers of *human nature* and the *motivational drivers* of the human animal. They mistakenly believed that what they saw in a person (with their eyes) was all that was there; even while they, themselves, knowingly projected a false image about themselves concealing who they really were and their intentions. The managers mistakenly assumed that they had the measure of everyone they encountered by their own superficial visual observations and from an analysis of some tangential interactions. And we all have been guilty of this... its egotism and arrogance on our part and it's a mistake. We discount the intelligence of the masses and because of our own superior mindset, we assume that the unwashed masses lack the level of sophistication and deception that would be needed to cloak and mask their true natures from us. We assume that they are exposed and naked for all to see. And it's not until sometime later that we find that these false assumptions have repeatedly been the reasons for our failures. The common man is no different than you, and we all project multiple and distinctly different public images of ourselves dependent upon whatever social or professional hierarchical setting we happen to find ourselves in. It's like we're all wizards, living in Oz, each of us hiding behind a curtain, projecting an *aspirational* image of our greatness, or at the very least, our importance. It would be a mistake for you to underestimate us, we are extremely intelligent, and if you choose to treat us like idiots, it will be to your own peril. We don't let anyone see who we really are, much less our managers, our superiors, or anyone else we consider as being competitors. We keep ourselves cloaked and never allow anyone to get close enough to pull back our curtains and expose the total being; our true nature. We are human, and as a consequence of that, we are also prideful, craven, deceptive, un-contented, grasping, vindictive, and selfishly disposed creatures that are fully engaged in an unannounced war with our own kind; no different than you. We, like you, are in a constant battle for turf, superior recognition, and dominance within the group. And we hide our war machines behind those curtains and project an aspirational image of altruism and civility. It is the self, the Ego, and our sense of entitlement, and the things that drive them that also drive our aggressive, competitive and combative nature. And, if you are a manager directing people, or just interacting as part of a group, it would be to your advantage to know who and what you're actually dealing with, when you deal with us. Man's ego and his sense of entitlement are your primary opponents and the ones you'll have to develop effective strategies around. Throughout the course of this book I will be talking a lot more about the human ego, its drivers, and its various manifestations. And it will be incumbent upon you to devote a considerable amount of time and resources learning as much as possible about man's ego, human dynamics, and human motivators just to be able to compete in this unannounced and unrelenting war for dominance. But even that won't be enough, you'll have to be trained in different strategies and techniques that will allow you to avoid the open combat, the petty rivalries and constant backbiting that are always underway whenever two or more people come together anywhere on the planet. You'll have to stay mindful that the human element has and will always be the wild card in your every undertaking, and your opponents are as intellectually astute as you. Call it what you'd like, posturing, intellectual jousting, gamesmanship; it doesn't matter what you call it, as long as you see it for what it is, and it is psychological warfare and the battle for supreme dominance. And because you're human, interacting with humans, you'll have to learn to play this game. So the question becomes, are you going to *just* play to play, or are you going to play to *win*; the choice is yours.

Have any of you ever given any real thought to what it means to be a manager of people? When you say you manage people, just exactly what is it that you are actually managing? Let's take a closer look. Man is a complicated species and a lot has been said and written about us being a social animal, but if that were the case, then why are we so confrontational and difficult to manage? When I look at man on a more primitive level, I find it difficult to describe what I see in man as social. In fact, I believe that I could put forward a rather strong argument to suggest that man is actually an isolate, a loner, preferring to live in his own little world where he has total control of his immediate environment and everything in it. He only ventures out to gather supplies, to mate, and to mark his territory. In addition, and as I noted above, I see him as cowardly, self-centered, cruel, greedy, and immoral. And, I am by no means the first to make that assessment[1]. In the presence of nature or some other animal, man is content with himself and his position within nature and he doesn't compete for territory or dominance. But in the presence of another human being, man becomes stressed and immediately becomes territorial, competitive, and extremely protective of his public image and his rank or status within nature or any given hierarchy. Like other animals on earth, man is warlike and is constantly battling for dominance over his own kind. If he is successful in battle, he subordinates his opponent, if not; he becomes subjugated, who at the first opportunity will try to reverse his position. If a third individual is introduced into the group, the struggle for dominance starts anew and won't end until a new hierarchy has been established. This battle is being played out every day and everywhere. There is nothing you can do to stop it, we're hardwired to compete and we can't disavow our natural tendencies. And managers, we are predators and you are not immune from our infighting; just let us detect weakness in you, any insecurity, self-doubt, or believe you to be a fraud (a pretender), we'll resist and won't follow you, and that will cause you to fail.

I won't argue with the experts as to our social nature, but if we are so social, then why is it that every encounter starts another round of combative posturing and gamesmanship. And when I look at those behaviors that purport to be of a social nature, I see them being more a product of fear and self-preservation than gregariousness. I recognize that I may be splitting hairs here, but I don't think man is social (in the truest sense) at all. The word *"social"* implies a level of compassion, generosity, and emotional linkage that I just don't see in man. I think a more appropriate word would be *"communal"*. And I think we are communal because we are timid, weak, and afraid to be left alone on our own. We join groups and have created civilizations to protect ourselves from people just like us. We know that in larger groups we can ward off a single night raider; we can gather more food and water than a single individual, and the group will provide

---

[1] Niccolo Machiavelli; in his work, The Prince, put forward his description of the nature of man. He wrote…"men generally that they are ungrateful, mutable, pretenders and dissemblers, prone to avoid danger, thirsty for gain. So long as you benefit them they are all yours…they offer you their blood, their property, their lives, their children, when the need for such thing is remote. But when need comes upon you, they turn around"…

for us and protect us should we get sick or become injured. So I would say that we are communal, but not yet social. But even then, there are problems just being communal; because just by joining groups puts us in direct conflict with others where there is an established hierarchy and a rigid hierarchical structure where everyone is competing to be *the top-dog*. And when our smaller groups join other groups, together they create larger and larger societies, and in order to maintain peace and tranquility, large societies will establish societal codes of conduct, ethical rules of behavior, and restrictive laws complete with defined sanctions. And while we've had to surrender some of our freedoms and suppress our primitive natures to benefit from the safety and protection of the group, we have also had to reconcile ourselves with the fact that we can no longer rape, rob, and pillage like we could before joining the group. And for some of us, the jury is still out as to whether or not that was a worthwhile tradeoff. But being part of the society does little to restrain our baser and competitive natures, we are still aggressive animals and we are doing our best to keep our animalistic tendencies behind the curtains and under control. We have to work very hard to just stay civil, but we are also prideful and still territorial and will revert in an instant to any threat to our position in the hierarchy, any challenges to our projected image or to our survival within the group[2]. Managers, this is what you're managing and this is your challenge when working with people. Their public projections show them to be social, altruistic, self-sacrificing, trustworthy, honorable, moral, and compassionate, but don't assume that that's what they are, that is merely the image they project and possibly the person they aspire to be... *there is a difference.*

If any of you are having difficulty accepting any of this you should seek counsel from an expert in human and/or animal behavior, or you are free to reject it outright. This is not an indictment of man, but a description of man's baser and competitive natures, and there's more. Man is competitive by nature and will compete to survive and to improve or, at the very least, maintain his place in the hierarchy. Look deep within yourself and try to find the competitive beast that resides there; it's in all of us. If you can't find it, try looking again, but open your eyes this time.

In any and every interaction with people, you'll need to stay aware that you are always working with all three maturity levels of man, though you can only see one. The primordial baser animal

---

[2] We are evolving as a species but I don't see a time when we will be able to separate the animal within from the intellect. If you subscribe to Darwinian thinking...survival of the fittest...our aggressive animalistic behavior may very well be a survival mechanism and could help to explain why modern man survived while all other humanoids died out.

is at *level 1*. Whenever man is made to feel insecure or believe his survival is threatened, for example his life, his financial stability, his mate and/or offspring, his membership within the group, etc., man will revert to his in-born *fight or flight* mechanism in order to assure his survival. At level 2, man's survival is not at stake but his place within the group's hierarchy is always under threat from those coming in from the outside and from those within the group trying to move up. As a consequence, man is constantly in a battle for position, domination, recognition, and adoration within the hierarchy; and there is never a truce in this battle. When we get to level 3, the image projection level, and the level at which the manager is interacting with the individual, man displays his aspirational self; the self that allows him to join and stay a part of the group and without which he would likely be rejected or exiled. This is the level where man pledges his allegiance to the group and its mission. He does everything to hide the baser being at level 1, and does as much as possible to conceal his competitive peer infighting at level 2. It's the aspirational being that you are formally communicating with. Everything from team-building and motivation, setting expectations, training, planning, preparation, execution, and coaching and counseling is communicated to the aspirational projection of man's ultra-ego. But you'll have to remember that when you communicate to the aspirational being, the animal and the competitor are also listening. And so far as what you communicate, by words or actions, does not threaten man's fundamental stability or survival, the animal in us goes back into its corner and lies back down behind the curtain. The competitor within us, more often than not, will have difficulty accepting your role of authority within the hierarchy and in the workplace; we simply have a natural aversion to anything or anyone having authority over us. When the manager communicates to our aspirational selves our competitive selves interprets every word looking for anything that could be perceived as an insult or even a minor slight to our honor or to our standing within the group, anything that could justify our narcissistic desire to pushback and resist. Because of this, skilled managers stay mindful of the 3 different and distinct beings and levels of maturity in man, and make every effort to be as clear, crisp, and concise in their communications in order to avoid unintended and unnecessary interpersonal conflicts that can arise as a result of flawed or failed communications.

Confrontational Peers:

In establishing your place in the hierarchy and lessening the likelihood of a challenge to your position and authority from the start, a manager has to exhibit at least one quality that will set you apart from the rest of the group. There must be something that is, or will quickly become, overtly apparent to the group's members as to why you were chosen for the position above everyone else; why you merit the leadership position. It could be anything, but it needs to be legitimate and not contrived. It could be a set of specialized skills, a superior knowledge of the work being done, organizational acumen, and/or an ability to work with a diverse group of people. Clearly, it would be ideal to have all these qualities, but most of us will arrive at our new position having only one or two special skills that were just sufficient enough to allow us to meet the minimum job qualifications, and that won't be enough. Special skills alone will only allow you to win the position, but they cannot and will not assure your future success. This is particularly true if someone else (or others) in the group believes that they were equally qualified and meritorious to have been promoted to the position, but were passed over for you.

Initially, I had not planned to get in to a detailed discussion on this topic this early in the work. But I will, because I've recognized that I would better serve the new managers by helping them understand the environment there're entering and helping them avoid pushing some dangerous, though innocuous looking buttons that could cause them to fail. I have already stated that the new manager must demonstrate some legitimate attribute that lets the group know that they were selected and installed due to their merit and not nepotism or politics. Even then, there will be those that, because of pride or envy, will be reluctant to follow and would like to see them fail. If you are that manager, you will be dealing with the darker side of human nature and we may as well start exploring it now. Here are two examples that will illustrate the problems you're likely to face if someone you have to manage doesn't see you as a leader, but an equal...a peer:

Example #1:

In the military, you will seldom find two college graduates in the same infantry platoon, one serving as the platoon leader and the other as a regular infantryman. The reason for this is because the military recognizes that having a second college graduate in the command of someone he might consider a peer could become disruptive to the fighting force and could jeopardize the safety of the men and the success of the mission. The rank and file would see the platoon leader (an officer) as being more knowledgeable then themselves; having a college degree and having been briefed on the mission. They would see that he is 3 to 4 years older than they are and age is often equated with wisdom. He may or may not be thought of as a skilled war fighter but he is frequently looked upon as an older brother that will protect them when things get tough; and with that, he normally wins their trust and compliance. On the other hand, the other graduate in the platoon (an enlisted man) may not be able to see anything remarkable about the platoon leader that sets the platoon leader's qualifications apart from, or above, his own. For example, he may consider their educational backgrounds as being equal, and because they are likely to be close in age, he wouldn't see any reservoir of wisdom in the platoon leader; he would consider their life experiences and level of maturity as being equal. As a result, he will likely be unwilling to invest any trust in the platoon leader and will find himself questioning every decision the platoon leader makes. His actions and repeated questioning would be clearly apparent to the other members of the platoon, and if left unaddressed, could cause a noticeable drop in morale that could lead to the entire platoon becoming dysfunctional, and that could put human lives and the success of the mission at far greater risk.

Example # 2:

This is more of a story than a matter of fact, but I've included it as one of the examples because I wanted you to see that management and peer infighting has been problematic from the very start; even as far back as the first people.

Have any of you ever heard the story of Lilith? It's an ancient tale that can be found in some of the very old an obscure heretical text as well as in some Hebrew mythologies. According to the story, Lilith was Adam's first wife and was created by the Creator at the same time as was Adam, in the same place as was Adam, and from the exact same earth that Adam was created from. So, by all accounts, she was equal to Adam in every respect. Lilith saw no qualities of Adam that were superior to her own and she saw no reason why she should blindly follow him and allow him to manage, dictate, and control their lives or to rule over her. So it would be safe to say (according to these texts) that the first people were pretty much a dysfunctional couple. I don't know how long the dysfunction was allowed to last but needless to say, something had to give. Lilith left the garden and never returned after she mated with the Archangel Samael (arguably a superior being to both Adam and Lilith). And, Adam's second wife Eve, was deliberately made from lesser stuff (Adam's rib) so she would never have a voice or a claim to equality. While the story of Lilith is a myth, suffice it to say that it points to a fundamental characteristic of mankind; the desire of one person or people to dominate over and dictate to another. You've seen it as sibling rivalry among your children, in adulthood, and among the elderly in your local nursing homes. The battle must be fought and the outcome decided. And in the end, there can only be one victor and one vanquished; it's man's nature and a universal imperative for all of us in the animal kingdom.

Both examples were put here as props in order to convey the simple fact...that you must have, or quickly develop, some characteristic or quality that is apparent to all you man-age that makes you deserving of your position; otherwise you are assured of being chal-lenged. And, if it hasn't happened to you already, it will. In both examples (and this is only speculation on my part) neither the enlisted man nor Lilith was able to set aside their egos. Blinded by ego, the enlisted man could see no quality that would set the platoon leader apart from (or above) him. And because of his inability to get beyond his ego, he would have likely suffered periodic bouts of envy, anger and damaged pride. His silent rage would have eventually bubbled up and manifested itself as passive-aggressive behavior, and/or even open opposition and insubordination, which would have been apparent and disruptive to the entire platoon. You would naturally expect this scenario to end badly, and if allowed to persist, it would have. That's why the military provides leadership training for their leaders and tries to avoid this type of command and report-ing structure, but it's one that you might have to deal with at some point in your career. With respect to Lilith, it was clear to both her and Adam that she was his equal. Adam had no quality that could set him above her or that could merit her obedience. She refused to voluntarily subordinate herself to someone she saw as an equal, a peer, so she left the garden.

These two examples only point to a real need of managers to be able to demonstrate a clear point of difference between them and those they manage. It's also important to note that in these examples, things were destine to go badly for subordinates that challenged manage-ment. But the reverse is also true; companies can ill afford to replace their entire workforce and governments will not replace their dysfunctional armies, they will however, replace their ineffective managers and generals.

Let's go back to Adam for just a minute, and let's assume there were no Lilith and no Eve, just Adam alone. Let's take him out of the garden, where everything is provided for him, and put him in a real forest (out in nature) where he would have to fend for himself. This Adam would have no interest in status or pecking order because it would be apparent to him that he could kill and eat some animals, and if he were not careful, some of them would kill and eat him. His single concern would be survival not who should be the leader. Adam would have to rely on his intelligence, his skills and cunning to navigate his world. If he is to survive he has to hone his skills and rely on his own unique intellect and physical capabilities just to get through the next day and night. For him, there is no higher point of reference, just a retrospective from where he started to where he is today. His successes were successes and his failures were failures and each provided valuable information. He sees himself for who and what he is and can accept what he sees, although he might envision a time when his skills and abilities will be far more advanced than they are today. Upon careful examination, this is a clear reference to the two primary components of the Super Ego; *the phenomenal self* (the conscious self - who and what you are) and *the ideal self* (the aspirational self - who and what you want to be). And because Adam is the only person that is or ever was, doesn't uncouple him from human nature and the baggage that comes with it. His wiring would be no different than our own, and while he may not be aware of the Id or ego, he is grounded in reality and is both aspirational and self-aware. His struggle for survival is with nature and his position in nature is fixed and unchanging.

Now let's go back over what we know: Adam's single concern was his survival, self-preservation. He would have had successes and failures along the way that would have caused him great satisfaction (pride) and disappointment (rage and anger). He was aware of his abilities, and while satisfied with his progress, he would have aspired to be more (greed). As he looked to the skies, he would have marveled at the birds' ability to fly and wished that he could as well (envy). I recognize that no one would be around to write them down, but by my count, Adam is well on his way to committing most of the *Seven Deadly Sins*; it's his nature, it's human nature, it's our nature.

Adam has seen the constant squabbling among the forest creatures over food, nesting sites, and mates. He has seen young lions drive out the old and assume their position of status within the pride's hierarchy. He has also witnessed the dominance of the alpha male and female wolves and saw how they controlled the pack at the site of a kill, and saw how they always got to eat first. None of this had an effect on him because he was not a competitor with the animals in the forest; furthermore, the resources that are available to him in the forest are abundant. Now, let's bring in Lilith with no changes to Adam. Just remember that Lilith and Adam are equal in every respect but they are not identical. Lilith resided in another part of the forest (higher on the mountain or farther down in the valley, it doesn't matter which), and she developed those skills and abilities that have assured her success and survival in her native environment. Because Adam and Lilith are from the same forest they have developed (in isolation) many of the same survival skills. Adam's human intelligence and unique qualities and capabilities of which he was so proud, are no longer unique to him. What's more, Lilith had other skills that Adam lacked that could improve his existence and vice versa. And Lilith had the ability to bear children, something Adam could never hope to do. Adam's place in nature had been fixed and unchanging. Now, for the first time, he begins to feel challenged by an equal and begins to become insecure in his place within nature's hierarchy[3].

Let's try to imagine what might be going on with Adam; psychologically. I would expect that he would be wrestling with change. We, as a species, have never found it easy to adjust to change and the introduction of another human being into his world would have to be considered earthshattering change, and he would surely have felt threatened by it. After all, things were just fine before Lilith showed up. He had always been the most intelligent creature in the forest, and was confident in himself and his abilities. He had realistic aspirations, which he knew he could achieve with time. So yes, he had things to be proud of, and from time to time, he would have been a bit envious of the birds and the other animals' abilities. And when things didn't go well he would sometimes get a little angry or maybe even suffered a little rage. But that's what being human is all about. However, with Lilith, he finds himself in conflict, comparing his skills and intelligence to hers and competing for superiority. As he would learn more about her abilities he would have become more and more envious of her and even hostile toward her. He could accept the birds' ability to fly and the other unique abilities of the other forest creatures because they were different,

---

[3] In a real sense, nature does not allow equals to reside in the same place at the same time. She always provides some point of difference (regardless how small) that ultimately allows one to dominate over the other. Go back and take another look at the lions, wolves, and forest creatures, there are always winners and losers.

they weren't human. They didn't challenge his position as Lord of the Forest; Lilith did. He saw her as a direct competitor to his status and the resources within the forest (despite the fact that they were in abundance). He no longer felt special and privileged. In fact, Lilith's ability to bear children made him feel inadequate, subordinate, and superfluous. Whether real or imagined, Adam likely saw Lilith as a threat, not only to his position in nature's hierarchy, but a threat to his very survival. It would have only been a matter of time before their competitiveness would have escalated into all-out war in the forest; the same would have been true if Lilith had remained in the garden. And, according to the myth, the situation from both Adam's and Lilith's perspective became impossible and Lilith escaped from the garden, never to return.

This has just been a snapshot or a basic description of man's competitive nature. And for you, if you ever hope to manage man, you'll have to understand man. And toward that end, we will be exploring some of the many facets of man's nature (your nature), in one form or another, throughout the entirety of this book.

Reaching Perfection:

Having identified the Holy Grail of Management (above) the question becomes, "how do you get there"? My answer to you would be…"you don't". The quest for the Grail is just that…a quest. We will work to develop skills that would bring us as close to the ideal manager as possible, but none of us will ever get there. So for starters, let's be realistic and set a goal that's achievable; and right away we can take perfection off the table. None of us is a deity, therefore, there's no point in striving for something that will only end in failure. We can still all work to become increasingly more competent, efficient and effective as managers. The goal that we set for ourselves should be *excellence in managing* and not *perfection*. And in the early stages of our development, we'll often have to be contented with being *a pretty-good manager,* but we will continue to improve by working at it. And with our knowledge of some of man's baser and competitive drivers and the knowledge that it is *"we"* that will have to change and adapt to him, we will be able to use the tools, tactics, and strategies in this book to be able to step forward and lead man in such a way that he can follow, and will follow.

But before we can actually lead or manage anything or anybody, we'll have to have a sense of confidence and assurance in our own worth and merit. Man won't follow a weak pusillanimous leader or a leader he does not fear or respect. We will have those discussions on fear and respect farther into the book, but for now, we can talk self-confidence, self-worth and self-esteem.

Chapter # 5:

Self-confidence, Self-worth, and Self-esteem

Generally speaking, we have all admired and often tried to imitate those people we saw in society that seemed to be born leaders. They tended to stand out from the rest of us and had a way about them that caused us to want to be around them and follow their lead, even when they didn't have a position of leadership. They seemed to be a central hub for human interactions and it all appeared to be so natural for them. Those that were managers or leaders, and those that went on to fill management roles, seldom (if ever) appeared to find themselves at a disadvantage with respect to challenges to their leadership or authority. Why do you think that is, and what makes them so different from the rest of us? I would imagine that there's no one thing that makes them consensus leaders; it's more likely to be a combination of their apparent, as well as subtle character traits. If you were to step back and take a good long look at them, you'd find that they all appear to have very highly developed social skills. They appear to be comfortable around people and confident with themselves and their own relative status in the group and in their abilities. They don't appear to be ego driven and rigidly coiled to contest every point of contention like the rest of us seem to be. They all seem to have self-worth and self-confidence and don't appear to seek out the limelight as most of us do. We're always on a mission of self-promotion and aggrandizement, seeking out the limelight wherever we can find it and doing whatever is necessary to assure we get a place *out-front* and on *center stage*. We struggle for the favorable attention and admiration of the group even when we don't believe it has actually been earned. But unlike the consensus leaders, we lack their self-confidence and self-worth and are fragile and uncertain of ourselves. We don't trust, and often don't even like ourselves because we don't believe in our own merit; and don't believe that we can ever really measure up to the expectations of the hierarchy. What's worse is that we're afraid that any minor change in conditions or shift in the wind could expose us as being pretenders and frauds. So we do everything we can to keep ourselves guarded and protected from discovery. In every interaction, we're on offense, and we try to position ourselves to take advantage and get the upper hand whenever and wherever we can. We take apart every communication looking for any slight, even when there is none. We keep ourselves in a heighten state of fear and anxiety because we're unable to see, much less appreciate, our own unique talents, intellect, potentials and abilities. We are shortsighted and are just competing for status, and our status within the group is all that matters to us. We are so afraid of losing our place in whatever hierarchy or social arrangement that exist, and fearful that someone else's comments, inputs, or contributions will get them more favorable recognition than ours that we will do whatever is necessary to keep ourselves propped-up and keep others down. This is part of our daily combat, and we have even accepted sabotage as a useful and acceptable tool of our trade. But remarkably when we are around those charismatic people, we holster our weapons, put aside our false pretense and become more civil, docile, and restrained. The question becomes, why? I'm sure that psychologists have studied this and have come up with some really good theories. But from what I can see, it appears that we don't see these people as peers or subordinates; combatants that are competing for the same limited resources (status and recognition within our immediate hierarchy or social group). They are somehow different and we don't feel threatened by them or feel compelled to prove ourselves and defend some arbitrary position or point of trivia. Instead, we tend to gravitate to these enigmatic personalities and find ourselves quietly seeking their approval and kinship. We see them as being bigger than us, as people we can trust, and therefore we don't crowd them out, but make room for them, and give greater credence to their counsel.

What makes them different, and appear to be a cut above the rest of us is that they are not competing, at least not in the traditional sense, they have already taken control. Many of them appear truly altruistic and more positive about life and are more generous with their assessment of others; preferring to see the glass being half full as opposed to half empty. They know what their unique abilities and talents are, as well as their limitations, so their confidence comes from self-knowledge and self-worth. We, on the other hand, tend to rely on the voices in the crowd to determine our merit and those voices can often be harsh. When they look into a mirror, they get a true reflection of themselves (self-awareness). When we look we don't see what's really there, we only see what we've been told. The crowd has control of our thinking, and one day it elevates us into the rarified air of greatness and pride, and on the next plunges us into the depths of despair and self-hatred. This is a battle for peer and hierarchical recognition, and it's one we simply can't win. The difference between us and those that don't compete is that they recognize that the battle is lost before it even begins. While we wallow in irrelevant minutia and one-upmanship, they have chosen to stay above the fray and trust who they are. We are unsure of ourselves and feel that we always have something to prove.

A manager, any manager, that wants to maintain their position in the group and have their staff follow their lead has to stay above the fray and not get caught up in the tit-for-tat back-biting that's always going on around them. And though your leadership style may not be magical or charismatic, it should be clear to all that you are comfortable in your own skin, confident in your abilities, and in charge. I think that this would be a good time for you to look into a mirror and record what you see. Like I mentioned earlier, we seldom see what's really there; we swing from one extreme to the other. There's nothing great about any of us, so when we stand there after having made a major contribution to the betterment of mankind, we should be happy and proud of our accomplishment. But if that accomplishment was made over 15 minutes ago, it's already fading, the roar of the crowd is already subsiding and within a week, the world would have forgotten about us, and moved on. And that reflection will be lost in the mirror forever. Conversely, when we have a setback or a failure of any type we tend to punish ourselves beyond reason. We see a 2 point setback (on a 1 through 10 point scale) as a 7. And if we had a 6 point failure we would have to throw-out the linear scale and replace it with a logarithmic one before we could determine how much and how far to kick ourselves. Successes and failures should not be viewed in isolation, but as a single part to a greater body of work. Accolades are fleeting and so is failure (though the residue of failure seems to linger a bit longer) and in the end, no one can afford the emotional toll that they take. You have to judge yourself fairly and find ways to be comfortable with who you are *"now"*, and realistic about who you want to become. When I look in the mirror, I see a middle age man that is about average looking (though my mother loved me), not very tall; and maybe I should shave today. A man that has had significant success on the professional level, by some peoples standards, and hardly any by the standards of some others. I am a critical thinker, a generalist, and people say that I have an easygoing personality style. I am a husband and a father with adult children and some grandchildren. During the course of my life, I have tried to be a benefit to others. I am not handsome, young, tall, or rich. I don't speak

17 languages, nor am I an expert in any field. According to my wife, I lack charisma and often have bad breath. But when I look into the mirror, I see the actual person, I don't look to find some stylize, unattainable *Greek God*... he won't be there, but neither will *Rumpelstiltskin* or any other troll or ogre for that matter. I am who I am, and that's what I have to work with and work from. All-in-all, I am far from perfect, but so is everyone else. There are clearly some areas that I could and should improve upon and others where I just can't justify making the investment. So in the final analysis, I am really not a bad person and I can live with the person I see in the mirror and I'm comfortable with that. You are no different. But before we move on, notice that my work or job made up only a small part of who I am. If you can find comfort and a base-line for who you are, you can find it in what you do. So just stand there for a minute longer, let yourself get beyond the self-aggrandizement or self-hatred (whichever the case may be), because if you ever hope to find success in managing other people, you'll need to be comfortable with that person in the mirror. The charismatic people we are trying to emulate have already done that and have found their own self-worth, their confidence in who they are and their own level of self-esteem.

Now it will be left to you to determine your own merit. You'll have to look deep inside yourself and recognize that you can never be all things to all people or ever measure up to your perception of society's expectations. You'll have to accept what you find and build upon it. And confidence, self-worth and self-esteem will come with practice, experience, knowledge acquisition and training. You'll have to learn to march to the beat of your own drummer and not be intimidated by the chorus of drummers that are herding the masses. It is my intent to provide you the knowledge, skills, and training that will allow you to determine your own merit and self-worth, build upon your level of confidence as a manager and a person, and help you to cultivate a personal level of self-esteem that should flow from that knowledge.

In addition to this book, there will be other forms of management training that will be available to you. Let's take a look at companies of various sizes and wealth and consider the types of management training they might be able to provide, as well as what they will need to do in order to retain their highly trained workforce.

Chapter # 6:

Management Training

We have all, at one time or another, been a boss; whether over younger siblings, every time the neighborhood kids wanted to play with our toys, or during our terrible two's. Just think about how we acted then. Now think about any boss you've known; do you see the similarities? I'm going to go out on a limb here and say that the vast majority of us have already earned our certifications to be bosses; yes, I think we all know how to do that. But when it comes to managing, for most of us, this is a new experience and we're going to have to get some help if we ever hope to be successful at it. Managing people is an unusual activity for a majority of people in any population, and it will take training and practice before anyone can actually get good at it. Training can come in a variety of forms, for example, having observed and adopted techniques from leaders or peers that have been successful managers, working with good role models or mentors, getting experience and opportunities to increase your managerial confidence and refining your skills by leading small groups of people or leading projects, reading books and taking courses on the subject, or even the ever popular *on the job training* (OJT), also known as *trial by fire*. Many times with OJT you have no other choice other than to just dive right in and either sink or swim. If you don't have a mentor to help guide you or have not prepared in other ways, you're likely in for a very bumpy ride. Unfortunately, due to a lack of *succession planning* in many organizations and the high cost of formalized management training, OJT has become the method of choice for most companies. Ideally, it would be in your best interest, as well as the company's, if you (being the new manager) and all current managers were provided the management training you needed prior to assuming the positions, as well as, ongoing skills training to assure that you kept current with best management practices. In a perfect world preparatory and ongoing continuous educational and management training would be the norm, but our world is far from perfect. For example, the time that would be needed for formal training and the capital cost associated with such training would be impractical for all but the largest and/or riches organizations. Even then, the companies that could afford it would have to carefully assess their specific training needs, as well as, who should be trained, and even, how?

Today's workforce is transitory[4] and if any company invests time and money to formally train their management staffers, they will also need to find effective ways to retain those individuals once they've been trained. Because, without a meaningful and attractive retention program in place, there will be little incentive for their formally trained employees to stay with them; they could easily market their skills elsewhere, and some other organization would reap the benefits of their investment. There are two important takeaways here: the first being… management training and continuing skills training, of any kind, are essential to the ongoing viability of any company. Because formal training is the most costly (in both time and capital) smaller organizations should look to optional methods for providing the necessary training. Options include, but would not be limited to: apprenticeships, mentoring programs, on the job training, correspondence courses, internet programs, in-house seminars, or even a good book on the subject. The second is, because a company has invested time and resources in order to provide training for their employees, they will have to protect their investment by developing an attractive retention plan to keep their employees from moving on to greener pastures. And while *transparent succession planning* is not the norm at most companies, I believe that it's worth looking in to. I have little doubt that training would be mandatory at most organizations, if they would just take the time and did the analysis to compare the costs and benefits of preparatory training and continuing education for their staff to the negative costs associated with consistently launching untrained and ineffective first-time managers and/or not providing the training that weak and unskilled managers need. The costs of training will show up on the balance sheet as a single line item that will be more than offset by increased productivity, higher employee morale, faster turnaround times and a stable workforce. The negative costs for not providing the training can be measured in higher rates of absenteeism, flat to declining productivity and higher employee turnover rates. Without appropriate skills training, you and most other managers will turn into bosses and that will negatively impact the entire operation.

---

[4] There are undoubtedly many reasons for our mobile workforce and possibly key among them are advances in technology, job insecurity brought on by constant restructuring within companies, and a demand for a better quality of life (in and out of the workplace) by employees and their families. An in-depth analysis of the actual causes of the transitory workforce is really beyond the scope of this work, so I will leave it here.

Chapter # 7:

The Manager and the Boss

Success, going forward, will be based in large part on what you are attempting to achieve, and key to that is having a full and very clear understanding of the differences between being a boss and being a manager. If your intent is to be a boss, this material has very little to offer you. But if your intent is to become a manager (ostensibly a good one), then there is value for you here. Let spend a little time to really understand the differences between what it means to be a boss and what it means to be a manager. In our everyday lives we tend to use the terms interchangeably. And if we looked to an authoritative resource (e.g. Webster's or The American Heritage Dictionaries) you'll find just enough overlap that it's really not clear how best to pars out the differences between the two. And while the differences appear negligible in translation, in the workplace (where the rubber meets the road) the distinction between the two couldn't be more different. Think of it this way, a boss exercises direct power and control over their staff, and a manager exercises indirect power and control. Bosses are needed primarily to oversee simple projects, usually of very short durations or projects that require people to perform simple and repetitive task. Bosses often rely on fear or some other form of intimidation to control their workforce; for example, it could include anything between docking their pay, giving unpaid time off, up to and including the loss of their job. Bosses are best used to push or drive the workforce. For example, bosses are in high demand where you have a captive work force; correctional and penal institutions come to mind. Here, the employees (inmates) are forced to do exactly what they are told and the downside for not following orders is usually severe. The military is probably the best example of a successful organization that relies, primarily, on the boss in its normal operations[5]. But then, we also have to concede that the workforce in the military is in fact a *quasi-captive* workforce. There should

---

[5] Like most organizations, the military has a command structure in place. But very much unlike any public enterprise, the chain of command in the military is rigid, each person in the chain is a commander (a boss) and there is very little opportunity for discussion once a decision is made; and everyone, from that boss down, is expected to follow the command.

be no question that the boss's presence is a powerful motivator of a captive and quasi-captive workforce doing physical work. But as soon as the boss steps away, you'll find that there is a measurable drop in motivation and productivity. In fact, there is a direct correlation between the motivation of any worker and their productivity to the proximity of the boss. The manager, on the other hand, provides leadership and direction to an unencumbered workforce in an environment that is free, open, and non-threatening. The overwhelming majorities of people in a free and open workplace are already self-motivated and already want to do a good job; they define themselves and measure their self-worth, in large part, by what they do. They need to have a sense of satisfaction in their work that roles forward and helps facilitate satisfaction in their lives. Successful managers service that need by sharing power, control, and the responsibilities of the department with them[6]. In that way, the staff becomes true stakeholders in the work product. Their motivation and productivity is not determined by the physical location of the manager but by the pride that they take in their work and the knowledge that they have made a meaningful contribution. So, just to be clear; the boss maintains all the power and control and proves to be far less effective than the manager that shares power, control, and responsibility with their reports. The bosses approach will always fail in a free and open organization where people are able to come and go as they choose. But unfortunately, and with new managers, the bosses approach is almost always tried. When people are bossed, they don't exercise their intellect in the workplace; they make no personal connection to the work, take no ownership or pride in the work product, and have no loyalty toward you or to the organization. If you ever hope to tap into the full potential of your workforce, you'll have to move beyond the notions of *Management and Labor* and start seeing your people as partners and stakeholders in your enterprise. And, in order to get the most out of your people, you'll have to open your eyes and start to appreciate their true value. When people are properly and effectively managed, the organization will benefit from their desire to contribute and add value to the work, but if they are bossed, they will do exactly what they are told; no more, no less.

---

[6] Important here: while you share the department's responsibility with your staff, you also share every success with them. But on those rare occasions when things go wrong, the manager has to step up and take full responsibility for any miss-steps. Scape-gloating sends one message to your staff and another to your management: you let the staff know that they are expendable and will be *thrown under the bus* at the slightest threat to your career. As a result, you lose their trust, loyalty and their willingness to take future responsibility. This becomes a major loss for you as they are no longer self-motivated, become less productive and no longer work as a team. While management is aware of the failure, they also see a manager that does not take ownership for their own area of responsibility. This will significantly limit your career growth within that organization.

If any of you are already in Management, then you should already know that you have to exercise caution in hiring in order to avoid hiring the wrong manager because there is a significant downside for making a bad hiring decision. I will talk to that next.

Chapter # 8:

Promoting or Hiring the Wrong Manager
A word of Caution to the Leadership

As was stated; managing a group of people is an unusual, and in some cases unnatural activity for most of us, you would only have to look around to see that whenever and wherever one person is made responsible for managing another that, at that very moment, the new manager finds that their managerial toolbox is either empty or wholly inadequate for the task. Most new managers lack (both) the *hard* and the *soft* skills required for success in their new position[7]. They tend to adapt an idealized set of normative practices and behaviors that, at first blush, they believe should work...but they don't. And the new and/or unskilled manager quickly finds that due to the unpredictable (fickle) nature of man and the changing dynamics in the workplace, they have quickly gotten out of their depth and have lost control of their operation. Recognizing that they are flailing and floundering, they make every effort to conceal their failings from their manager. And, it's at this point where many of them start down one of two paths. The first is the path of the *Maestro,* the second is the path of the 3rd *World Dictator;* and, to their misfortune, neither path will serve them for long or provide the skills they lack. When they slip into the persona of the Maestro they transmit an air of confidence intended to assure their managers that their promotion was the right decision. But in reality, they have already surrendered their leadership and control to their subordinates and they become the lone actor in a slowly developing tragedy. The Maestro is a *pretender*, a *fraud* that may well be technically competent and have superior knowledge of the workplace, but is totally lacking in any ability to lead and direct people. Often, this is an individual that wants to be liked and accepted by everyone in the hierarchy (superiors, peers and subordinates) so as a consequence, they are reluctant to ruffle feathers for fear of alienating anyone. They

---

[7] Hard skills are basic management standards, expectations, strategies, techniques, and tools. While soft skills are diplomatic, persuasive and seductive, interpersonal people skills.

may also have no concept of the power and authority that has been afforded to them in their position, and even if they did, they wouldn't know how to use it. They are totally reliant on the generosity of the aspirational nature of man to sustain them and their position...but it won't. They are the embodiment of the untrained orchestra conductor. They look the part, they enter the stage, wearing a tuxedo with white gloves with baton in-hand, they step to the podium, taps twice with the baton, raises their hands and the orchestra begins to play. What is not immediately apparent to the audience (or to their superiors) is that the Maestro is already lost. They aren't conducting or leading anything or anyone and each of their subordinates (orchestra members) knows it. The longer the orchestra plays, the more difficult it is for the Maestro to keep up. They are trying and failing to herd cats. And before long, people will do what people do best; express their own individuality. They will no longer play as a well-tuned orchestra but as 80 individual soloists. Because of the Maestro's lack of leadership skills, and their desire to be accepted and liked, coupled with their inability to understand and execute power and authority, and their total lack of knowledge of what drives the human animal, the Maestro fails and creates chaos in the theater and in the workplace.

The other path often traveled is that of *His or Her High Exulted Excellency* (the 3rd World Dictator). This is the selfish, egotistical manager that, regardless of their lack of skills and training (and for the single purpose of promoting themselves) becomes the *Tyrannical Boss*. Many times, in a last-ditch effort to save their positions, the Maestro tries to cut across to this path in a failed effort to gain more time and get some level of control of their staff. But, it's almost always too little, too late. And in any event, both paths will ultimately lead to failure and a significant disruption in the workplace. But the disruption that is caused by the Tyrannical Boss is many magnitudes greater than those caused by the Maestro. The Maestro is seldom respected by their staff; the staff sees them and knows them to be a fraud *("the Emperor has no clothes")*. The Maestro is often tolerated because they don't threaten the livelihoods of their staff, and as a result, they don't make themselves feared or hated, so there is only a marginal negative backlash to their appointment; and, in some cases, they might even be well liked. But product quality and productivity will ultimately suffer under their leadership or lack thereof. The impact of the Tyrannical Boss, on the other hand, is far more destructive and disruptive to the organization. They are never respected because everyone sees them to be a person without ethics, morals and even honor. They impart fear into the organization by directly threatening the livelihoods of their staff. Their every action is seen as self-serving and self-promoting and no one is able to trust them. As a result, they are not only disrespected and feared by their staff, as a result of their own actions, they have made themselves *hated*. I recognize that some of you are very prolific readers and are able to consume volumes of information at a single sitting. But I want to slow you down here in order for you to think about what I just said…"they have made themselves *hated*". Let's take a minute to think about what that might mean. Most of us, at one time or another, have come across someone that we felt we couldn't trust; either because we thought they were self-serving, unethical, superficial, amoral, dishonorable or any combination or all of them. In most cases, particularly if we had to work with them, we found ways to cope with their character flaws and we were able to tolerate them…if only for short periods at a time. With respect to fear, here again, we can all point to someone that could get our full attention while simultaneously sending a chill up our spines. For many of us, the first attention getter was our fathers. So having a little fear is not always a bad thing. If you trusted your father and saw him as an ethical, moral, honorable and evenhanded (fair) person, that little twinge of fear would have been coupled with respect and oftentimes wrapped in love. We only have to look to our Judicial System to see a similar parallel; we have established a society based upon the rule of law. And because we have established specific sanctions for specific violations we tend to follow societies rules in an effort to avoid the sanctions. And while our judicial system is still a work in progress, we believe it to be ethical, moral, honorable and evenhanded; we rely on it to keep us safe. So, while we have a healthy fear of being caught up in it, we also respect it because without it, there would be *anarchy*. Now, let's look around the world to governments and judicial systems that are both feared and considered (by its people) to be corrupt; being unethical, amoral, dishonorable, and unfair. These governments and judicial systems are viewed in the same light (but on a larger scale) as our tyrannical manager. They are self-serving and have made themselves both feared and hated. Now, as you would expect, *here comes the revolution!*

Before every revolution there are clear signs of civil unrest. It starts in the streets where the citizenry makes and sends up a list of requests that become demands. Usually they will be petitions for basic human rights, fairness and equity, and freedom from tyranny. As the petitions are always certain to be ignored, they are followed-up with minor protest and (maybe some) public works strikes. These are usually put down (using force and intimidation) and before long, the people's distain and hatred overflows into the streets in the form of riots, burning, looting and sabotage. As the situation spirals further and further out of hand, even the weakest among them finds the courage to resist; even your sweet little old grandmother would be out there throwing rocks. Now, they are in *full revolution*. Anytime you couple fear and intimidation with distrust you'll breed hatred. And, whenever any manager makes themselves hated, your operation will suffer, and suffer dearly.

There is an additional point to be made here, one that is either obscured or invisible to some managers and leaders of people... and that is *"you don't manage or lead by divine rite, but with the permission of those being managed or led[8]"*. Just look around the world and throughout history, Kings and Queens, Emperors and Potentates, and those who have appointed themselves President for Life, found that out far too late to save themselves from the masses. Every manager should keep this credo rattling around somewhere in their heads if they hope to maintain their positions. That concept is either unheard of by the manager that becomes the Tyrannical Boss or it is totally rejected by them. And here again, this manager might well be technically solid...but they are also likely to be socially crippled. Because they are ego driven and their sole objectives are self-aggrandizement and self-preservation, they underestimate or completely reject the importance of interpersonal skills and the needs of their workforce. I would, very much like to be generous here and make some concession for this type of manager. I would like to give them the benefit of the doubt and pretend that (maybe?) they are *"unknowingly"* headed down the wrong road with respect to their approach to the job and their staff, and once they recognize their mistake, they will change or correct their course. But we have all seen this manager before, and if there's one thing we can all agree upon is that they know exactly what they're doing, who they are promoting and to what ends. This is the manager that is incapable of change or adaptation because they are self-righteous and knows it all. Their callous disregard for their staff and others (often bordering on contempt), is not an aberration, like any 3rd World Dictator, it is no accident, it's real. As like with the Maestro, initially all outward appearances look right. They assure Management that they are up to the task, but right away, they start politicking and blowing their own horn by making promises of loftier efficiencies and increasing throughputs because "now they've got the right person for the job". When they meet with the group for the first time, they are normally well received (save a bit of trepidation by a few of the members). The group wants

---

[8] Take a look at the United States Declaration of Independence paying particular attention to the second paragraph.

them to be successful because, in their view, if they succeed they all do. And anyway, they look like someone they could trust.[9]

In order to achieve their desired ends, of self-promotion and total control, this manager will typically take one of two tracks (dependent upon how secure they see themselves within the organization). The less confident manager will take a slow and methodical tract while the confident manager will take a fast (*in your face*) intimidating track. While they will use the very same tools for the same purposes, they use them at different times. The manager taking the slow track uses deception as their first tool. They'll settle in quietly, learning people's names, their areas of responsibility and (most importantly) any weaknesses they might have that they could exploit at a later date. They might appear overwhelmed with the new job and seem victimized by Management for requiring the higher efficiencies and increased throughputs that they, themselves, committed the group to but has not publicly taken ownership or responsibility for. They will be open to any and all suggestions and brainstorming sessions to find the best path forward. Once the path is clear and they are reasonably confident that there is nothing else of value to be learned from their staff, they will neatly fold-up and put away their *Dr. Jekyll* identity and come roaring back as *Mr. Hyde*. The staff will, at first, be shocked and surprised but they are not ignorant or blind; they will be able to see exactly what their manager has done and is doing. The manager has used *deception* and has preyed upon their generosity, candor and vulnerabilities to make themselves strong and to put their staff at their mercy. The manager has violated their trust and shown themselves for what they are. Now, as Mr. Hyde, they will introduced *fear and intimidation* into the equation in order to secure absolute control. They seem to be oblivious to the fact that they have just introduced the last component needed to bring about hatred, and has just started a clock that is slowly counting down to revolt and their own undoing. They will adopt all the best ideas and suggestions offered by their staff, and present them as their own. Now, they seldom, if ever, ask for any inputs or suggestions. Instead, consumed by their own ego, they truly believe that their staffers don't really have anything else of value to contribute and that their ideas, from this point on, are the best ideas. All of you have seen this before, "*it's*

---

[9] But then, consider misplaced trust and the mythical beast Geryon (a hideous winged monster that had three bodies and faces and was subsequently destroyed by a poison arrow shot by Hercules as his tenth labor). Because Geryon had 3 different personas, you would never know who you were really interacting with. Another description portrays Geryon as the embodiment of **fraud and malice** because you were never able to see his whole body, just his face, and his face was the face of a just and honest man. Though he was a monster, he concealed his true nature from you until it was too late.

my way or the highway". They are quick to take personal credit for every success, but when things go wrong, they run out of fingers assigning blame. No matter the size of your organization, from a major corporation, too a tiny start-up, this manager, their management style, their lack of compassion, and their lack of professional ethics are a major threat to the future success of your business. Fortunately, and in most cases, Management becomes aware of the problems by-way-of a decline in productivity, low morale, poor workmanship, apathy in the workforce, higher employee turnover, and in the worst cases, outright hostility and revolt. This is also about the time that the Tyrannical Boss begins to make excuses for the worsening performance of their department. Again, they don't take personal responsibility but, almost always, attributes it to performance problems with specific subordinates. And, as you would expect, the subordinates that they single-out are generally those that are the weakest and most vulnerable within the group, as well as those that they have been unable to intimidate or thoroughly subordinate.

Let's move on now to the manager that takes the fast track. For this manager, the first tool to come out of their bag is *magic*, followed very closely by *intimidation*. This manager is likely to have come in from outside the company and has a stellar resume (on paper). They would have presented themselves to Management as an agent of change. And by bringing their knowledge of their former company with them, they hit the ground running. Here comes the magic. Before this manager even gets to their new office, or finds out where the restrooms are; they would have already offered 15 suggestions and recommendations and made 5 changes to an operation that they know absolutely nothing about. The most amazing thing here is that the Management Team will just stand there like bobble-head dolls, *gap-jawed* and *in-awe*; never questioning the logic or practicality of the new manager's recommendations and changes, just blinded by what they perceive as their new *superstar's* instant knowledge and insight into their operation. Think about this: Machiavelli wrote…*"for men in general judge more by their eyes than by their hands; everybody is fitted to see, few to understand. Everybody sees what you appear to be; few make out what you really are. And these few do not dare to oppose the opinion of the many…"* This manager is completely reliant on that human peculiarity. Their *razzle-dazzle* is intended to impress and deceive, and it does both. But if Management would stop for a moment and look at their actions objectively, it would be easy to see that it was nothing more than a *cheap parlor trick*, and upon further analysis, they'd discover that their recommendations and changes did little, if anything to actually benefit the organization. They may have even been harmful. But now, having reasonably impressed the Management and feeling even more confident in their new position, this manager (mindful that razzle-dazzle and parlor tricks have very short shelf-lives) moves quickly to gain absolute control by *intimidating* and *dominating* their staff and *weakening* and/or *undermining* (in the eyes of Management) any of their subordinates or peers that they see as a competitor or a threat to them. This manager breeds *fear* within the organization. And while they may have been originally brought in to make improvements, they are really a merchant of destruction. The methods that they use will ultimately prove damaging to both your organization and your employees. They will start with a series of one-on-one meetings with staff. These meetings are ostensibly intended to get to know the staff and to find out what each of them does. But covertly, they are looking for any scrap of information that might show personal weakness in the staff or in any of their peers. During the meeting, you'll find most of their questions rather innocuous and about the job, but a few of them may appear to you to be a bit odd or curious, in that, they would seem to be soliciting general background information about you, your coworkers and/or their peers. While they will play down the relevance of the questions, each staff member will leave the meeting a little more suspicious of the manager and a lot less secure in their jobs. After a few of these one-on-ones you will begin to see what appears to be, an inner circle forming around the manager; a small group that seems to have a much closer relationship with the manager than anyone else. There is usually nothing professionally remarkable or outstand-ing about any of these people, except that among them are those that tended to be some-what self-oriented and opportunistic long before the new manager took the position. These are the new manager's minions, their eyes and ears throughout their little kingdom. Almost everyone sees this change, and with it, trust in the new manager is lost as more and more *direct control* is exerted; ideas and free speech are suppressed or censored and any direct links to Sr. Management (by staff) are truncated. Talented and creative people flourish when they have the freedom and liberty to do so. Your new superstar has created a controlling environment filled with fear and distrust, and your best people won't tolerate it; they will be the first to leave you. Your superstar may have made themselves hated. And while people might tolerate fear, character flaws, and idiots, *they will find themselves compelled to react to hatred*. And if Sr. Management had been disengaged or had not provided a sufficient level of oversight, the cost to the company for making a bad hiring decision will begin to cascade. Employee morale will be the first to go, followed by workplace apathy, then a reduction of product quality and productivity. You can also expect to see a breakdown in team dynamics as well as an increase in absenteeism. Let's stop again, take a minute to figure out what this could costs your company. There are administrative and relocation cost, initial in-house training cost, the cost of the damage to the morale within your company, the cost of an apathetic workforce, measurable drops in the quality of workmanship and productivity, the cost of losing your best employees, the cost of trying to bring peace to a dysfunctional organization, the cost of the severance package needed to rid your company of your superstar, and the productivity opportunities that will be lost just trying to get your organization back to where it was prior to that manager's arrival. If Sr. Management is vigilant and involved in their operation they can stop things before they get this far. But they must be willing to admit that they've made a hiring mistake and also be willing to move quickly to correct it. Unfortunately, it has been my experience that even with *hard evidence* and the involvement and recommendations from Human Resources, Sr. Management allows the situation to drag-on and become more costly to the company before they are willing to step forward and end it; to admit a hiring mistake was made and take corrective actions. There are no shortages of examples of where Sr. Management has failed to act in the *present* in order to stave-off catastrophic damage to the organization in the *future*. Your problems with this manager won't go away or get any better. You need to take unambiguous and decisive actions when the need for such actions are upon you. What if Presidents Truman and Obama had not fired (or allowed them to resign) Generals MacArthur and McChrystal respectively? Their egos, vanity and apparent disregard for the US Constitution and for the Office of the Presidency could have destabilized our democracy and we could 'now' be subject to the dictates of a military junta. I know that I could have used a better example here, but I have been carrying this one around for the last few days and I didn't want to lose it. Suffice it to say, Sr. Management has to be willing and able to step in and take action while there is still time to cut your losses. No one wants to fire someone they just hired or recently promoted, it reflects badly on everyone and it comes at a cost and it's painful for all involved. But by avoiding the pain early-on and ignoring the problem hoping it will go away or trying to conceal it, will only make matters *exponentially* worse. Sr. Management has to stay vigilant in order to identify trouble spots and to correct them while they are small. For example, an illness is difficult to detect in the early stages when a small amount of treatment or effort can cure it, but if left untreated, the illness spreads and its symptoms become far more pronounced and are very easy to recognize. But by then, it has gotten much more dangerous (or even fatal) and can only be curbed or treated with very intensive, drastic and expensive methods; that's if you are lucky. Do you see the parallel here?

Needless to say, there are some individuals that, for whatever reason, are not and will never be good fits to your organization and should never be considered for management responsibilities. That's why employee screening programs and succession planning processes are so important.

In the next section, I want us to take a look at you and try to determine where you fit, with respect to the 4 most common *"Operating" or "Personal Management Styles"*. The importance of this section is to make you aware of the differences in the way you and others operate and how you can benefit from modifying your style in order to accommodate theirs.

Chapter # 9:

The Style Assessment
Operating Style Descriptions; How to approach them and
what you should avoid

Managing and management is a process, and in order to stay current and relevant a manager
has to maintain enough flexibility in their particular management style to be able to change
and adapt to the changing requirements of the client, the demands of the company, the
needs of their workforce, and the political dynamics that are a constant component of every
enterprise. In addition, a manager has to keep a close eye on their own management and
career objectives so they are not lost or put on a back burner. Earlier, I asked that you determine what your objectives were, to write them down, and develop a realistic, flexible action
plan around them with specific milestones and timing to help you stay focused. Believe me,
they will help you achieve your goals, or at the very least approach them. So if you haven't
already, now might be a good time to jot some things down.

Before we can start any heavy lifting and build you into a better manager, we'll have to take a
look at your current management style and decide where we should begin our renovations,
modernizations, or if need be, total demolition followed by all new construction. Now, as you
would expect, this is going to be difficult. But this is the way I plan to go about it, since I don't
know who you are and where you fit within the standard model for management styles we
will approach the problem this way. First I want you to do an assessment of your manager,
and other managers you've known or have reported to. I will give you as set of characterizing
examples for each of the 4 basic management styles and you will try to decide how closely
your managers compares to them. Then (and this is the tricky part), I want you to try to be
as honest as you can with yourself and compare yourself as close as possible to the manager
whose style is closest to yours or to the style description that matches the way you believe

you operate; *the way you currently operate…not how you would like to operate*. If you can get some honest and reliable feedback from a relative that really knows you or, better yet, from your subordinates, peers and/or your manager, your results will be more relevant to your actual operating style. The last point, don't be surprised if your subordinates, your peers, and your manager all see you a little differently, we tend to modify our styles dependent on where we find ourselves within a given hierarchy.

Identifying another person's operating style and learning to adjust and modify your style to accommodate theirs is an essential component of people management. I would recommend you take a training course or a seminar from a qualified expert in the field in order to develop and perfect this skill.

<u>Operating Style Descriptions:</u>

"Analytical Style"   This person is likely to be very formal in their interactions with peers, staff, as well as with management. They are not much on small talk and are particular and precise in their phrasing; seldom if ever making a general or unsupported statement. They use information and data in decision making and stays focused, *working slowly and methodically* to arrive at the best options for the path forward. They will want to know *what* the problem is and will *ask* for more and more detailed information and data in order to provide you support. They will also *ask* you how you would like to proceed. Their primary driver is to be *right*. Their office is probably stark and their desk is most likely clear of everything but what they are currently working on.

"Dynamic Style"   This person is professional and business like. Their time is valuable to them and they *work fast* and make decisions relying on the available facts, their past experiences, and their gut-feel. They are not much for small talk preferring to get to the project at hand. They can often be found working in the trenches and getting their hands dirty. They speak in general subjective terms. They will want to know *what* the problem is and will take up and take over the project and *tell* you how you should, and how they will proceed. They are multitaskers and I expect their office will be in disarray with paper and files stacked everywhere; but they will most likely know where everything is. They prioritize their work and focus on whatever happens to be important at the time. Their primary driver is to be *in charge*.

"Sociable Style"   This person is warm, very receptive and easy to approach. They value relationships and prefer to engage in social discourse before getting down to actual business. They are careful with the words they use; so as not to offend and is generally someone you would go to for counseling about a private matter. Their use of time is *slow* and they are easily distracted, they'll *ask* how they can be of service and *ask* how you would like to proceed. Their office is likely filled with personal items and the documents and files on their desk are in neat arrangement. Because people having the Sociable Style tend to be unsure of their place within the hierarchy, they will often use friendship and kindness as a way to build alliances within the group. As a result, they will be less interested in the nature of the project than in *who* else is involved. Their primary driver is to be *liked and accepted*.

"Animated Style"   This person is outgoing and outspoken. They are often thought to be a pivotal person within the organization and they seem to have an opinion or suggestion on every topic. They tend to be multitaskers and they *work fast* but have trouble staying focused on any single issue. Their office is often cluttered and they can't seem to find anything in it. They will do most of the talking and it will primarily be about current events or some of the local gossip. They are prone to make over-the-top statements that are largely unsupported and there is an emotional component to how they interact with the group. They will *tell* you how to go about solving your problem and provide directions and leadership for you. Like the person with the Sociable Style, they will also want to know *who* else is involved, but for a completely different reason. They are overtly competing in the hierarchy and want to make sure that their contributions are seen and appreciated by the senior people in the organization. Their primary driver is *to be important*.

Which of these management styles do you believe is the most like your own? What did your relative say, your subordinates, your peers, your manager? Are the results similar or different? Which style is considered to be the second best description for the way you operate?

There is no one management or operating style that is better than the next; all can be equally effective as a means to an end. What this shows is the style that you find most comfortable and natural for you to operate in. Your base style (or primary style) is your operating comfort zone and the second style is your supporting style; the adaptive style that supports the base style, but is subordinate to it. Therefore when you want to express someone's style, you do it this way: supporting style/primary style. For example, my style is Analytical/Dynamic; my primary style is Dynamic and my supporting style is Analytical. There are a number of professional organizations that provide excellent training in the area of personal management styles and I would recommend them for anyone wanting to learn more. But my intent here is not so much that you understand your own style, but for you to be able to recognize the styles of others; particularly the styles of peers and managers. Determining their management styles (comfort zones) and being able to adjust your style to accommodate their needs in order to lower the stress level that accompanies every human interaction. There is always stress (even when you can't perceive it) because there is always some form of posturing occurring. You have to take control of the environment and prevent the natural stresses from being perceived as a threat; a challenge to them personally or to their little bailiwick where they have control. And the only ways available for you to do that is to not have contact with them at all, or to give them what they need to lower their stress levels *up-front*. When a person feels threatened they will automatically go into their "Defensive Styles"; a natural reflex designed to protect themselves and their place within the hierarchy. There are always signs, but we are usually so caught up in what we are doing or saying that we either miss them or ignore them completely. Can any of you remember a conversation you've had with someone that didn't go well? Can you recall when you thought you may have been losing them...you know...around about the time you thought you could see shutters rolling down across their eyes, when their faces began to flush red with blood, when they stopped making eye contact, when they began checking their watch (even though they weren't wearing one), when they started to squirm around in their chairs, when their eyes seem to glaze over, or when they crossed their arms and moved back against the wall; getting as far away from you as possible. When you see these signs you need to back off and let it go. You have lost your audience. These people are about to enter their Defensive Styles; this is where all the pissing happens and no one wins. So when you are working with any individual it's always very helpful to have a sense of their base management or operating styles so you'll know how to approach them, while creating as little stress as possible.

How to Approach Them and What You Should Avoid:
Analytical Style:

Approach this person with a problem that requires solving. It's important for them to feel intellectually superior to others, but don't expect a quick turnaround because this individual is methodical and works purposely, but slowly. And don't expect a hard solution or answer to your problem because they will only report to you what the data shows; any decisions and recommendations are left up to you. Remember, this person's primary driver is to be right so they are unlikely to commit to any of their results so long as there is any chance, any chance at-all, that they could be wrong. This is obviously and exaggeration, but it might be said that "Analyticals predicting the end of the world would be less concern about the event than making sure their calculations were right".

From what we have concluded about the person with the Analytical Style, they are likely to be uncomfortable with the social graces, aside from a standard greeting; they may even be socially cripple, so you should avoid excessive small talk. They can't be hurried along, and they will resist any attempt to do so. Don't press them for a definitive answer because they are unlikely to give you one, they will always need more and more data and, even then, will only give you a set of probabilities and options. In their mind, their position within the hierarchy is secured by their superior intellect and rational problem solving abilities. Therefore, you should refrain from any-thing that would cause them to feel they had become irrelevant or superfluous to the project because you were unable to wait for their input and have moved on without them. Any of these will cause them to revert to their Defensive Style where they will *avoid* you and the project. They will no longer trust you and will be reluctant to work with you or your group in the future.

Dynamic Style:

Approach this person with a task (something that needs doing). And while this person is capable of making small talk, they are more interested in the project or task in front of them. Don't waste their time; they would rather get down to business. They only need to know what the task is and any particulars. After they've done a topical assessment, they will tell you how they want to proceed. They will listen to your comments and recommendations and adjust their approach based upon their merits, but will reject recommendations that they deem off target or counter to their thinking. Their primary driver is to be in charge (the project leader, the boss).

You should avoid excessive details unless they are critical to the success of the project, and you should avoid any challenges to their knowledge base or their decided path forward.

They see their place within the hierarchy being secured by their ability to solve any problem and overcome any obstacle and whenever they perceive a challenge to their position they'll revert from the Dynamic Style into their Defensive Style. In their defensive style they become *autocratic* and *dictatorial* (it's my way or the highway). But fortunately, once the dust settles, everything goes back to square-one and there are usually no lingering effects of the confrontation, which cannot be said with regard to those having other styles.

Sociable Style:

Approach this individual with a complement and social small talk; they are easily intimidated, so you have to lower their stress levels as quickly as possible. They want to be of service to you and be accepted by you and your group so they will often assume a subordinate position to yours, even when they out-rank you. Be patient and let the social particulars run their course before getting to the purpose of your visit. Remember, this person values personal relationships above all else and their primary driver is to be liked. So they will ask how you would like them to help and ask you how you want to proceed.

I need to add a word of caution here because this person can be supersensitive and difficult to read. Their perception of themselves within the hierarchy is largely determined by their level of self-esteem and that level is primarily determined by their interpretations of human interactions; "you". So you need to watch for any signs of stress in this person and how you say what you say.

Avoid any displays of dominance or pressure because they are viewed as personal put-downs or slights. And, a slight of any kind, regardless of the size, lowers their self-esteem and self-worth. They will collect every slight as if they were small pebbles or rocks and put them in a sack that they carry around on their backs. And, over time and over a number of collaborations, the accumulation of slights will eventually get so heavy that they will drop the sack and you along with it. They won't want to have anything else to do with you; *forever*! All of this will come as a surprise to you because they didn't show you any apparent signs of discomfort or stress. Yes, you worked together and you got what you needed. But you failed to recognize that when someone with the Sociable Style reverts to their Defensive Style, they *acquiesce*. They let you have your way and just give in; then at some point, when they've had enough, they simply reject you and are done with you.

Animated Style:

Approach this person with an objective and some social small talk. They are naturally outgoing and friendly but highly competitive. They see themselves as an indispensable member of the team and the go-to person for strategic and tactical problem solving. So they will usually have an inflated view of their position within the hierarchy. They will want to direct and coordinate the activities of the project or the group. They are happiest giving advice and telling others what they need to do. As with those with other operating styles, this person can be of great value to you and your organization provided you give them what they need. And for this person, their primary driver is to be important.

Avoid a nose-to-nose confrontation or a public contradiction of views; it will cause this person to lose face and diminish their standing within the group. They will have lofty and grandiose ideas, which are beyond the scope of the project, so you'll have to find non-threatening ways to keep them focused on the project at hand. When this person reverts to their Defensive Style, they are very likely to suffer an emotional outburst where they will verbally *attack* anything and anyone around them. And unlike the person with the Dynamic Style, this one will hold a grudge.

All this may seem to you to be a lot of unnecessary work just so you can navigate through your day; identifying style types, developing strategies, tactics and diplomacies to work some kind of magic on people, and I can't argue with you, your right...but that's the way the game of human interaction is setup. And if you want to be a successful manager or leader of people, than you'll have to know how to play the game and win at it. You have to stay above the posturing and backbiting and build alliances with your peers and managers so you can better control your environment. When you give people what they need to reassure them of their place in the hierarchy you become a supporter and an ally, to which they will owe a debt. But if you can't rise above yourself and your own ego, you will remain a competitor and be forever mired in a pointless battle for turf and supremacy within the hierarchy. And as a result, you wouldn't be able to build beneficial alliances with your peers and manager. And because of that, any ability that you may have had to move up in the hierarchy would have become a lot more challenging, if not outright impossible.

The Four Primary or Base Styles

Operating Styles

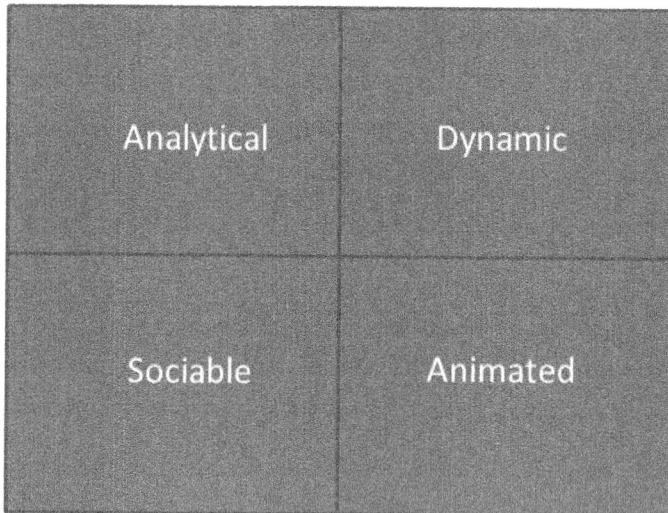

Analytical	Dynamic
Sociable	Animated

Panel # 1

The 16 Secondary or Supporting Styles

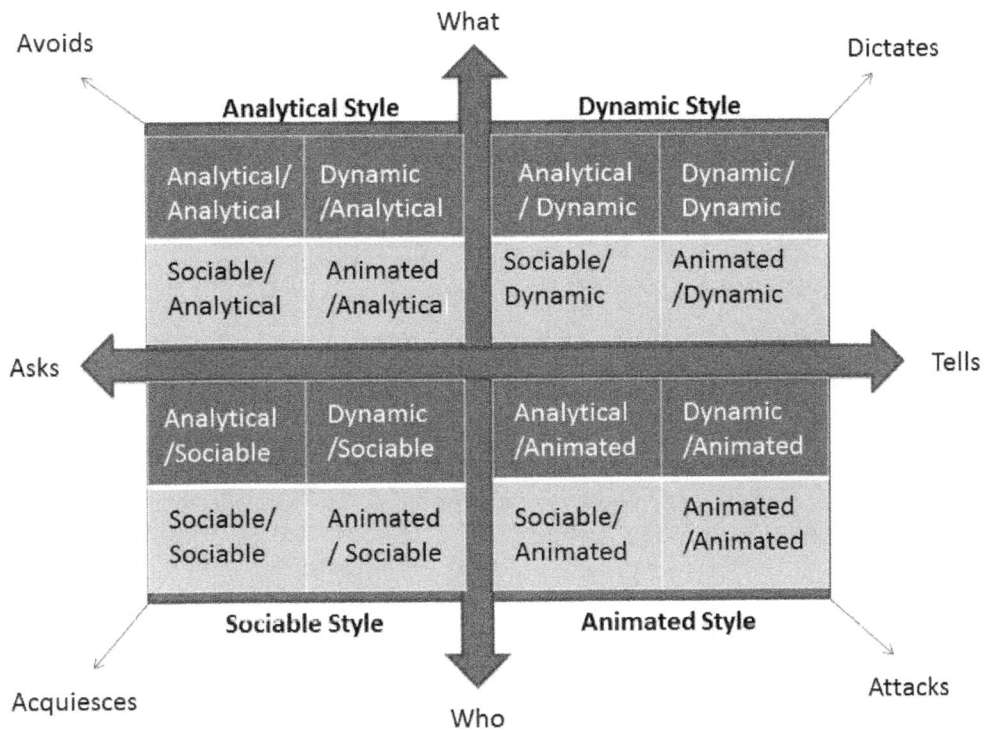

	What		
Avoids			Dictates
Analytical Style		**Dynamic Style**	
Analytical/ Analytical	Dynamic /Analytical	Analytical / Dynamic	Dynamic/ Dynamic
Sociable/ Analytical	Animated /Analytica	Sociable/ Dynamic	Animated /Dynamic
Asks			Tells
Analytical /Sociable	Dynamic /Sociable	Analytical /Animated	Dynamic /Animated
Sociable/ Sociable	Animated / Sociable	Sociable/ Animated	Animated /Animated
Sociable Style		**Animated Style**	
Acquiesces			Attacks
	Who		

Panel # 2

How You Should Approach Them And How They Use Time

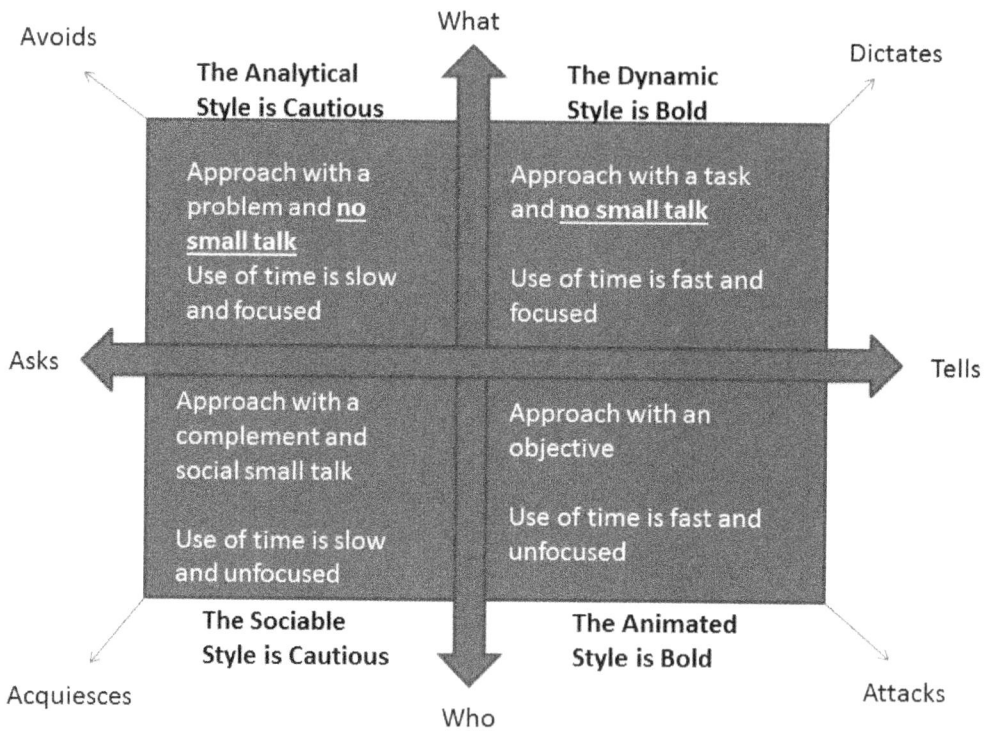

Avoids

What

Dictates

The Analytical Style is Cautious

Approach with a problem and **no small talk**
Use of time is slow and focused

The Dynamic Style is Bold

Approach with a task and **no small talk**

Use of time is fast and focused

Asks ←————————————————————————→ Tells

Approach with a complement and social small talk

Use of time is slow and unfocused

Approach with an objective

Use of time is fast and unfocused

The Sociable Style is Cautious

The Animated Style is Bold

Acquiesces

Who

Attacks

Panel # 3

How Decisions Are Made And What Their Needs Are

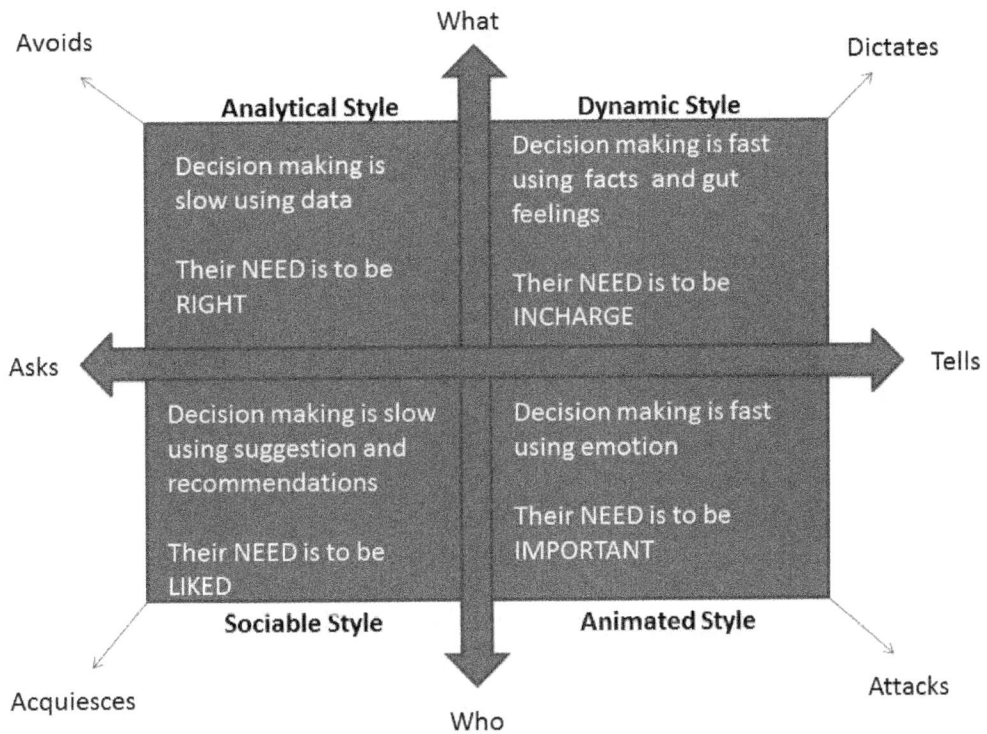

What

Avoids

Dictates

Analytical Style

Dynamic Style

Decision making is
slow using data

Decision making is fast
using facts and gut
feelings

Their NEED is to be
RIGHT

Their NEED is to be
INCHARGE

Asks

Tells

Decision making is slow
using suggestion and
recommendations

Decision making is fast
using emotion

Their NEED is to be
LIKED

Their NEED is to be
IMPORTANT

Sociable Style

Animated Style

Acquiesces

Attacks

Who

Panel # 4

The Differences in Their Outward Demeanor

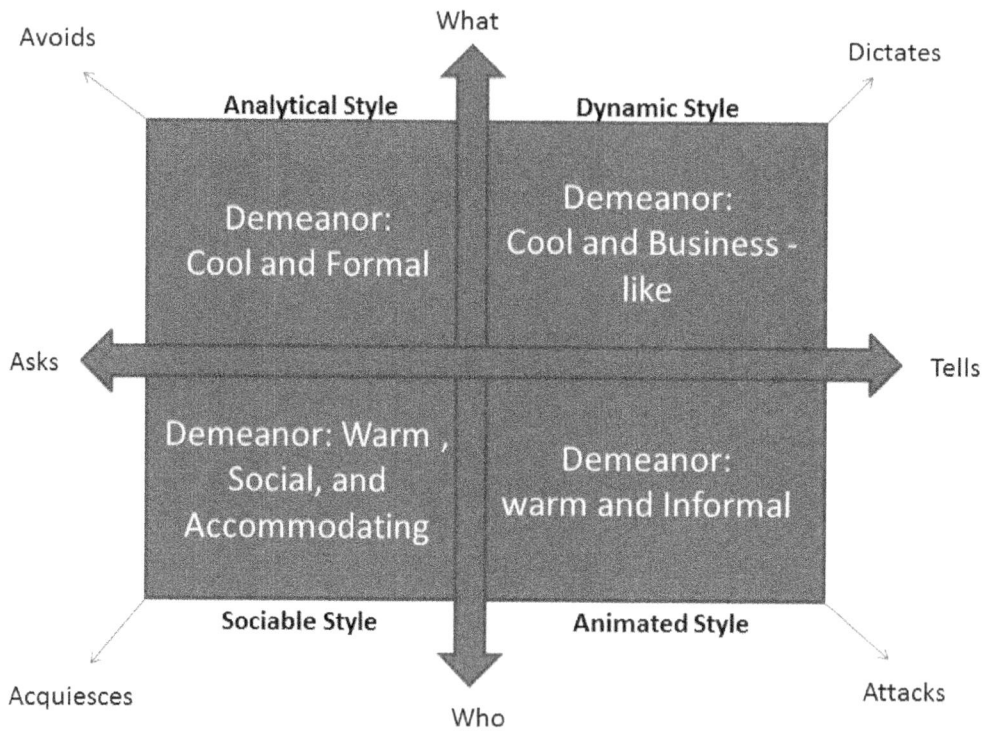

Panel # 5

What to Expect From Their Defensive Styles

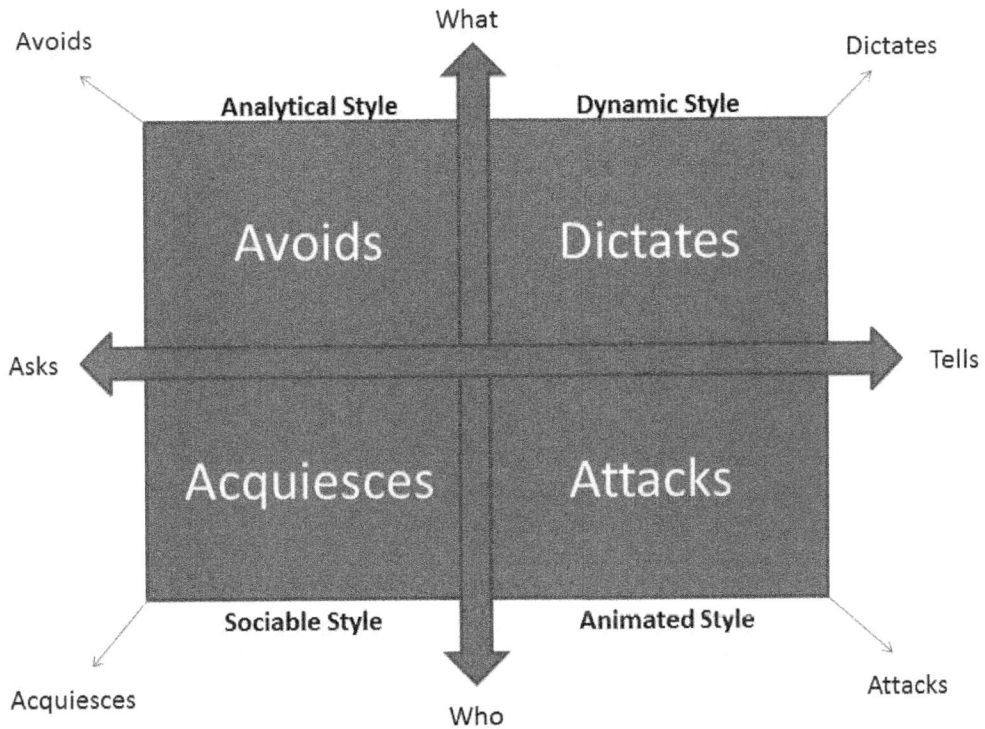

Panel # 6

Don't file this section away and consider it done, your subordinates have the same operating styles, supporting styles and defensives styles as your peers and managers. And while they may not be able to challenge you 'outright', they will express any displeasure with you in more subtle ways. Therefore, as their manager you'll have to work out what their styles are and find ways to service their style needs. In addition, you'll have to stay mindful of their aspirational needs as well. You already know they have hidden baser and competitive drivers, but what motivates them to come to work and do good work every day? If you've forgotten, go back and re-read the section on "The Manager and The Boss".

We are going to be talking more about the different operating styles as we move through the book, but we'll return to it in earnest when we get to the section entitled "Managing your Manager".

A Recap Before Moving Forward:

In order to become a successful manager of people you will be required to develop and exercise a considerable amount of intellectual discipline. You will have to be able to change your approach to your people and the work. Your approach will have to be objective and professional, not subjective, emotional and threatening. Step away from your ego and give them what they need from you in order for you to get what you want from them. If you're working with peers or superiors, let your *Analyticals* feel that they are right and intellectually superior, let your *Dynamics* have a sense of being in charge, let your *Animateds* have a sense of importance, and let your *Sociables* feel that they are welcomed and a valuable part of your team; they need to be liked. When working with subordinates, stay mindful that they have similar needs and you'll have to find ways to service them as well.

In Chapter #1, we agreed that the Holy Grail of Management would be the ability to lead people in such a way that they can follow you, and will follow you, and achieve the desired objectives. In Chapter #3, I noted that it fell to you to make the necessary changes and adaptations because "Man" will not change or adapt to you. And in this chapter, we examined 4 of the most common operating or management styles and learned how to accommodate the needs of others in order to facilitate their compliance or to create an environment where they would be more receptive to following your directions or honoring your requests. In each instance, your level of success will be determined, in large measure, by your ability to step forward and take deliberate actions in order to control the environment and the human interactions that are playing out.

The next 4 chapters are intended to broaden your strategic and tactical knowledge base with respect to some specific management tactics that will prove to be complimentary to what we have already covered. We will be studying some Ways to Win, techniques to Resolve Conflicts, Situational Leadership, and the interrelationships of Power, Responsibility, and Authority. Upon completion, we will be ready to move off into our Case Studies and our First Scenario.

Chapter # 10:

Ways to Win

Take a moment to think about what winning means to you when it comes to human relations and interactions. Now, let's look at some ways to win, either by force or by persuasion. Once we do, then you'll have to decide for yourself which is the best way to win based upon a given set of conditions; your current situation, and the best possible outcome for those involved. We can all agree that there's no best way to lose, but you'll find that winning in the wrong ways can and will ultimately result in a loss because, winning in some ways is better than winning in others. The way you win "today" will greatly influence your winnings and/or failures in the future. We all know, and for those that don't, management is really a full-contact pursuit. It's getting people to do what you want them to do when they would rather do what they want, or do nothing at all. You are the manager, and in addition to your title you also have some degree of position power, authority, and political power (influence) that's available to you in order to help move things along. But you have to recognize that your position power and authority is finite and is likely well defined, but your political power is an intangible and it is what you make it. Therefore, I would hope that you would use your raw position power and authority both wisely and sparingly because they are self-limiting and frequently leaves an offensive residue behind. Instead, and whenever possible, you should use the power of influence to encourage people to move in the direction you want them to go and to do your bidding. Staying focused on your win will require you to climb-down off your ego and be generous in your interactions with people. Based upon their individual styles, you'll give them what they need as unique individuals to help reduce the stress of the interaction and to help them feel whole. Remember, if you want to be successful and get the win, you're the one that has to change and adapt because man cannot turn away from his competitive nature. Let's, just for the sake of argument, say that you are weak and insecure and your ego won't let you get above the fray. If that were the case, you'll find that you'll have to join every battle for fear of losing face, losing status, and your perceived place within the hierarchy. You won't be able to resist the battle because you'll always believe you have something more to prove. Let's see how far you can get with the little position power and authority you have. Well, for starters, whenever you go nose-to-nose with anyone, you burn-up a lot of your resources and come away being added to another person's list of enemies. When you go nose-to-nose with a subordinate you'll win, but you would have also intimidated and dehumanized a person that you'll need in the future and likely have cause them to see themselves being at much lower status within the hierarchy; not a positive thing. In addition, you may have quite possibly destroyed their trust in you and lost their respect. No doubt, you would have silenced them and got the win, but don't assume that silence infers compliance. You have been silenced yourself, and you already know that your silence did not transform you into a convert. Just try to remember that *"you have not converted a person simply because you have silenced them"*. It's far more likely that what you have done was to create an enemy within your own house. Equally, if you go nose-to-nose with a peer, no one actually wins because you are likely evenly matched. You will retain your place within the hierarchy but you would have expended a considerable amount of your limited resources, lost some valuable political support and created an enemy just outside your house. To go nose-to-nose with your manager is just a losing proposition so I don't have to explain that one. The paradox here is that *if you feel weak and insecure, you will always join the battle in order to prove that you are not weak and insecure*. This is yet another reason you have to learn to be confident and self-assured. If you want the win, you'll have to decide which is the most important, the win or your ego. Put another way, you have to ask yourself, what's more important, to build and develop social and political alliances or is it more important to you *to be right about it and in control*! Combat and confrontation are a waste of time and energy. Throughout your career, you'll encounter people at all levels who will, at every turn, exercise direct power to get their way or to advance their own positions. Cooperation and collaboration are foreign concepts to them, as well as the skills necessary to build and maintain important social and political alliances and/or to move the project forward. They are driven by vanity and pride, and for them, a win is being *right about it.* And, more often than not, they're not. Would you consider confrontation, intimidation, and domination a win for them, or is it just short term psychological gratification? If you glance back over the different operating styles you'll find one where there's a need to be *right* and another where there's a need to be *important.* There is a subset within each of those styles that will always rely on their direct powers to mask their own shortcomings and insecurities. Not to lose track of where I'm going with this, I'm only actually talking about the exercise of power in order to obtain a win; using direct power or indirect power. So far, I have been talking the use of direct power, and when it is used. By definition, direct power is confrontational and partisan, therefore it's impossible for you to stay above the fray when you use it...you will get dirty. I guess you can probably gather from my approach that I believe direct power should be used only when the stakes are high and other alternatives have been exhausted; and you would be right. But there will be times when you have no other choice, when you have to get that win by getting everything you wanted (the whole 9 yards) or at the very least, come away with what was critical and essential for you. I will talk about that later. But for now, let's talk about how you would go about using indirect power. Consider this example, which do you think is better, to be the Emperor on the throne or to be the power behind the throne? There is no right answer to this question, but your success might depend on how comfortable you feel in either role. The use of indirect power provides a base for you to secure much greater wins through your ability to influence your peers and your leadership than by anything you might be able to do using your limited direct power. Your peers and managers are the Emperors on the throne, and you need their support if you are to grow your career or even survive in your current position. Earlier in this work I compared management to combat and just above I reminded you that management is a full-contact pursuit; it's not for the faint of heart. You are a single manager with a rather small powerbase, so in order to survive; you'll have to find ways to amplify your powers and resources. And the best way to do that is to build *honest professional and ethical* alliances with your peers and managers; you can't go it alone, your department is not autonomous and it cannot operate in a vacuum. And if you alienate your subordinates, peers, and superiors you'll quickly discover just how limited your direct powers are and how tenuous your position has become.

Now, in order to advance my own argument, I am going to use some situational logic that is at once realistic and self-serving. And while my position is bias, it helps me to demonstrate the power of influence and building important alliances, as well as teamwork. You are always free to reject my premise.

Consider the Emperor, any Emperor or for that matter, any King, Queen, President, Prime minister or Dictator. What do they really know about the masses they govern...I would say, not a lot. Then, what do you think they consider being the most important thing in the world to them...what about selfishly maintaining their positions? They know that they are being challenged on all sides by the many pretenders to the throne; they also know that they govern with the permission of those being governed. So what do they do? They surround themselves with people they trust and can rely on; advisors. These advisors come with all different names; High Priests, King's Counsel, Private Secretaries, Cabinet Ministers or Secretaries, cronies, and on-and-on. They are the power behind the throne; the people guiding the Emperor are the actual decision makers. They take the pulse of the people and keep track of the important day to day activities and events that could negatively or positively impact the government. From the very early days, till today, these individuals were already powerful in their own rite, well before becoming an advisor to the Emperor. They had standing armies, great wealth or large tracts of land, or large groups of political or religious followers. The Emperor needed these people and their political support and guidance to hold on to the throne, and in return, they needed the Emperor to implement their legislation and laws in order to retain their power and wealth; power begets power. Let's look at who usually makes up the Presidential Cabinet in the U.S.A., among those sitting around the table are former Governors, Senators, Bankers, Generals, Educators, Captains of industry and the President's most trusted confidantes. The President and the advisors go to great pains to govern, placate, and pacify the masses in order to keep down all forms of dissent and to advance their own agendas. And as a result, they maintain the status quo and the reins of power, making them the true winners in society, not the masses.

There are 2 truths that can be distilled from this, and the first is how power is amplified through the formation of alliances and the second is that the powerful are self-serving. The Imperial Credentials appear to provide almost limitless powers to the Emperor but in reality, the Emperor has very little independent powers and authority on his own. So he has to surround himself with the wealthy, the wise, the powerful, the influential, and the violent in order to consolidate all the powers at the top. But the Emperor's ability to exercise those powers are not absolute, he does not rule by *Divine Rite*. The Emperor's advisors (his allies, counselors, ministers, secretaries or his gang) will always try to limit the Emperor's powers, less they be turned against them; something the Knights Templar should have thought of as bankers to King Philip IV of France. By limiting his powers, they keep him in an ever-present state of imminent peril where the slightest misstep, shift in the political winds or at any time the masses won't follow, could trigger a coup d'état, marking an end to his reign and his undoing. A classic example of this would be how King Dionysius allowed Damocles to sit upon his throne[10]. Damocles could only see the opulence and seductive trappings of power from his sycophant position in the King's Court. But from the throne, Damocles quickly learned that with great power and responsibility comes great risk and begged the King to allow him to step down. And the second truth is when you consider each of the Emperor's powerful allies, you won't be able to find one among them that is selfless or altruistic; they are all self-serving, for them, everything is *"quid pro quo."*

So let's get back to us and how we want to win. What choices do we have? We can choose to be the Emperor on the throne (at considerable risk to us personally) or we can choose to be an advisor, the power behind the throne. To put it a bit clearer, we can choose to be the puppet, or the puppet master. Which would you rather be? In reality, we are both. When we are operating at our departmental level, among our subordinates and peers, we serve as the Emperor. We align ourselves with our most skilled, trusted and dependable staffers and peers to carry on the work and to provide us with timely feedback and guidance to prevent things from going off the rails and putting our careers at risk. We use them to maintain our positions. In return, they will expect a certain level of freedom, respect and recognition, job security and management (and or peer) support when things go wrong. Like it or not, they are pulling your strings. And likewise, when you operate at your level and above, your peers and managers rely on your support in order to move their projects to a favorable outcome in order to preserve and advance their own careers. This time you are the one pulling the strings, and as a consequence of your nature (man's nature) you would have some expectation of some form of reciprocity. That's just the way things are. After all, how many of you can honestly standup and say that you put in the long hours and go the extra mile for your peers or your managers because you are just a good guy and really didn't expect anything in return? I thought so. And for those that had the audacity to standup, go back and take another look at the objectives you put down at the beginning of this book, and try to decide why you are reading this, also try to determine if you can truly be honest with yourself and if you actually want to become a manager. Before leaving this section on getting wins through powerful alliances, there is something else you need to know. You should never align yourself with the unscrupulous; regardless of their power, they will always bring you down as a manager, as well as a human being. There has to be a professional and ethical reason for the

---

[10] From Greek Mythology, "The Sword of Damocles"

alliances you make, and even then, some will try to get you to put your power and reputation on the line to further their private and unethical agendas. You need to prepare for this and expect it because, it will happen!

Now let's look at the last way to win that I noted above; getting everything you wanted, the whole 9 yards. This win is heavily dependent on the stakes involved and the situation. If a total win is vital to the preservation of your position, department or any of your personnel, then get it. If the total win is at the expense of a powerful and committed adversary and you need it, then get it. If the total win is needed to restore your reputation or the reputation of your firm, then get it. In these and other similar situations, you have to decide when you need to get the whole 9 yards. But when you do, you need to recognize that you no longer have any friends or allies along that road and you will never be able to travel down it again. So you have to weigh the situation and the stakes to be certain that that's the way you have to proceed. You just need to be aware that when you focus all your direct powers, authority and political resources to take it all and leave nothing, it amounts to *rape*; and regardless of the justness of your crusade, the enemies you make here, will be enemies for a lifetime. I could never take a total win off the table, and neither should you. But when the stakes are not that high and the situation allows, negotiation is a much better way to get that win[11].

When you negotiate you have to put your ego aside, there is no room for it. You'll also have to stay objective and focused so you don't lose sight of what's critical and essential for you to come away with. You also have to bring your scales with you to the negotiations so you can balance the weight of your cost (what you have to give up) to the weight of the value (what you get in return). In a successful negotiation the negotiating parties reach a consensus (a middle ground) where everyone walks away with a partial win and no one feels as if they have been exploited. The majority of your alliances and partnerships will be built upon the ways you choose to win, either by your use of direct and dominating power or through influence and persuasion. Both methods have their place in your toolbox; the key is for you to choose the right one at the right time.

---

[11] A word of caution: remember people with the Sociable Operating Style need to be liked. So when negotiating with them it is important for you to have a real sense of what you are asking of them and weather your request is reasonable and fair. You have to closely watch their body language to determine any levels of stress. Because they have a need to be liked and accepted, they will subordinate themselves to you and give you everything you want; leaving them stripped bare and naked. This is not a win for you, but a loss. Don't inadvertently turn a valued ally into an enemy.

Chapter # 11:

Conflict Resolution

Conflicts are inevitable and largely unavoidable, even if you ran away to a cloistered monastery, conflicts will find you. Wherever there are people, there is bound to be conflicts. Remember Adam, when he was alone in the forest, there was nothing to be conflicted about, but as soon as Lilith showed up, so did conflict. We've been talking about ways to avoid conflict from the very start. And because they are unavoidable, the smart thing for us to do is to develop a strategy that will help us approach and resolve the conflicts we encounter as rationally and reasonably as possible, and without getting caught up in all the emotion. But for us to do that we'll have to climb above the petty day-to-day squabbling over turf and the constant posturing; we'll also have to tone-down the brawn and tune-up the brain so we can win most conflicts through negotiation and compromise.

Let's pull out everything we know, or think we know, about negotiating and compromising. We also need to drag out those emotional injuries and hang-ups that would make negotiating and compromising impossible (trust issues, pride, anger, envy, vanity, prejudices and anything else you've got back there), Let's also look at how you perceive your work and your job in order to determine how that might affect your decision making process and how you would approach the negotiations. Then we have to consider your career and what you think you need in order to be successful. You'll need to take a realistic look at how any current compromise might affect you now, and in the future. Now, at least from an intellectual perspective, you're ready to enter the negotiations. But the question becomes, are you ready emotionally? I've asked you to lay out all your extraneous baggage so you can see what you're carrying around and what is likely holding you back and preventing you from rising above the noise and confusion of the masses. These are your *"Hot Button Issues",* the very same buttons your opponent will be looking to push. You'll have to set them aside and not allow them to follow you into the negotiations, if they do, you will most likely lose.

Conflicts come in all different shapes and sizes and many seem to arise out of nowhere, while the causes of others are clear and unmistakable. But in any event, whenever there is actual conflict, you can bet that everybody involved is already operating in their defensive styles, even you. Conflicts in the workplace, burns up a lot of valuable time and human resources; they strain otherwise stable relationships and alliances and negatively impact individual morale. While conflicts may be unavoidable, you do however have choices; you can choose to get fully emotionally engaged and sit-down across the negotiating table and hash out every point of disagreement until it becomes clear that a third-party mediator has to be brought in because you and your adversary can't find any common ground. Or, you could choose to become the adult in the room and take control of the situation. The first thing you'll have to do is to bring down the temperature in the room. You have to control yourself and not allow your buttons to get pushed. It's easy to get caught up in the competition and posturing for superiority in the hierarchy; it's natural and even expected, but it doesn't help resolve the issue. Next, you have to control the emotions of your opponent. Your opponent may be marinating in their own emotional juices and may be all but blind to reason. They may even be dragging their chains over some old but festering, unrelated injury, which they have yet to reconcile; and until they do, it will manifest itself as part of their psychological and emotional baggage. This would be the same baggage that I asked you to pull out and set aside. In their defensive style, they won't be able to get beyond their emotions. You, on the other hand, have three tools at your disposal that can be used to bring them around and disarm them so you are more likely to come away with a win instead of a loss or a stalemate; which is also a loss. The first tool is to distance yourself from your own emotions, it's difficult to make your best decisions when adrenaline is coursing through your body and blood vessels are bulging on your forehead. Put things in perspective and see them for what they are. You have to develop self-control and become an unbiased thinker so you can see things clearly and not through the toxic prism of emotion. Throughout my career, I have had to rely on one of the basic tenets of Stoicism to help save me from me. It goes something like this, *if a situation, in and of itself, is not life threatening, don't allow emotions to elevate it to a position where it does become a life threatening event*. The second tool that you should have is professionalism. There is a professional code of conduct and it includes professional courtesy, ethical behavior, and mutual respect. You have to maintain your level of professionalism at all cost during a conflict, everyone on the other side will be feeling around trying to find any buttons they can push that would expose any of your vulnerabilities. And if they do, and you act out emotionally, you'll lose the advantage of professionalism and join the battle; then, they win and you lose. Your third tool is your understanding of the different operating styles. If you know their normal style of operating and you can see how they are operating in their defensive styles, you can control, or at least modify, their behavior by catering to their needs (needing to be liked, to be in charge, to be important, or to be right). You can cater to their needs without giving them what they want. By not getting emotionally involved, remaining professional and courteous and satisfying their style needs, you would have helped them to get beyond their pride and anger so you can get down to the real meat of the conflict. You, on the other hand, should have already centered yourself, long before any conflict could arise and have become confident and assured of your place within the hierarchy. You should fully understand the requirements of your job and have made an objective assessment of your powers, your areas of responsibility, and your actual authority in those areas. Conflicts arise wherever responsibilities and authorities have either not been established, have not been clearly defined or where they overlap. The best way to resolve this type of conflict is for you to take the high road and collaborate with the other party, working together to get beyond the present disagreement. Then after things settle down, get back together and negotiate and document the roles and responsibilities in that area in order to avoid a future conflict. It may require input from your manager and theirs if you can't reach agreement on your own or if it becomes a dispute over turf. Conflicts will also occur when individuals or groups are competing for limited resources; for example, people, equipment, space, services, capital, etc.,. In these instances, you may not be able to be as generous with your opponent as you would like. You have an area of responsibility in which you are expected to perform on time and within budget. You have a staff that is using the available tools in order to get the job done. And, it's your responsibility, and their expectation, that you will be a strong negotiator and use every available and ethical means to get first shot at the needed resources. This could get ugly but you still have to stay above the fray and stay professional in order to win. However, if things go against you and you don't get the needed resources, you will have to communicate that to your management and staff and get agreement on adjusting your deliverables and timelines if they were dependent upon resources that were not forthcoming. This needs to be made clear so you and your staff are not held accountable for something you could not control. There are many other types of conflicts you are likely to encounter in the workplace and we can't cover them all. However you have the tools in your possession to help you sidestep those that are trivial and win the majority of those that are relevant to your success. But there is another type of conflict you need to be aware of, and it is one you should avoid, or if possible, ignore. There are individuals in every organization that go to great lengths to call attention to themselves. They do everything within their power to be in the center of things, and they believe that the best way to get the attention they crave is to constantly be embroiled in every kind of *visible* dispute or confrontation. They are self-promoting troublemakers. In their minds they believe they are demonstrating their value and importance to upper management, that without their constant intervention everything within the organization would go awry because no one else in the organization has their commitment to the job and dedication to the company. You know who they are, and so does upper management. If they report to you, it becomes your responsibility to get them under control because they are negatively impacting the organization at large. If they don't report to you, it becomes someone else's problem; but you still have to keep your distance because they see every interaction as an opportunity to self-promote at the expense of everyone else.

You also need to be aware and be able to recognize that there are some conflicts that are unwinnable. And if you find that that's the case, it's best to cut your losses and give ground if it will minimize further damage. Even when your opponent is a rational individual, in some instances common ground is unattainable; you simply have irreconcilable positions, or you and/or your opponent have a private agenda that is causing the impasse.

Chapter # 12:

Situational Leadership
The Developmental Continuum

The Maestro and the Tyrannical Boss are probably the two most extreme examples of bad managers you are likely to encounter over your career; but what about the remaining managers (you included), what kind of manager are you? When you look at those managers you've admired and try to emulate, what is it about them that draws you in? When I ask myself that question, I find that I am struck by their ability to maintain an even keel and remain extremely flexible under some of the most adverse conditions. They remain confident and stay cool under fire. But even more impressive is their ability to communicate to, and manage, people with vastly different operating styles and knowledge levels intuitively. They know each of the individuals on their staff, their development levels, their motivators, and their limitations. And when it comes down to human interactions, they know that one approach does not fit all. They tailor their interactions, assignments and directions specifically to the individual and not to the masses. On a broader stage this is considered *Situational Leadership*, and these managers know that if they are to get the most out of people, they have to lead them in such a way that they can follow and *will* follow their lead and directions.

Let's be clear here, there are any number of reasons why managers fail, and without trying to explain them all, it comes down to a lack of performance on their part; because work didn't get done. And when you distill why the work didn't get done, it comes down to one of two reasons: you or your staff were *unable* to do the work, or you or your staff were *unwilling* to do the work...in rare cases it can be a combination of both. Needless to say that from a senior management perspective the whys are unimportant, the fact is, you failed; and that's how you'll be judged.

Let's take a good look at these two causes of failure; *unable to do the work* and *unwilling to do the work*. Every manager would like to think that their staff is always ready, able and willing to take on any assignment. But in reality, that is not always the case. Other managers believe that they can push any project through to completion with the sheer force of their will and dominance over their staff...that approach won't always work either. What will work and serve you far better is your understanding of your staff and where they fall along the *Developmental Continuum*. Okay, now what the hell is that!??! Well, it's something we are going to make up to give us a visual reference so we can track where each of our staffers are with respect to their productivity and job performance. It will help us get a better understanding of what their development needs happen to be and let us know what we have to do in order to meet those needs. For example, if your staff is both willing and able to do the work they don't have any developmental needs, they only need leadership. But if your staff is able to do the work but is unwilling to do so, they will need to be motivated and managed. If you have a staff that is willing to do the work but is unable, you have to provide them the tools and training they need to get the job done; another opportunity that requires you to manage. The last possibility is a case where you have a staff that is unwilling and unable to do the work. If that were the case, then you would have a real problem. You'll likely never find a situation like that (outside of a correctional facility) but if you did, it would require you to become a boss. You would have to pay close attention to every action at every step along the way. In addition to close oversight, you would have to provide a sufficient amount of training so the staff will know what is expected of them and when. And in addition, you will need to provide some form of incentives to get the staff to do work that they wouldn't otherwise do. We will talk more about motivational incentives when we get to the chapter entitle "The Responsibilities of the Manager", in the section entitle "Adapting Man to Your Needs".

To make it a bit more visual, I've put our Developmental Continuum into a table so we can get a better handle on what we need to do in order to meet the needs of our staff, so that they can follow and *will* follow our directions.

Developmental Continuum:

Stage of Development	Developmental Needs	How to Manage at this Stage of Development
#1. People in development stage one are both able and willing to do the work at hand.	None	Don't try to manage or boss these people, they will resist you. They require Leadership; someone that defines the task and any particulars along with the time frame for completion. Then they need for you to get out of their way so they can do the job. You need only monitor their progress.
#2. People in development stage two are able to do the work but are unwilling to do so.	An employee at stage #2 requires motivating. There may be any number of reasons why people would be reluctant to do work. The work could be considered menial and beneath them, tedious and unimportant, dirty or even unsafe. If the employee has been in the job for a while they may no longer find the work stimulating or challenging. Or, the employee could be experiencing a personal crisis at home.	This person and their productivity will have to be managed. Because every situation is different, you as their manager should work to find the right motivational drivers to get this person up and running. Dependent upon your amount of latitude within the organization, you could offer cross-training to a different job, provide some additional incentive, coaching and counseling, or anything else that you deem to be fair and reasonable that will motivate them. But in the final analysis, this is their job and there should be no doubt in their minds that you have a clear expectation that they will do the work; otherwise, you will have to plan for a different kind of discussion.
#3. People in development stage three are willing to do the work but are unable to do so.	An employee at stage #3 requires training and/or the essential tools of the job before they are able to make a contribution. As a manager, you have to determine the level of training that is required, how that training should be provided and who should do the training. The manager also has the responsibility of providing the right tools that are needed in order to allow the employee to do the work. Tools can be anything from computers and databases, equipment such as hand or machine tools, a pad and pencil or just some placed to sit-down to do the work.	People at stage #3 have to be managed much closer than those at stage #2. While they are very happy and willing to do the work, they don't have the knowledgebase, familiarity and expertise with the work or the tools to be left on their own. For those of you that are micromanagers, this is where you can shine. You should give these employees clear step-by-step instructions on how to proceed with the work. The work should also be compartmentalized so they can check-in with you after completing one step before going on to the next. Remember that you are working with the aspirational being while working with this employee, so you should be constructive and generous with your positive feedback. **A note to the micromanager:** *This is the only time or place where micromanagement is welcomed, you will be resisted and reviled everywhere else.*
#4. People at development stage four have no place in the workforce. They are neither willing nor able to do the work.	If you have an employee at development stage four, your problems are many. Their development needs are both training and motivational. But the amount of work that will have to be invested exceeds all reasonable expectations for any manager. Cut your losses and move on.	These people require the over site of the Tyrannical Boss; for example, in a prison setting, and even then, they will have to be handled with chains.

Development Stage #1:

Our visual representation of the Developmental Continuum shows us that the ideal employees (those that are at development stage #1) don't require a manager; a manager will
only get in the way. They are looking for leadership; someone that defines the objectives,
expectations and determines a time frame. Then, they want the leader to get out of the
way so they can do the work. This is the stage of development that every manager should
be working to get all of their employees to. For the most part, if you have been mindful of
your employee's aspirational needs, as well as their hidden competitive and baser natures,
most of your employees will reach development stage #1. But in the real world, things
don't always go as they should. How many of you have seen or have been part of a group
or department that was highly tuned and running like a well oil machine, and then, have to
deal with a change in management? You feel that you have just gotten your current manager trained so they stay out of the way, then within short-order they take a promotion
or have moved on in their careers. And, before you can turnaround, a brand-new jack-ass
hits the ground; you could be that jack-ass! We have all seen it…time-after-time; the new
insecure manager comes in and mucks-up the works by imposing themselves on the work
or into the processes. The manager underestimates the intelligence of their most skilled
and motivated people or they determine that they have to get their fingerprints on the
work; else senior management might think that they are not effective or is superfluous to
the process and not needed. Experience has shown me that when you dive headlong into a
situation that you know little about you usually get the *wrong* first impressions, make bad
decisions, and ruffle feathers that will be difficult to put back in place. You have time, the
department is not going to self-destruct; it will run on autopilot until you have a chance
to get the lay of the land, understand the process, get to know the staff and their levels of
expertise, find out who the leaders are and who follows. Successful managers stand back
and monitor the progress of their staffers and only make themselves available to them
if there are questions requiring guidance or if help is needed to resolve issues with the
work; they never micromanage. They know that motivated, skilled and knowledgeable
employees need to have a certain degree of freedom and latitude in their work in order
to maintain their pride and self-esteem. When the micromanager curtails that freedom,
morale suffers and the workers will become apathetic and will move from development
stage #1 to stage #2.

Development Stage #2:

In the example above, I have assumed that your staffers were all at development stage # 1. But the approach I suggested would also be valid for a mixed staff (those at development stages #1 & #2). If there are morale problems among your staff, you have to give yourself the time needed to identify where and what they are. You can't make snap judgements and move off in a direction or take actions that were not indicated. If you do, you will step in it every time. And when the *new* manager steps in it, it takes a long time for the odour to go away; and, everybody will know it. So take your time to understand your department, your people, and your job before attempting to put your mark on your department. But when your tenure is not new and you notice a loss in morale or employees becoming apathetic you have a responsibility to them and to the company to do everything that is fair and reasonable to get things back on track. Your employees are your company's most valuable resource and in most cases it takes very little to stimulate and re-invigorate your people and get them to move from development stage #2 back to stage #1. But you have to stay vigilant and not allow a small slight or wound to fester and turn into open revolt. In most instances, you will only be working to motivate one or two employees at any given time; but, managing with the soft skills is a process that is always on-going. There is just one other point that I would like to make here, that is, as their manager you should have a wide degree of latitude in what you can do to improve morale in the workplace, but I would stay as far away as possible from any non-work or personal matter the employee might be experiencing. These matters are usually very sensitive and sticky and you are not qualified to handle them. Your job is the company's work, not social work. The company expects both you and your employees to perform your duties and maintain productivity regardless of the state of morale. Managers, you don't get a free pass because morale is low, however, if productivity suffers because of it, you might get replaced.

Development Stage #3:

In a dynamic work environment employees are moving between one development stage to another based largely on how they see themselves within the company's hierarchy; how they perceive they are being treated and their perception of their own self-worth. The majority of your employees should be at development stage #1. But they can move from stage #1 to stage #3 and back to stage #1 without ever having to go through stage #2. At stage #3 the employee is willing to do the work but is unable. We like to think of a stage #3 employee as a new hire; very eager to do the work but lacking the training to do so. And while this is true for new employees, the majority of stage #3 employees are your best performers (at stage #1) that have been given the opportunity to train in a different area and take on new responsibilities. Training and an opportunity to take on new skills can be a powerful tool that the manager has at their disposal that can move a stage #2 employee to stage #3 and back to stage #1. But the reverse is also true; we can't lose sight of the fact that there is an on-going competition among our employees, and if a stage #1 employee believes they have been passed over for training and recognition in favor of someone else, your stage #1 employee could quickly become stage #2. Therefore, the selection requirements for higher skilled and even management jobs should be *out in the open* and available for review by your entire work force. The qualifications for consideration should be clear and should include: the current needs of the company, the employee's performance and length of service, attendance, current skill sets, related work experience, formal education, and the employees desire to transfer to a new work arrangement. The selection process must **never** be influenced by nepotism, race, religion, creed, color, national origin, gender, or sexual orientation. If an employee or group of employees believe that they have been unfairly treated due to biases in selections for training and career development, they become problems for the company. They lose faith in the selection process and start to resent you (their managers), their work, and eventually the company. This is clearly not a condition that contributes to, or is compatible with the creation and maintenance of a stable, productive work environment.

Development Stage #4:

Any further discussion around managing people at development stage #4 is beyond the scope of this work.

To Recap:

Managers fail because they don't perform and they don't perform because they are ineffective managers. The type and quantity of work that passes through a department or organization is, for the most part, relatively stable and unchanging, but the human dynamics are always in a state of flux due to competition and posturing. Therefore, a manager has to be able to tailor their management style and approach to the situation and development stage of the people involved. At development stage #1 leadership is required, at stage #2, motivational management is called for, and at stage #3 the manager is required to provide the necessary tools and/or training for the employee to be a success. If you manage to the situation you will succeed and your operation will run smoothly, but if you are out of step and try to lead employees at stage #3 or try to train employees at stage #1, or any other counter indicated combination you will create confusion and you will fail.

Now let's move the discussion to Power, Responsibility, and Authority.

Chapter # 13:

Power, Responsibility and Authority

Many managers fail because they don't take full advantage of the power they have been given, others fail because they abuse their power, and yet some others will fail because they did not understand the full scope of their areas of responsibilities, and still others fail because they have accepted responsibility but was not given the authority needed to succeed. Any, and all, of these failures will put your career into a tailspin. Managers have the responsibility for making things happen and getting things done. Things just don't happen spontaneously, they require some form of ignition, some force in order to get them moving in the right direction; that force is power...*managerial power*. We will talk responsibility and authority farther down, but let's start our discussion with power.

Power:

A lot of very smart people have devoted their lives to the study of the forces that we collectively call power. And while there may be many different schools of thought and conflicting thesis's on what power actually is, there seems to be some agreement that there are only "4" different types or branches to the tree of power. The four distinctive types of real power are: *Position Power, Financial Power (or Economic Power), Political Power and Physical Force,* though in some venues, there is an argument for a fifth power; *Perceived Power.* Perceived power is the illusion of power. Perceived power, while not universally considered to be a real power, does have its impact in our day-to-day lives as well as in our workplaces and social settings. It is manifested in the larger than life images we project of ourselves so others will believe that we are higher in the hierarchy than we actually are. Perceived power can mimic any of the 4 actual powers but it has a very short shelf-life. Though, if perceived power is projected at the right time, in the right place, and to the right audience, you can control a given situation by causing people to believe that you actually have one or more of the 4 real powers. We will talk more on perceived power later.

For demonstrative purposes, let's start at the highest possible levels of power, where all the real powers have their origins and where there is no need to project perceived power; and that would be at the Nation-State level. At this level, Kings, Queens, Prime Ministers, Presidents, and Dictators have all four powers concentrated in a single location. They can raise armies in order to go to war and subjugate an external enemy or direct their armies to put down internal insurrections (*physical force*), they can levy taxes, exploit natural resources, nationalize industries, and stockpile capital resources in order to finance their armies and to commission large public works projects (*financial power*), because of their high rank they can appoint others to high ranking positions of power and authority in order to carry out their agendas (*position power*), and because they control the nation's media, they can control, or exercise significant influence over national propaganda which allows them to control what the populous thinks. The ability to control *"group think"* allows them to placate the masses and keep them in line and willing to follow their leadership (*political power*). The next step down is the state and local government level. Here, the powers remain consolidated, though weaker and not as absolute; they can still be challenged on the national level and instead of armies, state and local governments have established state militias or guards, and police departments to respond to local emergencies and to maintain law and order.

The third step down is where we find the corporations and the independently wealthy. The corporations and the independently wealthy have far less power than the nation-state or local governments and any ability to exert physical force has been taken away completely (except in failed states where War Lords have their own personal armies). Albeit on a much smaller scale, corporations and the independently wealthy still have a significant amount of financial power, position power and political power within the arenas where they compete. In a free society, corporations are the driving force behind domestic and international commerce. And like everything else, the real power, particularly financial power in a corporation is concentrated at its top, at the level of the Board of Directors, the CEO and Sr. Leaders. When we get down to the level where we are, and where we operate (level four), most of the real power has been either taken away or greatly diluted and all that remains are position power, political power and very little financial power. We have a small amount of position power and even less financial power because, in the scheme of things, we operate in a very small domain relative to the size of the greater organization. Our political power is generally limited and only extends to our subordinates, peer groups, and our manager. So let's scrape all our real powers together and see what we've got...we have position power that was given to us by the company that allows us to supervise the work of other employees. If we have any responsibility for hiring or departmental budgeting, we would also be able to claim some small amount of financial power. But we should note at this point that our position and financial powers were given to us by the company. Our political power (if any) is wholly dependent upon our ability to lead and influence, build alliances, and garner trust so that others will follow. Our level of political power is limited to our own little bailiwick and those in our immediate surroundings. But it is critically important to note here that political power (*people power*) is by far the strongest of all the real powers. It is not something that is given or bestowed by divine rite; it has to be carefully cultivated and kept current and relevant. I will leave for others to argue the powers they believe to be the strongest and most important, but from where I stand, there is no question. Those that have devoted their lives to the study of power and its acquisition will all agree that once you have acquired one of the powers in a dictatorship, a monarchy, or a democracy, it becomes that much easier to acquire them all. I would argue that you could lose your mighty army and still retain your wealth, position and political influence. You could lose your wealth and retain your position, your army and political influence. And in many cases, you could even lose your position and retain your army, your wealth and your political influence. But once you lose the support of the people, *your political power*, you lose it all. Just look around the world, whenever the people lose faith or confidence in their leaders they rebel. And when they do, no amount of force or money or august titles can save them. Managers, you have been given position power and some financial power, but you have to acquire your own political power. And, that is the whole purpose of this work and other works on the subject; to help you learn the interpersonal skills, techniques and strategies that have proven to be fundamental to the development of political power. But, I say again, you must use common sense in order to gain and retain political power. Just one more thing for the novice manager: *Yes*, your company fully expects your department or group to run smoothly, therefore, it was not set up or modelled on a democracy, it is expected to run like a quasi-dictatorship, with you at its head. If you thought otherwise, just look around and count the number of times anyone decided to take a vote on how, or whether to do the work at hand. Just remember that dictators and quasi-dictators will continue to lead and even flourish as long as they have the support of the people. You just have to avoid making yourself hated!

Responsibility:

Let's move on to your areas of responsibility, which is another area that causes managers to fail. When managers take on the responsibility for an area they don't always fully understand the true scope of their assignment. Frequently they are given an abstract top-down and very general description of their responsibilities from someone in Human Resources, their manager or someone the manager has assigned. But in each case the information will be conveyed by someone that has a detailed knowledge of the performance expectations and the areas of responsibilities. The person will likely talk in 'corporate speak' and only address the most obvious requirements of the job while avoiding any detail. You will also be given a generalized job description that won't make the scope or requirements of the job any clearer. You need the details. No one is expecting you to ask for details during your initial walk-through and orientation, and let's face it, you won't know enough about the position to even pose the right questions anyway. But you need to find a way to get your head and your hands around your new job. Therefore, during your initial orientation you should let your manager know that you would like to schedule a second or even a third meeting to go over some of the finer points of your responsibilities. Don't just sit there smiling and nodding your head as if you have everything under control because people will believe you and come away thinking that you're a fast study and is up to speed on everything; and you won't be. You're not that smart. Here is the danger...some responsibilities are apparent and intuitive and that's where you'll naturally focus your attention. But other responsibilities can be obscured and go unnoticed until they get out of control or cause you political damage. Consider this; during the transition between one manager and the next, some parts of the department can run for a while on autopilot and in other cases some of your department's responsibilities would be picked up by other managers to prevent any losses in productivity. And while you have focused your full attention on the obvious and apparent, those things that were put on autopilot have been getting further and further off course. They only get brought to your attention, and you become aware that they are your responsibilities, when they become a problem for the company. The other possibility is where other departments and managers have provided support and have filled in by taking on some of the responsibilities of your department during your transition. Once you get your feet on the ground, they will expect you to start taking back those responsibilities. But if you didn't know that they fell under your jurisdiction you won't take any action. Then, more often than not, these peers will probably not say anything to you, but they will complain to their managers and yours. In both these instances, the first impression you made was to lead people to believe that you had everything under control. Now you have made a second impression because you really didn't know the full scope of your area of responsibility. I wonder how much either of these missteps will cost you in political capital.

This has only been a discussion of responsibilities as they apply to the physical scope of the job or assignment. We have yet to discuss the tremendous responsibilities that come with managing, directing, and controlling the human being. But we will have those discussions as we move through some of the person-to-person interactions between the manager and their staff, the manager and their peers, and the manager and their manager.

Authority:

Let's turn our attention to authority. Authority is the life's blood of all of the powers, without it, you really don't have any powers at all. Authority is the permission that allows you to use a given power. It originates from the very top levels of the organization and is born alongside the powers within the organization. Authority does not change as you move down in the organization, you either have authority or you don't. What does change is the degree of power you have at any given level. Authority places limits on when, where, and how you can use your powers. It's intended to act as the initiating force that commissions work, and it also serves as a company safeguard, established to prevent the misuse of power. Nearly all companies have some form of written documentation that sets out a *Code of Conduct*; a set of company guidelines, a set of best practices or some other system established to prevent the abuse of power by unauthorized means. In the absence of anything written by your company, there are well known ethical standards, social norms, and established labor practices that have been established and are intended to help us avoid unauthorized abuses of power. But we do it anyway, and that causes us to fail as managers and as human beings. Power corrupts, and if we lose control, our baser and competitive natures will overwhelm our aspirational selves and before long we'll find we've misused our position power and/or financial authorities and have garnered the loathing of our subordinates, peers and probably even our manager. Managers rarely, if ever, recover from a selfish misuse of their authority. Once it's discovered, it destroys just about all the political capital that you may have banked; and without political power, you're just an empty suit and just in the way.

We have looked at what authority is, and how it can lead to failure when it is abused. So now, let's talk about authority and career suicide. Whenever any manager accepts responsibility for any department, project, or any undertaking without having the authority to exercise the powers necessary to bring it to a satisfactory conclusion, they would have failed long before ever getting started. You should never accept responsibility for anything without having the proper authority to exercise the powers needed to get the assignment done. I know that some of you are currently reporting to weak managers, deceptive, and micromanagers that will assign you responsibility for various projects but won't give you the authority you need in order to *independently* see them through. Whenever that happens, they are setting you up to fail. If they keep the real power and authority at their level, you are left impotent and subject to the whims of your subordinates and peers. Your subordinates and peers aren't blind; they can see that you have no power or authority. And beyond the common courtesies that they would afford to any figurehead, you're just in the way, and all but ignored. They will circumvent you at every turn. Your manager will bypass you, leaving you out of the loop and go directly to your staff and peers. Your manager will even countermand your directions in order to assure that even those staffers living under rocks knows who is really in charge. And none of their actions will be recorded or documented so they could be referred to and attributed to them later. Go back to the mirror we were looking in earlier…and take a good long look; you're looking at *the Fall Guy, the Designated Felon,* but you probably already knew that. But did you also know that there is no way for you to win, short of refusing the assignment. And of course, that would lead to additional complications for your career. But what are your other choices? Your weak, deceptive, and *"Alpha-dog"* micromanager knows precisely what they're doing; they're keeping you at a disadvantage and in your place. They've got you where you're not a threat to them, and in a position where there is not even the slightest possibility of career growth. If your project is a success, your manager will step forward and accept the recognition, and if it fails, then it was your failure because…it was your project. But regardless of the outcome, at your performance review there will be a few positive bullet points followed by a large section detailing where you were deficient in the areas of management and leadership. Note that you were given the responsibility but never the authority to either manage or lead. As you come away from the review, you should forget about your promotional prospects because they just went to zero. Your manager is concerned with their own career growth, not yours. I know that this is a very difficult situation to find yourself in, and *"No";* there are no easy ways out. But if you accept responsibility without having authority you are destine for failure. And for those that are wondering, *"Yes",* I'm speaking from experience.

At this point, I think that we should have enough of the basic background material and supporting management tools to go into our first Case Study. So let's move on.

Chapter # 14:

About the Author
Case Study #1

In this section, I will start by giving you a brief snapshot of my professional background because it will make an excellent segue into our first case study.

Though I am retired now, I've had what I would consider to have been, a very interesting, diverse, and rewarding career. My formal training was in the sciences, but I truly enjoy the arts and have always tried to make time for them whenever possible. I have held positions of leadership in some of the larger consumer products companies in the United States. I have held positions in Product Development, Quality Assurance & Control, Regulatory & Governmental Affairs, International Technical Services, and a few others. I stayed active in many of the industry trade associations and have been honored to have had the opportunity to serve as Chairperson on some select committees. I served as a non-governmental delegate on United States Delegations to international trade committee meetings hosted by governments around the world, and I was recruited by the Food and Agriculture Organization of the United Nations (FAO) to join them in a consultant capacity in Rome, Italy.

However, my professional career didn't start out on such a positive note. In fact, it almost crashed and burned before it could even get off the ground. The following is a recount of the challenges I was confronted with on my very first professional assignment.

Case Study # 1:

Reader, note that as we get into the meat of this case study it becomes an exercise in _Root Cause Analysis, Problem Solving and Decision Making, as well as Situational Leadership_. As we move through, you will see the problems, the cause of the problems, the decisions that were made in order to resolve the problems, and the managerial leadership that was used to turn things around. These, and similar problems, will become a recurring theme as presented in this case study, our first Scenario, and in Case Study #2, you'll need to study them and be able to resolve them because they *will* emerge at some point in your career.

My first professional job was at a company that was undergoing a significant cultural and technological transformation. They recognized that their future depended on their ability to recruit and retain a new breed of management level employee; people that were strong scientifically and technologically savvy. They realized that there was not enough time to grow the skills and technologies they needed from within while still staying competitive in their industry. So they undertook a major recruiting effort to bring in the talent that they needed from the outside. I was among those recruits and was a part of the first group put through what they called, their *Fast-track Management Program* (all college graduates). The training that we were given was intense; there was classwork, in-house and off-site seminars and internships. Once those were over, came round 2 and then round 3 of additional seminars, classwork, and more internships. The company made a considerable dollar investment in each of us before we were assigned to a field location; training took about a year. At the conclusion of my training I was assigned to a field location in the mid-west. But when I got there I was surprised to find that the amount of animosity and hostility directed toward me was palpable; I was not wanted. There was nothing personal about it or special unto me, all of my classmates, at every location were confronted with the same level of resentment; this went across the board. Quite a few in my class decided that the amount of resistance they had to endure just wasn't worth it and many left the company before completing their first year in the field. I was poor, had a family with a mountain of debt from school loans and less than a thousand dollars in the bank; so I didn't have that option. I had to stick it out.

It turned out that there was *absolutely no support* for the program that I was part of (this Scientific and Technological Renaissance) anywhere in the field. In fact, the reverse was true; the field locations were diametrically opposed to it. The corporation and field were like a house divided and we represented the first shots in the culture war. People, in general, don't respond well to change, and when that change is likely to have a negative impact on their security and their place within the hierarchy, they immediately confront and resist it.

And there I was, the new kid on the block and the manifest object of their contempt. I was resented by my staff because I was an outsider. One of my senior staff members was all but consumed with rage at my arrival…I found out later that historically supervisors and managers were promoted from within, and I was appointed to the position they felt was rightfully theirs. I was disliked by my manager because he saw me and the company's Fast-track Management Program as a direct threat to his career prospects, because he was not part of it, nor did he support it. Things were tough and would only be getting tougher. Even though my name was embroidered on my lab coat, my manager and the old guard (other managers at the facility) and even some of the hourly employees would refer to me as *"The College Boy"*, and no, it was not said with any degree of reverence.

When a company undertakes to change its culture, it's generally a slow and painful process. But when change is imposed rapidly and from the outside, while it is achievable, it will likely have far more devastating consequences. In this case, the company's leaders felt they had only two alternatives; they could choose to move quickly and incur all the expense and disruption to the organization, or they could elect to try growing their needed scientific and technological resources organically, thereby risking additional losses of market share and further damage to their brands. The company made a business decision and opted for the former. As a consequence, me and my fellow recruits were the first to hit the ground at the field locations, where we represented the opening salvo of the company's culture war.

A very large portion of what I've learned about human nature, human motivators, and the deceptive nature of man came from working with my manager at that field location. And I don't say that with any sarcasm or cynicism but it's truly ironic that the man (an old guard manager), the person that did everything he could to discredit me and the Fast-track Program; the one that tried to get me fired and the program cancelled was one of the best teachers I ever had (save Miss McNeil, my kindergarten teacher). He opened my eyes and taught me about trust, honesty, honor, ethics, and morality, and he was totally devoid of all of them. Up until that point in my life, I had never seen such a master at work. He was the most deceptive, self-serving, craven little urchin I had ever seen. He would do whatever was necessary to promote himself while grinding his staff under his boot and simultaneously stabbing a colleague in the back. He was remarkable, and while he could never be trusted, for anything, he truly impressed me. When I looked at him I saw the Cheshire Cat from Alice in Wonderland, a big wide smile and a mouth full of teeth. But behind that smile was the body of a serpent with a rattle at its end. Now while I'm being somewhat dramatic here, I don't want any of you to read this and start comparing your guy to mine; that's not why I put this here. You will find a little of my guy in everyone you meet, but rarely will you find it all concentrated in a single individual. My guy was remarkable, he was a case study in *pride, avarice, gluttony, fraud, envy, entitlement, deception, and narcissism*. And on top of all of that, he was extremely intelligent and very shrewd. I was convinced that if he were a chameleon, he would have had no trouble doing *plaid*. That was my assessment of my manager and the environment I found myself in as a very weak and vulnerable newcomer to the professional stage. And while I have been a bit facetious in my description of him, I really don't want to understate the important role that man had in my career and my life. In fact, were it not for my exposure to him, I don't think I would have enjoyed the level of success that I've had over the course of my career, and I'm certain I wouldn't be as attuned to the baser nature of human beings as I am today. He was an excellent teacher and all I had to do was to stay out of his reach and just observe him; and for that, I am grateful. Lastly, without my experiences with him, I wouldn't have been able to write this book. I will say again, people do their best to only reveal their aspirational selves and they try to hide their competitive and baser beings. But when you come across someone that is either unable or unwilling to hide their selfish depravity, don't be repulsed by them and turn away, study them and learn from them; they are displaying what others are concealing. You will never get anywhere near that level of learning from any books, training courses, or seminars.

Now let's get back to me, so let's see...ok, now the stage is set, you have all the background and the setting to what almost cost me my career. I came on-board under the conditions mentioned. And under the circumstances, I thought I was doing a good job. I thought, while not being a "great manager", I thought I was doing "ok". I would come in in the mornings and assess the work and special projects for the day's activities, assign my staffers to specific jobs and then I would retreat into my office where I would spend the first 2 hours on the phone with suppliers, contractors, and with headquarters staff. I would spend the next 2 hours doing paperwork while hoping to be able to get through it without interruptions, but there was always an issue or a crisis that pulled me away. After lunch I would walk back through my department, in-route to the sanctuary of my office. And in my mind, if no one flagged me down about a problem, then there were no problems. I would complete my paperwork, catch up on missed calls, and then at around 3 o'clock, I would head off to whatever meeting was posted to my schedule (production, quality, safety, management, etc.). When I returned around 5 or 6 PM my dayshift staff would have left for the day and the second shift would be on duty. I would ask my senior technicians if there was anything that I should be aware of or if there were any problems, and if the answer was no, I would head back to my office. If there was a problem I would come up with a quick fix and then head back to my office. I would check for any new messages, posted notes and missed calls so I could have them top-of-mind for the next day. Then I would leave for the night. Does any of this sound familiar to you...is this how you're managing, or think you're managing? I was naïve, and based on my management training, my book learning, and my lack of understanding as to what a real manager's responsibilities were, I thought I was doing a good job. I was the Analytical Services Supervisor and was frequently responsible for the Process Control Analytics as well. But when you take a look at my day, I would only devote about 30 minutes on the floor in the laboratory, while the lion's share of my time was caught up in the company's bureaucracy. I wasn't managing anything, my department was on autopilot and I was asleep at the switch. I didn't wake up until about 8 months later when I received a phone call from my manager, while I was on vacation. He called to inform me that my microbiology technician had been caught manufacturing test results for materials he should have tested but didn't. Maybe it was my paranoia, but even through the telephone I could sense that Cheshire Cat grin getting wider and wider and I could have sworn I could hear a slight rattle in the background. In an analytical or scientific lab, there is no greater offense than falsifying data. My technician had forfeited his job, **full stop**, there's no need for further discussion here! Falsifying or manufacturing any type of analytics is a career capital offense punishable by the career death penalty. And, this is directed to those of you that are new to management and to you want-to-be managers...though I was away on vacation at the time of the incident, it was still my responsibility for the accuracy of the analytics because that was my job, and because the microbiology technician reported in through me, it was my failing. And, as many of you would have already guessed, this represented another sizable nail in my coffin.

I cut short my vacation and returned to the facility. The first thing I did was to collect all the relevant information with respect to the investigation. Then, I took an axe to the time I spent caught up in the bureaucracy; cutting it back to less that 50% of my day. Then, I took a week and conducted a full scale audit of the entire laboratory and our records. When I had completed the audit and based upon my findings, if I had been my manager, I would have fired me on the spot. So, why didn't he? Well for one thing, the *College Boy* was part of the new program (that he pretended to support) and was relatively new in the position having only been in the job for less than a year. But I think it was something else, you see, there was a lot of desk pounding and ranting and raving about unacceptable performance and dereliction of duty before I had completed my audit. Then, it all tended to fade away once it became clear that most of the non-compliance issues that I found dated as far back as to his tenure in the position and persisted throughout his time as laboratory manager. Clearly, someone must have, or should have known about these problems and should have taken actions to correct them, including me. My guess is the corporate leadership may have known or suspected there were problems and that may have been why they wanted to bring in new blood in order to change the apathetic culture at the field locations. The results of the audit exposed a myriad of problems, both tangible and intangible. Among the tangible problems the audit found that people were poorly trained for the jobs they were doing, chemical reagents were being improperly handled, stored, and often times contaminated, equipment was improperly calibrated, or once calibrated the calibrations were made null and void by unauthorized and anonymous adjustments, records were poorly maintained (incomplete, illegible and/or improperly filed), samples were not routinely being pulled aseptically, many of the specifications and test procedures being used were outdated and no longer valid. The audit also showed that there was general dysfunction among the lab's personnel. Therefore, the intangible problems included a significant amount of hostility among the staff directed at each other, toward the company, and toward me and my manager. How could I have missed all of that?

Now, to make a long story even longer, I tackled the tangible problems first; it took about a month to get all the current specifications and testing procedures in-house and in their respective manuals and being referenced correctly. It also took about a month to get in a fresh set of calibration standards and chemical reagents. I had to rewrite job descriptions to better reflect the duties of each position as well as many of the standard operational procedures (SOPs), which took about 2 months. It took another month to make sure that everyone (on all 3 shifts) were properly trained to perform the required testing and to assure that records were being properly filled out and securely stored, the staff had to be retrained on how to handle chemical reagents, calibration standards, and to take aseptic samples. At around the third month I was ready to take on the intangibles. I arranged for an all-day departmental off-site meeting to address the areas of discontent and hostility. During the off-site, I discovered that there were a considerable number of problematic issues that ranged from conflicts between the laboratory shifts, disputes between the lab personnel and other departments, working hours and conditions, low morale, and up to and including my apparent lack of leadership and interest in the lab's day-to-day operations and its people. This was back in the days before laptops so we used posted notes and easels with those large pads of paper that we could tape to the walls. I acted as the facilitator and after an independent 2 hour purge we had covered the walls with paper and posted notes containing every complaint that anyone (about 40 people) thought was noteworthy. After eliminating the duplicates, we were still left with around 200, or so, complaints. Then we got democratic and ranked the complaints according to their significance and merit. We had to be realistic; we couldn't tackle all 200 so we had to agree on which ones were important enough to require action and which ones didn't. Using a show of hands and getting agreement from the authors of the complaints, about 75 were relegated to the back burner leaving us with around 125 to work through. Our next sort was to identify those items that were out of our control and could not be changed; about 30 items were identified that were principally structural and regulatory requirements dictated by a governmental agency or by the corporation. Then we compiled another list of about 30 items that were within my (or my manager's) jurisdiction to act upon. The list included grievances about the way the lab was set up, scheduling, workflow, leadership and employee recognition, the lack of timely communications, morale and team-building and training opportunities available to employees. The last list of actionable items for which we had agreement, and which was by far the longest, containing around 65 complaint items. The items on this list primarily dealt with how individuals went about their day-to-day assignments and the interactions between them, the need to demonstrate mutual respect, the need for more open communications between the shifts and with other departments, and the need to build greater trust through teamwork. It was clear to my staff that all the items on the list were firmly in *their* wheelhouse and they agreed to take ownership of those items and, with my support, form working groups to resolve them.

The off-site went a long way toward clearing the air, restoring morale and reducing the level of stress and hostility within the department. Frankly, it took a lot of weight off my shoulders and helped me find my actual responsibilities as a manager. At the start of the off-site there was general agreement that every problem in the lab, and everything that was wrong *was my fault*; all 200 issues. At its conclusion, people accepted the fact that some things were set in stone and controlled by regulations or corporate mandates and were out of our control. In addition, they began to recognize that most of the injuries they suffered were self-inflicted, not of my doing, and were well within their purview to correct. And when it came to all the problems they wanted to drop at the doorstep of management, the list, while important, was a lot shorter than anyone might have guessed. The final point I want to make about the off-site was that it gave people an opportunity to vent, to be heard, and it allowed them to get to know me on a more personal level; and not just see me as the guy sitting in the office.

I was able to have our forward actions from the off-site written-up and passed out to every-one about a week or so later. I reiterated my willingness to support the individual working groups where needed and if called upon. As for me, of the 30 complaints that were in my bailiwick, we agreed that 6 of them should be left as they were because they were essential to the lab's operation and we couldn't come up with any suitable alternatives. So in the final analysis, instead of having 200 complaints and grievances *that were my fault*, I was left with ownership of 24. And when you consider what they were asking, they were the things that separated the good managers from the bad, and I had been a bad one. For example, they wanted me to take an interest in the work and the people; provide mentoring and coaching and counselling; provide clear, transparent, and open communications; establish objective guidelines required for career development, and so on. And with respect to the other 75 complaints that were put on the back burner, well they really never needed addressing. Because by us dealing with the actionable ones, they seem to just evaporate and were found to be more personal irritants than legitimate complaints.

Needless to say, I began to spend the majority of my time on the lab floor with my staff on all 3 shifts. I began managing by walking around even before I knew there was such a thing. A manager has to be flexible and adaptable, be able to move from one activity, objective, or priority to another and back again with ease. They must also demonstrate an ability to con-nect with people. If you are managing equipment or systems, its "ok" to sit in your office, but if you manage people, it won't work. In my case, I wasn't a manager, I wasn't managing anything. I, like many of you had missed the orientation to Management 101 where you were given a detailed overview of what management entails and the true scope of your management responsibilities; particularly the part that deals with managing people. I either missed it or it was not clearly spelled out, or it was not covered at all. In retrospect, I don't think I gave it much thought at all. I came away from my orientation and management training thinking that, as a manager, I had two separate and distinct jobs. The first, and where I was to focus the majority of my efforts, was on the bureaucratic and administrative aspects of management. The second, the one that I put on and left on autopilot, was managing the people and activities of the department. I thought I was doing a pretty-good job; I was in all the right meetings, I took all the relevant training courses, and I tried to mimic the styles of other managers around me. But, I had abdicated the managerial portion of my job and was avoiding my staff...and they knew it. What about you...how are things on your end; have you found the right balance between the administrative and the managerial?

There is far more to this story but we don't have room for it here. However, there was one other hurdle I had to get over before I could drag myself completely out of the hole I was in. As I have already stated, the falsification of microbiological records was the trigger that got everything started. The corporate microbiologists had been complaining for years about their lack of confidence in the abilities of the micro technicians at the field locations. And their records showed that in side-by-side, split-sample testing the facility where I was located had one of the worst overall scores. Manufacturing and quality records showed that raw materials were accepted when they should have been rejected due to high micro counts. And a higher than normal amounts of finished products had to be put on "Hold" or destroyed as a result of microbiological contamination. The micro lab was really a dungeon, until that point, the worst I had ever seen. And none of our technicians had degrees because the testing they were doing would have been monotonous and unfulfilling to a trained professional. Yes, the corporate microbiologists had a very low opinion of the field staff. They wanted to shut down the micro lab and have all samples requiring micro testing overnighted to their labs at corporate or to have us contract with a certified micro lab in our area to have them do our testing for us. Neither option was acceptable to me or the Plant Manager. Either approach would have slowed down the entire manufacturing process and restricted the release of the finished product to transportation. In addition, it would have been an open admission that I had failed as a manager and was unable to get my micro laboratory to meet the company's minimum standards for analytical certification. There was already money in the budget to demolish the old micro lab, build a new one and replace the antiquated equipment. The plans for the lab had been drawn up years ago. But the lab's construction was always given a low priority in favor of any and everything that manufacturing thought they needed. My boss, by the way, let it happen year after year. The Plant Manager recognized the importance of keeping our lab work in-house and he expedited the micro lab's construction project. I then began fighting an uphill battle with the head of corporate microbiology to give us more time to sort things out. In the interim, I had promoted one of my junior staffers to the position of microbiology technician and provided her with the training she needed in order to do the job. But because I knew that my battle with corporate micro was more political than anything else, I had to come up with some way to get the head of corporate micro to buy in to what I was trying to do. So, as a consequence, I appealed to his vanity; I allowed him to get involved, take control and take ownership of my plan. I went to the local community college and met with the head of their microbiology department, explained the type of micro testing we were doing at the facility and my staff's level of formal training and asked if she would be willing to collaborate with my colleague at corporate to develop a 3 credit course, at the school, that would provide my technicians a sufficient level of training so as to be competent in doing the 6 different test that were required by the facility. The head of corporate micro bought into my approach and flew in to work directly with the school and designed the curriculum his self. I contracted with the school and put 5 of my technicians through the one time program.

The lab got built, the new equipment was installed, my technicians got trained, and corporate micro stopped criticising my people. It was a long slog to pull myself out of the hole and to right the ship that was my department, but I did it. Then, over time, most of the people at the facility learned to read, and began calling me by name, and stopped referring to me as *the College Boy.* Oh, I shouldn't forget, when it came time for our annual reviews, my manager had documented every one of my milestones and accomplishments; he didn't miss a single one of them. He gave them all a "Superior Rating" in the performance review; his own review, not mine.

This is real, this actually happened...the question becomes...what can you learn from this? I was under extraordinary pressures and behind the "8 ball" for over a year. I was recruited to the fast-track management program and given intensive training to do a very difficult job under difficult conditions, but somehow I missed that. I was brought in to step forward and lead, but I chose to hide in my office behind paperwork and administrative bureaucracy while avoiding all my responsibilities as a manager. The sad part is that the only person I was fooling was me and all of my staffers could see what I was doing.

Before I conclude, I want to take you back to just after getting the call from my manager: During my drive back from vacation I didn't know what to expect, I felt trapped, I had no money and had already sent out a flood of resumes, but I didn't have any prospects. So now that the *shit* has hit the fan I was in full survival mode, desperately looking for anything that could right my ship. I wasn't a kid; I was an older student with some degree of maturity on my side. But this was my first job out of school, and I knew I had stepped in it, and I knew I wasn't smart enough to make things right. I had no friends or allies and was out there *alone* just twisting in the wind. I couldn't see a clear path forward, until I thought about how I got myself into this mess. I joined the company's fast-track program. And as I thought more about it, I recognized that their training was intended to help me avoid these very problems. But when problems occur, the training materials and seminars were also effective in resolving the problems. Their training had been exceptional but after completing the individual courses and seminars, I just closed the books, put them in my bookcase, and forgot all about them; just as many of you have. But I realized that there was value in them, for example, this is a short list of some of the training and seminar tools that they provided for me in my management toolbox, and I had completely forgotten about: Management by Objectives, Situational Leadership, Problem Solving and Decision Making, Style Awareness, Conflict Resolution, Coaching and Counselling, Performance Assessment, Auditing, Regulatory Compliance and so on. So when I walked in to the facility on my first day back, if they didn't already have a *"Pink Slip"* waiting for me, I had an action plan and a strategy to resolve the current issue and any others that would have come to light as a result of my audit.

A critical review:

There is a tremendous amount of learning to be had here.

- I had no clear understanding of what managing people was about.

- I was naive about human nature and trusted when I should have verified.

- I didn't step up to lead.

- I was intimidated and retreated from my responsibilities because there was resistance and resentment.

- I set myself apart and above my staff.

- I didn't get to know my people and make a human connection.

- I ignored obvious signs of dysfunction and hostility among the staff and toward me.

- I didn't take ownership of my department and had no idea that things were out of control.

- I failed to use the management tools that I had at hand until after the problems were real.

- I chose the wrong role models to emulate.

- I was arrogant and unwilling to learn what I didn't already know.

Feel free to add to this list of criticisms; I am sure there are many more that can be sited. But this was a hard lesson for me, and I learned from it and made major changes to my approach to managing people and my areas of responsibilities. And remember too, I am retired; sitting at home enjoying my grandchildren. I am out of the game but you are still in it...how much of yourself do you see in the early me?

In the very beginning of this book I stated that I thought that the majority of management training courses and seminars were quite good but they tended to be reactionary. They just don't put as much weight, as I would like to see, on the causes of the problems and how management problems are directly linked to man's baser and competitive natures. To be a successful manager you will have to be successful at understanding human nature and what it requires.

Well, I'm about done talking about me, but I wanted you to know that I was successful in turning the lab around and building a sense of pride among my people, morale went up and stayed up, I was able to gain respect and acceptance, and I remained there for another 2 years before moving on. As for my manager, the world still cries out for justice. He moved on as well and though we moved in some of the same circles, we never ran in to each other again. From time-to-time his name would come up at trade association or industry meetings and from what I could tell, he was doing well. I understand that he had reached the VP level at some very well respected companies...well, so much for a good old fashion morality tale.

In this case study you saw that I was a manager without the slightest notion as to what my managerial responsibilities were, and it almost cost me everything. In the following chapter, I will present our first scenario, as well as Case Study #2. I will use them in an attempt to broaden your perspective of the duties and responsibilities of the manager while working in a dynamic workplace with people at different hierarchical ranks, maturity levels, and emotional drivers. And in doing so, I will present some additional management strategies, techniques, and approaches to management and leadership, that might not be intuitive or overtly apparent to the novice manager, but should be of benefit to the attentive reader.

Chapter # 15:

The Responsibilities of the Manager
Scenario # 1; Adapting to the Needs of Man; Adapting Man to Your Needs; Case Study # 2; The Six "Cs" Standards of Persuasion and Innovations; A Note to the Female Reader

In this section I will be talking about some of the duties and responsibilities of the manager that are not typically apparent from the outside looking in. Early on, we defined the manager's role as *being the leader* (the person in charge), *the one that has the final say and the person that will ultimately be held accountable in the event of failure*. And while that definition is a good one, it's actually only a 30,000 foot view of a manager's responsibilities and accountabilities. There's not a single word in it that would be useful in helping you manage your way toward meeting any expectations. This will be made clear as we move through our First Scenario and Case Study #2.

Scenario #1:

This is another example where we can study *Root Cause Analysis & Problem Solving and Decision Making.* Here again, as with Case Study # 1, pay close attention to how we solved the tangible problems before moving on to the intangible ones.

Let's imagine that you are interviewing for the position of Operations Manager at a company that makes *widgets*. During the interview, they take you on a tour of the facility and you see the people and the process in action. You say to yourself, this is going to be a piece of cake; how tough could it be, you're just making widgets. It's a straight forward process... raw materials are coming in through receiving; they are stored in the raw materials warehouse until they are needed in manufacturing. At the end of each day, the next day's manufacturing schedule is decided and the night shift picks and stages the required raw materials where they will be needed for processing next day's production. After manufacture, the widgets are packaged and sent to the finished goods warehouse for distribution. After seeing the operation first hand you walk away confident that you could do the job and you tell yourself, this won't be a problem at all. But in reality, you still don't have a clue as to what it's going to take to be successful in the job. You just took a walk through and only saw what they wanted to show you. You were given their 10,000 foot level myopic view of the operation. The only thing you know for sure is if you were the successful candidate, you would be responsible for making widgets. Let's imagine even further, let's say you got the job, gave your notice at your current employer, relocated and reported to work as their new Operation's Manager. After finishing all your paperwork at Human Resources you finally get an opportunity to get down to ground level and begin to understand the ins and outs of widget manufacturing. At the end of the first day things appear to be somewhat different than what you remembered from your tour during the interview. Then, by the end of the first week you begin questioning the wisdom of your decision to join the company, and start wondering what exactly you've gotten yourself in to. Because, for the last week you've had a front row seat of what was really happening on the ground, and it's a mess. Not just any mess, you took the job so now it's your mess. Welcome to management. You've walked into a department that is totally dysfunctional, out of control, and underperforming. Right off the top you find that the needed raw materials are not being ordered so they can be delivered in time to meet the manufacturing schedule. And frequently the materials that do arrive don't meet specifications or are damaged. There's no coherent flow to the manufacturing process and things are being done haphazardly and on the fly. The Sales Department has backorders and the company is losing sales for widgets that your department can't seem to fill. The absenteeism rate is higher than you expected and higher than what would be acceptable in any other organization. No one appears to be taking pride in their work or have a sense of urgency in meeting daily production quotas. Quality is marginal to poor and everyone seems to want to be somewhere else, just anywhere else, but at work.

This scenario is not outsized or atypical but is emblematic of what you should be prepared for when moving into a new position as manager. All it takes is just a moment of thought and you'd realize that if an operation could run smoothly on automatic, without glitches, there wouldn't be a need to bring in a manager. So just be prepared to have to fix things.

Now, before jumping in headlong to fix the problems here, you should take some time to fully analyze the challenges you have in front of you. When I look at them, I see them falling in to two categories; in the first category I would classify the problems as being tangible. Tangible problems are usually something you can get your hands around; and if you can get your hands around them, you can usually fix them. In this example they would include; raw material sourcing, the manufacturing process flow and controls, product quality, production throughputs, and attendance. The problems in this category should be addressed and corrected first. I would classify them as being critical, and the ones that will give you the biggest bang for your buck and give you the largest and fastest payback with respect to your productivity obligations. In addition, and relatively speaking, they would require less of a time and resource investment to implement. I don't want us to spend a lot of time on the tangible problems because they vary widely from industry to industry; and for the most part, once they are recognized, they are considerably easier to correct. We have to stay on point and be mindful that the focus of this book is to help you to learn how to manage people; an intangible process that is difficult to navigate and one that will result in unexpected and unintended consequences if great care is not taken. But because we have already identified some of the tangible problems in this scenario, and because there is a linkage between the problems in this category and in the next, I will briefly talk some of the solutions to the tangible problems so you can see the connections between them and those that I have called intangibles.

- The problems with raw materials seem to be related to communications. There does not appear to be adequate communication and coordination between those responsible for manufacturing scheduling and those that are responsible for raw material inventory controls. You need to assure that they develop a manufacturing schedule defining which widgets are scheduled for manufacture and what raw materials will be required during production. The manufacturing schedule has to be sent to purchasing in time for them to source the materials from suppliers and have them delivered prior to the scheduled manufacture date. You have to provide Purchasing with a set of measurable raw material specifications so they can communicate them to your suppliers to prevent their shipping non-conforming materials to your location. Lastly, if you are paying for raw materials that come in to your facility and are damaged, you have to change the terms of your contract in order to be able to reject any damaged and all non-conforming materials back to the supplier, at their cost.

- Next you would want to study the internals of the process; you have already found it to be ill-suited to meet the daily throughput quotas and the quality targets. You study the process flow and its less than fluid design, and then you solicit recommendations from your staff as to how they would like to see the process streamlined. With their input, you dovetail their specific suggestions with your overall perception of how the process flow could be optimized. Let's say you identified (for example) 3 distinctive parts to the process (P1, P2, & P3). You then document each part of each process and develop standard operational procedures (SOPs) and quality standards that are exclusive to that part of the process. For example; At P1, raw materials are received that meet specification tolerances to start the manufacturing process. Those materials are further processed according to P1 procedures until a P1 finished product is produced to a standard to serve as a P2 raw material. The process continues at P2 until a finished product is produced to a standard to serve as a P3 raw material. The final step at P3 produces a product that meets the finished product quality specifications for the specific widget selected for manufacture. You realign and/or redesign the manufacturing process to conform to the new process flow, and then you begin retraining your staff. After your staff has received their training for their part in the process as well as the SOPs and quality standards that are required at that station, you can begin your manufacturing process time studies. You have to complete those studies so you will know how much time is required at each step in the process in order to determine if the required daily quotas are reasonable targets. If the targets are reasonable, the results would also reveal to what degree your department has been underperforming.

- You have an apathetic workforce and a symptom of that apathy may be manifesting itself in your higher than normal absentee rate; there is no way of knowing for sure, it is too early to tell. But you have to communicate to your staff that regular attendance is not just desired, but is a requirement of their employment, and a reasonable attendance policy will be established, documented, and enforced. I recognize that you are new to the position and some of you might think this is a tough stance, and if so, think about it this way; you can't manage someone if they are not on their job. When people don't show up for work, the work is still there and others have to take up the load. The extra load, will in time, have a negative effect on morale which could lead to more absenteeism's. If that happens, your processes will be slowed down even further and your quotas will go unmet. You won't be able to deliver on your obligations to the company and that will put your position, as manager, at risk. And lastly, you'll have to recognize that a job is an opportunity that allows an individual to earn a living; it is not an entitlement protected by the Constitution. So you should expect to lose some people...but the likelihood is that they were already lost to you anyway.

In the second category you have your intangibles, they deal with personnel (people) and are less clearly defined and are the real focus of this work. You should never underestimate the importance of your intangibles, these are the ones that can cause you the most grief; and even cost you your job. So treat them with the same level of importance as you would a tangible problem. Intangible problems take time to identify and to work your way through, and short of cleaning house, starting all over from scratch and possibly risking throwing the baby out with the bathwater, there are really no quick fixes to these problems. Even when you can see the symptoms of these personnel problems, you still would have no idea as to what the root causes were, or how toxic they have become. But there are certain professional standards and operational guidelines you can put in place, and insist upon, that should keep most of the personnel conflicts at bay, or at least from deteriorating any further. Earlier I said that there was linkage between the tangible and the intangible, how many of you picked up on the process and personnel controls we developed and put in place *simultaneously* to resolving the tangible problems? If you missed them, go back and see how it was done. By my count, and with tacit support and inputs from the staff, we installed at lease 10, let's review what they were; we developed a manufacturing schedule defining which widgets were scheduled for manufacture along with required raw materials needed in time for Purchasing to source the materials from suppliers, we provided Purchasing a set of measurable raw material specifications to prevent suppliers shipping non-conforming materials to your location, we changed the terms of our purchasing agreements so any non-conforming or damaged materials would be rejected back to the supplier, at their cost, work station SOPs were developed, work station quality standards were established, finished product quality standards defined, work station time studies completed and established, employee training was conducted, attendance guidelines were established and enforced, and realistic daily production quotas were established and set as reasonable targets. By clearly defining the work, the process, and establishing guidelines all the employees now know what's expected of them, and no one had to be read the Riot Act.

If you'd just take a moment to do an assessment of what we have accomplished thus far, by most standards, it would be significant. You should be pleased because you have gained a level of control within your group and began to deliver on your responsibilities and obligations as a manager in the company. Your management should be pleased because there should be far fewer glitches in manufacturing scheduling, cost should come down, productivity should be up, quality should be up, and sales should go up along with increasing revenues. Just think about it, if you had not been employed by the company to manage the organization, but had contracted with them as a Management Consultant (with a far more lucrative financial arrangement) your job would be finished at this point. You would have fulfilled the terms and conditions of the contract and hit every one of their milestones. The company would be satisfied with your work and would have given you high marks for what was accomplished. And, they would likely recommend you to other companies in the industry. You would gather your things, collect your sizable fee and moved on to your next project...*just before things began to unravel and fall apart all over again*. There is no mistaking that a lot was accomplished in a short amount of time, but this was the easy part. And it's also where many managers let down their guard and allow themselves to become complacent. You aren't done; you've only bought yourself some time, all of your original personnel problems didn't just evaporate, they're still there. Remember, you only introduced standards and guidelines (process and personnel controls), your staff is still dysfunctional and apathetic, they have no commitment to the work or the company, they continue to have a sense of entitlement, and they would prefer to be somewhere else. These issues, as well as a myriad of others, that you're not yet aware of makes up your list of intangible problems. And if you don't move to address them, the safeguards you've just put in place will begin to breakdown. *This is where the work really begins and where you actually learn to become a manager, and a leader*.

I am going to move away from our widget scenario for the time being, so I can talk the man4268152_Balance and Controlstrategies, tactics, and tools) will help you to develop effective action plans for the resolution of many of the intangible problems we still have yet to address in this scenario. Let me move on to the new material.

Adapting to the Needs of Man:
The manager is responsible for the successful outcome of the project, the work, or the activity assigned; the manager is responsible and accountable for everything and everybody. Success

is the objective and the expected outcome. No one cares if key members of your team, or if no one on your team showed up for work today. They don't care if you got the project or job at the last minute and have to put in the longer hours to get it done. They don't care if you are wrestling with personal or personnel issues, or even conflicting objectives and priorities. Those are your problems, a good manager is expected to overcome any and all disruptions and distractions and consistently deliver on time and on budget. Now, the question becomes "how do you do that"; how do you consistently deliver to expectations? Well, you can't just rely on luck and hope that everything will come together in the end, because it won't. You have to rely on effective planning, preparation, personnel development, skills training, and your ability to lead to have any hope of success. You have to fill up your management toolbox with learned techniques and strategies that will help you. You have to use your knowledge of human nature, your interpersonal skills, your leadership skills, and your full appreciation and knowledge of what a manager's job *really* entails. And while you'll be hard-pressed to find all of the manager's jobs written down, those of you who are already managers should be able to identify with having to function in several of the following capacities on more than a few occasions. Managers, if you want to keep your work and your people moving in the desired direction, you will have to learn how to become a cheerleader for your people, a multitasker to keep all your priorities moving forward, a counsellor, mentor, and career guide to help people chart and work toward their goals, a director and leader; setting the goals and pointing the path forward, a trouble-shooter and problem solver to clear the chosen path and smoothing the way, a facilitator that provides the material, documents, and/or equipment required to do the job, a confessor and a trusted confidante that is discreet and respects personal space, a disciplinarian to keep everyone on track moving in the right direction and to keep the projects under control. Lastly, a manager has to be a defender and champion of their people; they will be reluctant to follow if they believe they won't be protected in their time of need. But being all these things is still no guarantee of success. I recognize that many of you are thinking that this is not what you signed on for. Well neither did I, and look at what happen to me. This stuff isn't written down anywhere and it should be, it should be spelled out in clear language that we can all understand, but it's not. They don't really touch it in the available training materials, or if they do, it's just implied or wrapped up in corporate speak. This will be a major part of your job if you are going to be managing people, and what's more, you'll have to learn to get good at it. I don't know of any shortcuts, and I hope I haven't said anything that would have encouraged that line of thinking because you won't find a panacea here. And while I can't say it with absolute certainty, I don't think you will find one anywhere. You can't lose sight of the drivers of human nature and your inability to lead if others won't follow. People are intelligent, complicated, and sophisticated beings; which makes managing them all the more challenging. We really can't be dictated to or ordered or bossed for very long before we start to revert to our baser instincts. And because of our intelligence we can quickly become very formidable adversaries and your biggest nightmare. Therefore, to keep us in check you will have to find ways to *handle* us, that is, handle us in such a way so we become willing and obliged to follow you and do your bidding. I don't want anyone to conjure up any images of mind control or Orwellian tyranny, but the fact is we all are always being handled, manipulated, and seduced by others in order to get us to do what they want us to do[12]. In a real sense, we expect it and even insist upon it. It may stem from our need for recognition within the hierarchy, our need to feel needed, or our need to feel important and special; as well as our need to feel protected and secure within the group. So we have an expectation that we will be handled using the acceptable norms in our particular work or social setting. We would expect a certain amount of consideration and deference to be shown to us based upon our social style, our relationship and/or rank within the group or to each other, and we expect that the amount of consideration will be in direct proportion to the value that you want to extract from us. Now, I don't want to get too obtuse with this, but I know that some of you are having difficulty visualizing this concept (this need in man). So let's just take a look back at your childhood; how many of you can remember saying to a playmate, or having a playmate say to you, *"if you do this or that for me, or let me play with your toys, I'll be your friend"*? Does this ring any bells? We haven't changed, we've just gotten older; we still curry favor and compliance by appealing to another person's vanity and self-esteem. We give them what they want and make them feel important, special, and pivotal to the successful outcome of whatever the project happens to be. This inflates their egos and their perception of value and worth within the hierarchy and they become obliged to honor our request. Just give it some thought; if you reflected back over this last month, who, or how many people did you handle, seduce or manipulate in order to get them to do what you wanted...and how many do you think used you? And just think about it, dependent upon what you wanted, there was likely no limits to the amount of social graces, recognition and

---

[12] This is just another reference to your need to develop the softer skills, interpersonal people skills. You'll have to learn the values of persuasion and seduction if you are to manage people. When you boss and force them, the benefits are both minimal and short lived.

respect you were willing to lavish upon that person (or people) in order to incentivize them to honor your request, and vice versa. Then, as a consequence of our nature, once you've gotten what you wanted, you may well have relegated that person (or have been relegated) back to the margins and forgotten about them until you needed their support or services again. You used them, or you were used, because that's what we do with each other. In a real sense, this is merely an expression of the **softer skills** (interpersonal skills and seductive and positive handling) and is one of the many ways in which we build alliances and political influence using indirect power. But when you're a manager, you can't afford to forget or marginalize your staffers once they've been a benefit to you because your reliance on them is on-going. So you'll have to keep some form of reciprocal relationship going. You'll have to know how best to handle and incentivize each of your subordinate so they will continue to be willing to follow your lead. Your position as manager may be the result of a promotion, an appointment, or as a new hire, etc. How you got there is far less important than what you do to stay there. Your position of manager was authorized by the company, but your position as leader has to be earned, and your ability to effectively handle people, good interpersonal skills and your ability to build and maintain alliances, will be essential to that end.

Your staffers need to see you as a committed leader. You have to earn their trust and be considered a fair and honest broker and a defender and protector of your people. In addition, you have to show that you take pride in your work if you hope to be able to instil that same sense of pride in your people. They take their lead from you and mimic what they see reflected from you in their work. And lastly, people are prideful, communal (or social) beings and readily form groups, clicks, and alliances around common goals, objectives and values. Therefore, you should use that natural tendency to build teams within your organization so people will feel that they've become part of a greater whole, working toward common and worthwhile goals. They find strength and security in numbers, and teams not only provide that, but also help to instil a greater sense of pride and confidence in its members.

I don't want anyone to think that my coverage here was in any way comprehensive, because it wasn't. Every situation is different and yours will require you to make decisions and adjustments based upon your particular needs at the time. The point that I had hoped to make was that the manager has to stay mindful of *man's nature and man's needs*; the manager should *only project their aspirational selves in any public setting,* and they will have to *keep earning their position as the leader of the group through alliance building and political influence;* your position is not static and can be lost if not continually reinforced. We will be talking more about man's needs as we move through the book. But for now, let's move the discussion to *your needs and man's nature.*

Adapting Man to Your Needs:

Every manager has to be realistic, man has to be controlled, *his nature is fixed and he will not change for you.* Guidelines, seduction and positive handling will only take you so far. Man could love you and see you as a wonderful person, but if he doesn't have a healthy respect and a slight fear of you, he will resist, rebel and try to dominate you. He can't help it, that simply his nature. Therefore, if you already know the nature of man and what to expect from him, you have to prepare yourself to curb and/or put down his baser and competitive natures. There're two sides to every coin, there is sunlight and darkness in a 24 hour day, and there are two sides to people management, making one whole. Up to this point we have talked about the things that you could do to better connect with your people and to provide them a supportive environment where they can work and grow as individuals. Now let's talk about the other side of the coin, because without it you're off balance. Some might consider this the dark side of management, but I don't, it is a necessary component of management and without it, you will fail. Managers have to be pragmatic about their job, their staff, and their environment. You'll need your people to seamlessly follow your lead and directions without their egos getting in the way. You all have a job to do, so everyone should just get to it. You don't need challenges to your authority or *Prima Donnas* disrupting the harmony within the organization. While failure falls on your shoulders as the manager, you need everyone in the group to share at least some of the risk; everybody needs to have some skin in the game. You are not there to coddle or babysit immature adults, but to complete the work at hand. It should be clear to everyone that walks through the door that they chose to be there and that they were the ones that consciously signed a contract of employment that spelled out the conditions of that arrangement. They agreed to provide specific human services in lieu of specified financial compensation, and you should have every intention of having them honor that agreement. No one on your staff is doing you any favors by being there. Neither you nor any of them are working for free; you are *all* only there for self-enrichment. This is business, and your company is not a benevolent foundation, they fully expect each of you to generate profits to their bottom-line. In a real sense, if any member of your staff doesn't fulfil the terms of their agreement with the company, it puts the entire operation at risk. Your job, as manager, is to make sure that doesn't happen. This is not a game, but you can expect some on your staff to want to play them and you should expect to be tested. Man always has, and always will, resist and rebel against authority because it personifies his lower position and status within a given hierarchy. You may be the greatest, most thoughtful and humane, considerate manager to ever grace their workplace. It will mean nothing to them. You will still be challenged and resisted, not because of anything you've done, but because of your higher hierarchical rank and status, and the authority that comes with it. Even the weakest in the group will try to determine how far they can push. This is a natural human reaction and there is little you can do to offset it. The resistance will always be there and will never go away. That's just another truth about the competitive nature of man.

Many managers have become frustrated, burnout, and have lost their positions because they lost their bearings. They lost sight of who they were, where they were, and what they were supposed to be doing. I want to help you and clarify any confusion that you might be having about your job and your position. You are a manager in a corporation; a corporation is not a democracy, but a dictatorship. And in a dictatorship, directions, decrees and dictates only flow in one direction, from the top down. You are a dictator, and if you find that hard to accept, you should think about another line of work, because you are destined to fail at this one. A manager is either in charge or they're not, *there is no middle ground*. The kindness, respect, and generosity that you 'rightfully' afford man are essential to the bonding process; but more importantly, it keeps down direct confrontation and open rebellion. But man is for-ever un-contented; he is greedy, grasping, selfish, disloyal, and cannot be trusted. Your gen-erosity won't make man love, or even like you; if anything it could cause him to resent and despise you. In our society, we tend to interpret kindness and generosity as signs of weak-ness, and that makes you prey. None of your employees hired you, the company hired you to take charge and manage a part of their operation that required supervision; you were hired to do a job, not to be liked. You can never lose sight of that, however, many managers do.

We humans are a deceptive species; we hide our true intent by putting forward the illusion of cooperation and project an image of ourselves that is both aspirational and altruistic, when in reality we are neither. So long as you benefit us, we will allow you to continue in that capacity; though our demands will become increasingly obscene. And when you are no longer of any service, we'll relegate you to the margins and move on to our next benefactor. When managers start to believing what they see of their staff with their eyes and not with their brains they start a slow migration from being a manager to wanting to be a friend (to be liked). Wanting or needing to be liked and accepted is a powerful driver in our nature as well as one of our greatest weaknesses. Weak managers often allow themselves to be seduced by their staffers in a vain attempt to gain acceptance and keep some degree of control in their department. But in reality, when you give up your position of authority as manager, and go pandering for praise or acceptance, you make yourself a peer and forfeit your control. You only make your bad situation infinitely worse. Before you were just a weak manager, now people will only follow your direction, not because it's their job, but as a courtesy or favor to you. And for each courtesy they will expect some form of exchange, and that will make you obligated to them. You need to stop here, open your eyes, and confront reality; you're no longer a weak manager, now you've become a prostitute, in service to everyone. When you started along this road, you set out for failure. Even if you tried to regain your position of authority and control, your people will rise up against you; they no longer see you as a leader, but a peer. And because of your already weaken state, you will lose. At some point, every successful manager reaches a crossroads, a point where they have to take a stand and begin to rationalize who they are, where they are, and what their job is. I can assure you that each of you will come to your individual crossroads of rationalization at some unknown time and in some unknown place, but you will get there. My intent, and my hope, is to help you get there sooner, rather than later.

I can't, in good conscience, go much further without letting you know that much of what I am writing in this section comes from a lifetime of personal experiences and from what I understand of Niccolo Machiavelli's book The Prince, and Ralph Waldo Emerson's essay Self-Reliance[13]. I will be moving between my personal observations and knowledge of man's nature and to some of the value that I've found in their works and will likely bastardize it all, but please stay with me.

When you get to your crossroads, you will have to choose how you want to manage going forward. There are many different shades of grey but really only three choices, you can choose the Yin (the dark), if you want your subordinates to fear you, or you can choose Yang (the light), if

---

[13] I would recommend you read both.

you want your subordinates to like you. Or take a balanced approach using equal parts of both, *Yin Yang*. If you choose to be liked, the discussion above will be helpful in letting you know what to expect. And if you choose to be feared, than a review of the earlier discussion about the Tyrannical Boss would be helpful. When Machiavelli addressed the subject; [whether it is better to be loved or feared or vice versa], he concluded that a Prince should do a myriad of positive things that would encourage his subjects to love him. Just as I recommended our managers should do through seduction and positive handling. It calms the masses and helps keep rebellions small or down altogether. But he also noted that man is selfish and fickle and loves as he chooses; therefore, a Prince cannot rely on man's love to maintain his rule or anything else he does not control. But because man is cowardly and timid and always tries to avoid pain, a Prince can use fear to control all those within his Principality, because the Prince does control how man fears. Therefore Machiavelli concluded that because man loves as he chooses and fears as the Prince chooses; a Prince should rely on what is within his control in order to secure his position, and if he can't have them both, the Prince should choose to be feared. The only caveat is that the Prince should try to avoid being hated. And, just to be clear here, Machiavelli was not advocating becoming the Tyrannical Prince, or a Boss. He was just helping the Prince to understand where he had the power to control man, and where he didn't. The same is true for you.

Where are your powers, and just as importantly, how do you plan to use them. If you are already a manager your array of powers should be clear to you. You should have the Position Powers that came with the title. I would hope that you have, and are growing, Political Powers among your peers, within your staff and with your management. You may also have some Financial Power, dependent upon whether or not you have any budgetary responsibilities. And finally, based upon the strength of your personality, you may also be able to project some Perceived Power. However, if you are new to your position, you may be less certain about the powers that came with it. But because of your title, you should have the Position Power that is required to do the job. You should also have some small amount of Political Power; a short honeymoon where your management, some of your staff, and other well-wishers tacitly support you while you're getting up to speed. In addition, when viewed from the outside, that tacit support may provide you an illusion of Perceived Power, making you appear to your staff and peers, more powerful than you actually are. But before you can begin exercising any of your powers you'll have to have your areas of responsibility clearly defined so you'll know where the boundaries are in order to avoid stepping into areas where you are not wanted or welcome. But most importantly, you'll have to know the limits of your authority in the areas where you have responsibility, this is essential for the development of your *leadership* tool box. Remember, never accept responsibility without authority.

Now that you know your areas of responsibility and the limits of your authority it's time to manage. However, before you can manage anyone, you have to get their attention. And, if we go back to our widget scenario, I would guess that based on the standards and guidelines we've already put in place; we've certainly gotten people's attention. All the work that we did to fix the tangible problems and the process and personnel controls we put in place was the work of a *good manager*. Although, all of the potential dangerous intangible problems are still there and the group is still dysfunctional. And, the jury is still out as to whether or not people will abide by the standards and guidelines; some have already decided that they were going to opt out. So you know that there's going to be resistance and pushback. You have already proven, by what you've already done, that you are a good manager. But this will be the first test of your *leadership*, and you will need to be prepared for it.

Volumes have been written about the qualities and character traits that make strong leaders, we have even pointed to some in this book. But in my truncated version of what makes a strong leader, I'll point to the single most important thing that they all had in common and fully understood; they knew that to be a strong leader, they had to have the powers and control to encourage people to decide that it was in their best interest to follow their lead. They knew man's nature, they knew that he is self-motivated and out for his own gain, and they also knew that man avoids pain. So they knew what you now know. You also know what your powers are and the limits of your authority. And you know that you'll fail if your people won't follow your lead. Strong leaders depend upon their knowledge of man's nature and how he will respond in order to preserve himself and his status. They set up systems to incentivize people so they can decide for themselves how they choose to proceed. The incentive systems they setup are nothing elaborate, in fact, they're quite simple, for instance, *"if you follow my lead, you get to keep your job, and if you don't...well, you don't"*. There's nothing complicated about that. Now it's up to the followers or your subordinates to determine whether they choose to opt out or to reconsider that notion. You can't decide for them, it's their decision to make. Some of you are thinking that this is a very cold and callous approach to leadership and management, and you might be considering taking a softer approach. That is, of course your prerogative, but this is a business, and you have responsibilities to your employer, to yourself, and to your family to honor your obligations and preserve your career and livelihood. Your objective is to raise the performance in your department to a standard professional level. Some people may not be able to make the transition and some others may refuse to, but your objectives remain unchanged. These are adults, and if you try to wet-nurse one, you'll find yourself trapped, wet-nursing them all. Furthermore, you can't make a person stay in a job that they don't want to be in, and you can't allow a person to stay in a job where they are not performing. So, for those of you that believe this to be cold and callous, let's take a closer look at your job and the controls your employer has imposed on you.

As a manager, you agreed to function in a specified capacity on the company's behalf, in lieu of some specified financial compensation; as did your staff. Therefore, so long as the company honors their agreement with you, you are obligated to honor yours with them. Your job requires you to facilitate the processing or completion of certain work products, and your staff's job is to do the actual work required. If for any reason you decide (by your actions) that you're no longer able or willing to do your job, than the company has a legitimate right (under contractual agreement) to terminate your contract and your employment. Am I being clear...is everyone following? My point is that, for you (as it should be for your staff) there are severe consequences for poor or non-performance. The consequences can take the form of a negative performance appraisal; and you are not awarded a merit increase, the loss of a promotion, disciplinary action up to and including termination. The company has introduced both positive and negative incentives in order to control your behavior and your performance. They have set up a system whereby they have clear expectations that you will meet specified milestones and deliver to target on a consistent bases. You are no different than any other human being, and your employer knows it. They already know everything there is to know about human nature, human motivators, and what humans avoid. They have all the powers and controls to incentivize you to follow their directions and to meet their expectations. Of course, you can always opt out. But now, you've got skin in the game and that's how you're being controlled. You are only there for your own selfish economic gain and are not doing your employer any favors by coming to work. In addition, your employer will always keep you at some level of *risk of termination* as long as you stay employed with them. In the view of an employer, and quite justifiably, your subordinates are subject to the very same incentive controls as you are...after all, you work for the same company don't you? As a manager and leader you have to pass on these incentives directly to your staff, just as they are; completely unvarnished. They need to know that they are just as accountable for the success or failure of the operation as you are, and that they will enjoy the same level of risk as you do. People will step up and preserve themselves and their fortunes; even if it means taking ownership of that small patch of the workplace that is theirs. When they do, they will begin to reject any subpar elements from other stations. Because they are being held accountable for their work, they will eagerly work with their managers and others to prevent subpar work putting them in a negative light. This is simply an expression of self-preservation when a downside risk is a real possibility. And for the optimist, this could be the first twinkling of job ownership, worker pride and the beginning of teamwork.

When we look back at our widget scenario and find that the organization was dysfunctional, people were apathetic, would have preferred to have been any place other than at work, and had a sense of entitlement. There may be secondary factors driving these intangibles, but from where I sit it appears clear to me that no one felt that they had any accountability for the work being done. No one felt that they were at any risk of losing their jobs and livelihood; therefore no one felt a need or had the desire to take ownership of their positions. And, as they saw no change or reason for change on the horizon, it gave them a sense of stability and entitlement to their jobs. Because there were no consequences for their actions or inactions and because there were no incentives to make things interesting and challenging, the people became disenchanted and disillusioned and got mired in their own stagnation. Man has to have hope, in order to thrive, and you can't have hope if you don't have change. The group was locked in self-hatred and self-mutilation because they didn't see their plight becoming any better. And if you had failed to lead, they wouldn't have been able to find their way out of the quagmire. And if they couldn't find a way out, they would have been more than happy to have made their problems your problems. What is your thinking now, do you still think the professional approach is too cold and callous? Maybe a better question would be…where would a softer approach have taken you?

I want to take us back to your needs as a manager and the nature of man. I think that a further discussion of them will be helpful to you in choosing your path when you get to your decision point; your crossroads. Though, when you get to your crossroads you can take whatever path and management approach you believe is most appropriate for you.

But before you do so, stay mindful that history is littered with the dead and rotting corpses of Kings, Queens, Emperors, Potentates, Warlords, Presidents & Prime Ministers, managers and the like, who failed because they didn't understand and appreciate the power of human nature and the motivational drivers of mankind; or they just ignored the warning signs. There is no need to repeat them again here, as long as you stay mindful of what they are. You're now at the point in your career where you have to decide how you are going to manage and lead your people, going forward. You could manage them with an opened and free hand, hoping that your appeal to their aspirational nature and your good deeds, kind ways, and interpersonal skills will be enough to inspire them to follow your lead. That is certainly one approach you could take, and if you were only working with mature aspirational people you would likely be successful. But you won't be, you will be working with all three variants of the human animal and the aspirational component is the one that we will project while hiding the competitive and baser beings. Even before you start down this path, you already know that it won't work. Yet you all, for whatever reason, convince yourselves that for you, it will be different; or it will be different *this time*. A manager has to be pragmatic and the adult in the room; they have to be able and willing to take tough and unpopular decisions. They have to chart the path forward and incentivize their people to follow them. They can't just go with the flow. If you are a weak manager, admit it; get the training you lack or find yourself a mentor. Don't think that if you get people to like you it will translate into them following you, because they won't. In my view, this approach to management would be an abdication of your responsibilities and it would constitute a total transfer of your powers to your staff, leaving them leaderless and without direction. You wouldn't be a manager, you would be a fraud; look at what happened with The Maestro. Without effective leadership, and within a very short time, a once impressive and unified orchestra descended into chaos. They lost the ability to make music, and could only make noise. This is what happens when no one is in control and everyone has a free hand to do whatever they elect to do. They move off in a direction of their own choosing or just simply sit there, doing nothing at all. They're no longer a group, but a collection of individuals marching to their own drummer. If you don't step-up and step-up early to take control, they will interpret your inaction as a sign of weakness. To them, that would be tantamount to tasting blood in the water, and they will feed on you and take you under. You can't allow your staff to control your destiny. This approach, and any variation on it, will fail every time. You'll have to be realistic and recognize that you can't manage or lead man without having a stick in your hand.

There is a segment of the management population that takes a completely different approach to management and follows a different path. For the most part, they are people that have marked a clear distinction between management and labor. They tend to be social climbers and they assess a person's value solely on where they rank within the hierarchy relative to themselves. They are extremely deferential to those with a higher rank, competitive with those of equal rank, and indifferent to those of a lower rank. They have an imperial mind-set and see their superiors as members of the *corporate elite* (the corporate gentry); with whom they would like to curry favor, and they see their subordinates as having little value and having emerged from the *inbred masses of the great unwashed*. They take their positions within the organization seriously and manage (rule) by what they believe to be is their divine rite. They have no desire to be liked or admired by their subordinates because they can see no value in it. Their objective is to promote themselves and their own careers and to move on to their next growth opportunity. The managers that take this path, more frequently than not, finds success and personal gratification in this approach, but it comes at the expense of those reporting to them. From the prospective of management, they are seen as being among their top performers and if they move them along quickly, few will see the damage they've done and are doing to the fabric of the organization (the front line employee). But, if they are forced to stay in their position for too long, they will begin to lose their totalitarian grip on their people and the people will revolt. Their draconian controls would be exposed and they would no longer be considered for additional responsibility or promotion within the organization. So, in the long run they also fail.

You will also find another, more familiar traveller moving down this path: this is often the next path chosen by the weak and insecure manager after the first or second or even third failure. Some come back while others leave management completely, opting for a less stressful career. But for those that return, they take this path, having finally come to the realization that their good deeds and good intentions were for not, that most people didn't have the capacity or inclination to recognize or appreciate their humanity and generosity. And, depended upon how frustrated, hurt, and betrayed they feel, they decide to take a track along this path that is punitive and one that would give them absolute dictatorial powers and control; the tract of the Tyrannical Boss. They do away with all of the pleasantries and have completely given up any notions of wanting to be liked or loved. Now they will put the full weight of their office on the backs of the people. They have lost faith in man's kindness and generosity and have had first-hand experience with the dark and selfish side of man and have vowed to never let that happen again. Now fear is their tool of choice and their sole commitment is to themselves. They are bitter and want revenge, and have decided that their staff is not worthy of their consideration and, from here on out, they plan to rule with an iron fist. And if possible, they will try to extract two pounds of flesh for every one that was taken from them at their last job. Clearly this is an over dramatization of this very sad and unfortunate approach to management, but it happens quite frequently. The problem is you can't hide this level of hatred and anger. Even, if they could back-off, way-back-off, the venom, it would still be difficult for them to conceal their resentment and distrust of their people; the staff would sense it and react to it. In turn, the manager would try to tighten their grip and controls through dictatorial rule and intimidation. And, this would be the point at which their best employees would begin to leave, the work would begin to suffer because the people wouldn't have a say in their work or a voice in the operation. Consequently, if the people don't have a say or a voice in what they did, they wouldn't take any ownership or pride in the work product. The manager wouldn't be able to hide the declining performance and Senior Management would have to step in, once again, in order to right the ship. So once again, they've failed.

I will admit that I had my finger on the scales and had already determined each outcome before we got started. So, in the spirit of full disclosure, I can't categorically state that you will fail if you choose one path over the other, but it has been my experience that you need both; the Yin and the Yang...one cannot stand without the other. I won't deny that you could find early success on either path, but in view of man's inherent nature, I am merely stating that your prospects for long-term success would be limited.

When you come to work, the work at hand is usually challenging enough, you really don't have the time or the inclination to spend the better part of your day coddling or bargaining with your staff to do their jobs, nor do you have the time to be locked in a pitched battle with employees fighting an undeclared war with you and the company. Many of you do this dance every day, catering to the needy and trying to keep from being broadsided by the disenchanted. It's probably been going on so long that you have deluded yourselves into believing that it's normal and just another part of your daily routine. And that's a problem, because it's not, or it shouldn't be; it shouldn't be part of any professional environment. Yet these little soap operas continue to be played out just about everywhere; and it's your fault. You have allowed this perverted culture to take hold and persist unabated while your attention was diverted elsewhere. Because we've been conditioned to accept them as an unavoidable artefact of management, we become blind to the negative impact they have on productivity and morale. Your needy people are needy because you enable them to shrink from their responsibilities by your constant attentiveness and unlimited support. Why should they grow into their own jobs when you are always there to do it for them? And how can they take pride in what they do, when they really aren't doing much of anything at all. Unless you are a manager in a sheltered workshop or have an employee with special needs, your constant support to these staffers is only hurting them and you. Your people are just as smart and intelligent as you are, you may be the manager, but you're not the only one in the room with brains. Once your people have been provided their necessary training, you should expect them to become proficient in their jobs. You should also expect that as they become more proficient and experienced, over time, they will become less dependent. If not, then you both have more serious problems that will have to be addressed. When you look at your war fighters and disgruntle people, their grievances could cover the entire gambit; you may have done something to offend them in some way, they may be having problems at home, they could be unhappy with their lot in life and had imagined that they would have been at a different point at this time in their careers, or they may just be very angry and very toxic people; we have those you know. If the cause of their anger is due to some action or inaction on your part you have to find ways to work with them to bring about a fair and balanced resolution; but if the cause is not work related, not apparent, or is beyond your ability as a professional manager to address, you'll have to leave it for them to resolve independently, but in a way that is no longer disruptive to the workplace. You have to stop this dance! You have allowed your people to construct an alternative reality whereby their underperformance can be justified because of their needs and/or disillusionment. These problems won't go away by themselves, they will continue to persist and get progressively worse if action is not taken. You have to make your people accountable for their areas of responsibility and expect them to act in a professional manner.

We didn't directly paint in any of these personnel issues or this on-going dance when we developed our widget scenario, but I don't think that it would be too much of a stretch if we were to say that similar personnel issues were playing a role in the overall dysfunction and apathy that was described in that scenario. I would like for us to keep our widget scenario in mind as I move from that imaginary construct to a real life example.

In our second case study, I will set the stage to give everyone the necessary background. But, because it would take too much time to fully flush out all the actual events and the different personalities involve, I have pared the story down, as much as possible, but tried to keep its relevance clear.

Case Study #2:

This is another case where *Root Cause Analysis & Problem Solving and Decision Making, and Situational Leadership* proved to be invaluable and ultimately saved the day. This case study builds upon what we've learned in the first case study and what we've learned in the widget scenario. But as you go through this one, I want you to study the interactions between the manager and her staff, the manager and her director, their management styles and how that effected their relationship and the productivity of the manager's department. And lastly, watch how power can shift, and how the manager went from being *the powerless* to become *the powerful*.

Several years back, I was working alongside a colleague that had about 8 to 10 reports. Her position at the time was Manager of Regulatory Compliance; I was the Manager of International Technical Services and we were both working for a very large multinational consumer products company. The Food and Drug Administration (FDA) had recently codified the Nutritional Labelling and Education Act (NLEA) and established specific guidelines for companies of various sizes to become compliant with the law within a specified time frame. The responsibility for bringing the company into compliance fell to my colleague and her group. I don't recall the amount of time the company had in order to bring all their labels and product information into compliance but I believe it was around 18 to 24 months. The company had around 5 or 6 subsidiary companies and even more private label brands, which would have brought the total to around 250 different products and around 2,000 labels for products with different sizes and configurations. In addition, the changes to all their product labels had to be done concurrent with the normal workload of the department. And that would prove to be a significant problem. The productivity in the department was already low and it was an on-going challenge to keep up with the labelling requirements for new product introductions as well as the routine packaging changes and promotions requested by Marketing and Sales. She knew that there was no way for her, and the group she had reporting, to make all the company's labels compliant with the new law within the compliance period. Her problems were many and instead of trying to talk through them all, I'll just list the major ones.

- She held a position where she had responsibility without authority. Her manager would often over ride or reverse decisions that she would make making her a weak leader in the eyes of her staff; they would often bypass her and go straight to him.

- At least 3 members of her staff were put there as a favor to some senior Director or VP; a clear act of nepotism. They would not have qualified for the positions based upon their own merit. They were unproductive, and she was stuck with them.

- The company placed a high value on employee quality of life considerations, both in the workplace, as well as time away from work. So people felt secure and entitled to their jobs and worked flexible hours, telecommuted, and even shared jobs so they could spend more time with their families. This was a trade-off between quality of life considerations and productivity... and productivity suffered.

- About half of her staff were needy and acted as if they could not put a product label or packaging graphics together using the computerized database and the regulatory documents available to them, as a consequence, there were a high percentage of errors in the work that they generated.

- There were no negative consequences for low productivity or for errors made during the generation of labels or packaging graphics, even though if errors were not caught before getting to the printer, they would have resulted in the high tens of thousands of dollars of losses for the company because packaging would have had to be discarded. She was the manager, and the responsibility for preventing that from happening was hers.

- She was already putting in 12 hour days, attending required meetings, catering to her very needy staff, and spending the better part of the evening going over every single label and packaging graphic generated by her staff that day; making corrections before they were sent out to the printer.

- While staff morale was not an issue, they took no pride of ownership in their work or tried to assure its accuracy because they knew that she would review their work that night and if there were any errors, she would fix them, and if not, the weight would still fall on her shoulders.

- Lastly, her manager was all but hostile toward her and I never could figure out why. The closest I could come was that he took her under his wing and was her mentor many years ago, and with time she had become a master in her own rite. As a consequence, he may have felt challenged by her regulatory expertise and may have seen her as his equal and felt threatened by her and possibly thought she was slated to supplant him[14].

I was an outside observer to what was transpiring in her department, but it was clear to me that the group lacked effective leadership. The people in her group thought they were doing what was expected of them; and upon closer inspection, they were. They were meeting the incredibly low expectations that she set for them. It was clear to me, and possibly any other third-party objective observer, that she was the fundamental source or major contributor to the majority of the problems confronting her. And if she couldn't get out of her own way, there would be no way for her group to meet the requirements of the law within the allotted time. Possibly, for a variety of reasons, my colleague had wrapped herself in a self-preservation cocoon. She could not rely on her staff to generate documents that were free of errors, and errors in the documents would result in substantial financial losses for the company; up to and including product retrieval from the market. As a result, she tried to control every step of their work; she micromanaged her entire operation. The employees could only take the work so far before checking back in with her. When she found errors, she would correct them without providing an explanation as to what was in error, and why; therefore the employees didn't get any learning. It was very much like giving a person a fish, but never teaching them how to fish for themselves. Because everything had to pass through her, she became the bottleneck in her own department. She was also getting pressure from her manager, as well as the Marketing and Sales departments because of the time it took to get anything approved. I was also one of her clients and needed her group to generate packaging labelling and graphics for my international products targeted for import into the United States.

---

[14] A reference to what happened with Adam and Lilith.

In her mind, she could only see that she was besieged with requests and demands that she could not possibly deliver against. And frankly, I agreed with her, she was a single person trying to do the work of 10. Of course it was impossible, but it was also her choice. At this point in the game, she was right not to trust the accuracy of the work generated by her staff; many of them lacked the basic training necessary to do the job. She found it very upsetting to see that her staff had no sense of urgency in meeting the compliance deadline and that they were not overly concern about the accuracy of their work, after all they didn't see themselves at any risk, only her. Periodically my job would require me to stay late into the night so I could be available by telephone to some of our sales people in the far east or to resolve import issues with a foreign ministry of health. On those occasions my colleague and I would talk in-depth about the box she saw herself in, and she could see no way out. I gave her the benefit of my observations and gave her a few suggestions. But what I had proposed would have required a radical change to the culture of her department and would have required her to actually step up and take control and lead her people. This was early in the compliance period and at the time she wasn't willing to make such a drastic move or to hear me tell her that she was the cause of her own problems. If you went back and looked at the different operating styles, her style would likely have been Sociable/Animated, with animated being her base style. People with the animated style have a need to be important and in the center of things; and she was. Her supporting style was sociable, and people with this style have a need to be accepted and liked; and she did. In my view, it was her supporting style that had and was preventing her from taking the action that needed to be taken to get control over her department and her people. It wouldn't let her ruffle feathers and imple-ment needed change because she didn't want to be seen as the *"bad guy"*. However, within a few months after she saw that nothing else was working, she became more receptive to my approach. Her rage and sense of betrayal by her staff was palpable and it was difficult for me to convince her that her anger was misplaced. That, her staff had done nothing wrong; they were only following her and her manager's lead and had settled into the laissez faire culture that they had created for them over the years. For her to confront them about their casual approach to their work and their low levels of productivity at this late date would have come as a surprise to them, and would have created considerably more problems in the group; without solving any. After a bit of brainstorming, we came up with a forward strategy that we called "TRA 2000". This was back in the early 1990's and everybody was adding a 2000 or the word "Millennium" to any new product or program. The "TRA" was an abbreviation for the name of her department (Technical Regulatory Affairs), and the "2000" was suggestive of where the department wanted to be professionally positioned in the year 2000. The title was aspirational and benign but it was also tactically deceptive and discreet. We wanted her staff to believe that they were being prepared to meet the company's regulatory challenges for now and for the future; and in essence they were. But from our perspective, TRA 2000 represented a new covenant, and new agreement with staff, and a change in the existing culture. The primary elements of the program included:

- Briefing her staff on the challenges that were before them with the NLEA and explaining what it would mean to the company and to the fortunes of the group, as a whole, if they failed to meet the challenge. This alerted them and helped them to understand that there was a real risk to their own livelihoods if they were not successful.

- She would only speak positively and optimistically about the program going forward and would not look back to assign blame for underperformance or poor performance. She would start everyone off with a clean unblemished slate.

- She would meet with each of her employees and go over the responsibilities of their positions, then rewrite their job descriptions so they were clear with defined expectations and performance milestones.

- She would provide training in a structured format for everyone in her department so everyone would have the same starting place and level of comprehension. I agreed to assist her with the training.

- She would provide on-going coaching and counselling to reinforce training and to help build greater confidence among the staff.

- She would do away with the automatic "Satisfactory Rating" on performance reviews and have her employees actually have to earn their rating.

- She would conduct an informal progress review with each employee every 3 months during the first year of the TRA 2000 program. This was used to help the staff know how they were performing to expectations and to help them recognize that the program was real, not going away, and was being followed. In addition, it helped to prevent surprises when it came time for the annual reviews.

- She would schedule weekly staff meetings to update her staff as to how well they were progressing to target; to share news and to promote teamwork.

When she put these forward actions to paper and stepped back to get a good look at them, she saw 2 problems with what she had written; the first was the proposed actions themselves. Almost everything listed (save the weekly meeting) was new and foreign to how they had operated to date, and it looked to be an additional layer of responsibilities on her plate when it was already filled to capacity. The second problem was there was no way her manager would allow her to roll this program forward. There was already a significant amount of tension between them and she knew that at the first sign of pushback from her staff, they would go to him and he would nullify any and all of her actions. By my assessment, he seemed to have had a Sociable/ Sociable operating style. All of the trappings for that style were there; his warm demeanour, his use of small talk, his desire to accommodate, how he made decisions, and his overwhelming desire to be liked. He saw himself as the receptive, understanding father of her group and tried to give the people in the group whatever they wanted. Another thing that led me to believe this to be his operating style was that people having this style would carry around a sack on their backs where they keep every slight or minor offense that you have ever committed with them, and one day, when the sack gets too heavy, they just drop it, and you along with it. This is what I suspect happened to their relationship over their long careers together.

Let's go back to the first problem, when she first looked at what she would have to do, it seemed to be overwhelming. But if you went back over the list you would see that there was nothing on it that was new or out of the ordinary for any manager, it was just new to her. With what she was already doing, she thought that there was no way for her to fit all of these in as well. My thinking was that she really didn't have to. She just needed to stop everything else she was doing and adopt a proven approach; after all, nothing she was doing was working anyway. There comes a time in every manager's career when they have to stop fighting the alligators and just drain the swamp; this was her time. And as for the time it would take to implement and maintain the new program; I thought an allocation of 5 days would be generous. Let's take a look at them, one at a time:

- No additional time can be allocated for meeting with your staff and making them aware of the importance of their work to the success of the company with respect to meeting the compliance guidelines for the new labelling law. The value of this meeting is to wake people up and make them aware that they too are stakeholders in the success or failure of this undertaking; they share in the risk.

- No time can be allocated for her suppressing her anger and sense of betrayal because she saw herself carrying the entire load on her shoulders and her staff seeming to be indifferent to her plight. Her anger was misplaced, and her staff was not at fault; her employee's productivity expectations and their current work environment was a creation of hers, her manager's, and the company. The staff did as little as was required to keep their jobs because they really never had an effective leader. If she were to explode and vent her frustrations publicly, it would have only confused and alienated her already confused group of people.

- All of her employees did very much the same job, but had a responsibility for different subsidiaries, so at best, 2 days would be plenty of time to rewrite job descriptions and set specific expectations and performance milestones for each employee.

- Everyone was given training on the new labelling requirements when the law was first introduced, so 3 days of additional remedial training should be enough to bring everyone to a satisfactory level of competence; and if not she would have deeper problems to root-out.

- No additional time can be allocated for on-going coaching and counselling to reinforce training; that is a major component of any manager's job.

- No additional time can be allocated for doing annual reviews or for communicating that ratings will be based upon an objective assessment of their performance with respect to goals. This is another incentive to help a person decide if they choose to opt in or opt out. A Satisfactory Rating would no longer be based upon whether or not they can breathe or if they had a pulse.

- No additional time can be allocated for giving your employees informal review counselling sessions. They need to know how they are performing to target so they're no surprises later on. This also keeps them mindful that they have skin in the game.

- No additional time can be allocated for weekly staff meetings; communication meetings are an essential part of every manager's toolbox.

This was her only option and she knew it, but even then, it would be a heavy lift and there were no guarantees that it would be successful, given the volume of work and the time constraints. In addition to all of this, there were powerful external forces at work that I will talk to later. But for now, let me tell you something about me. She had no idea as to who I was or what my motives might have been. I had only been with the company for less than 6 months and I had absolutely no skin in the game. Yet I was collaborating with her on taking a radically new approach to managing her group at the most pivotal point in her career. She would have to trust the new guy (who had nothing to lose) and take a leap of faith that our new approach would work, while risking the real prospects of being shut down by her manager. She was not in a good place. Ladies, it's okay to cry; men do it too, but we try to hide behind closed doors when we do. She had no other way out but she still continued to struggle with making the decision for weeks. Needless to say, we went through several boxes of Kleenexes during that time. At some point she found the courage to make the decision. She went home and had her husband dig out their Christmas tree ornaments; she selected 2 of them. The next day, she called me into her office and told me she was going to follow through on the "TRA 2000" program because, as she saw it, she had no other choice and nothing to lose. I told her that I would support her where I could, but it was not going to be easy. She looked at me and reached into her desk draw and put the ornaments on top of her desk, and then she smiled and put them away. I understood her message and saw that she was committed; after all, they were 2 of the biggest *brass balls* I had ever seen.

Now, that left us with problem # 2. Her manager would never buy in to any of her initiatives and he had virtually taken away all of her authority, as a consequence, she had no power. Therefore, she had to find and tap into another power source. Remember our discussion about power and authority. Power is always somewhere around you, and if you don't have any, you'll have to find ways to tap into someone else's. In this case, she was not the Emperor but if she played her cards right, she could very well become the power behind the throne. I'll have to give you some more background before this will become clear.

In the early 1990's the company was doing around two billion dollars in domestic sales. And, if any of their products were not in compliance with the Nutritional Labelling and Education Act at the end of the compliance period, they couldn't be put on the market for sale. This was a big deal, and I am sure that it was a topic of discussion or an agenda item during the company's Board meetings, and the Board would have been given assurances by its Chairman that all of the company's products would be compliant with the law within the allotted time. The Chairman would have required those same assurances from the President & CEO, and in turn the President would have required the same assurances from the Sr. VP of Research & Development (where the Regulatory Department reported). From my vantage point, it was clear to me that the Sr. VP of R&D was, by no means, convinced that the Regulatory Department could deliver to expectations. He knew that there was friction between the Manager and the Director and they were not working as a team. He was not impressed with the caliber or educational backgrounds of the regulatory staffers. He also knew that the group's Director lacked the leadership skills that would be required to meet the challenges of such an important project. So, prior to my coming on-board, he had assigned one of his VPs to act as a mentor for the Director. He also brought in an outside management consultant firm to work with the Manager, the Director, and their staff in order to identify and try to correct areas of dysfunction and to promote teamwork. Now, some 6 months beyond my interviews for the international position, I began to piece together the rationale for some of the peculiar questions I was asked during that process. When I interviewed, they were trying to determine if I would be able to take control of the department if one or both of the managers were no longer with the company; I had held the regulatory position at my former employer. When the pieces started coming together for me, I learned that the Director was required to meet off-site with the members of the consulting firm weekly, and he had to meet informally with his mentor at least twice a week. The manager and the director had to meet regularly with the Sr. VP to give updates on the progress of the group. And about once a month, all the staff, the manager and director, the outside consulting firm, and both VPs would meet for 3 to 4 hours in order to talk through any outstanding issues and to try to build better communication channels and teamwork within the group. I was in the dark about all of this because I wasn't included. My salary was being paid by the international company and I was housed in the research facility and the regulatory department because that was where all the technical documentation and resources were located. And while an organizational chart would have shown that I reported to the Director of Regulatory in the domestic company, my real bosses were my international clients and the Sr. VP of R &D. I was a one man band without any reports, and when I transferred technical data to the field or required a research expert to travel to an international location to solve a problem, I generated revenues for the R & D facility. From time to time the Sr. VP of R&D would call me into his office to ostensibly get an update on my current projects and to direct me to others within his organization that I could call upon for assistance. It was also on those occasions when he would probe me for my take on what was occurring with respect to the progress the Regulatory Group was making on the requirements for compliance to the labelling law. My responses to him were professional and objective, the man wasn't blind, and he was far more candid with me than I will be with you here. He wanted me to be prepared to step up, if called upon, to assure the successful completion of the project. I can't be certain, but I believe that it was during one of these meetings (after the manager had decided to go forward with the program) that I told him about the blueprints for the "TRA 2000" program. He was immediately interested and wanted a full briefing. He had been waiting for the Director to come up with some kind of a plan, any kind of a plan that would assure him that necessary steps were being taken to assure the success of the project. Unfortunately, he had been waiting for over a year. He arranged a meeting with all the managers in the department and requested that my colleague walk everyone through the proposed program. Though prior to the meeting my colleague briefed her manager about the program we had outlined so he wouldn't be blind-sided at the meeting. She also let him know that the topic came up in a meeting that I had had with the Sr. VP; that way, he couldn't accuse her of going around him. At the end of her presentation, the Sr. VP was fully on-board, which also meant that everyone else was too. I have to stop here to make something clear that I should have established much earlier; I was very fond of both the Manager and the Director and I worked with them both and took no sides in their on-going battle. But it was painful for me to see how quickly the Director ran to embrace the program once it had been embraced by the Sr. VP. And while he didn't techni-cally lie, his words could have very easily been construed to suggest that he had some role or authorship in the program's creation. He was undoubtedly under a great deal of stress. The Sr. VP wanted to be part of the initial launch of the program and suggested it be launched at the department's next group meeting with the consultants. I was instructed to attend.

Therefore, the second problem was taken off the table. My colleague went from being a manager with full responsibility and no authority to a manager with shared responsibilities with the full authority of the Sr. VP of R&D; putting it another way, she went from the power-less to the powerful. Our initial plan was to take a slow but deliberate approach to getting the program's approval. She and I had planned to have oblique conversations about putting such a plan together in ear shot of the Director so he could think it through and get involved and on-board early. If that had failed we would have had the same conversations so it could be overheard by his mentor (the VP of Technology). Our last option was to just by-pass the Director and present the plan directly to the Sr. VP of R&D, and that's apparently what I did. The Sr. VP had made it clear to me that time was running out, and I could sense that he was nearing a tipping point where he would be making some significant changes to the leadership of the Regulatory Affairs group in order to prevent a failure, *on his part*, to deliver the company's products fully compliant with the law within the allotted time. And I have to be honest with you; I had no desire to become a member of the Regulatory group, or to lead it. I didn't need nor want the drama. I didn't want the reports, I didn't want the chaos, and I didn't want to step into the middle of a mess that someone else had created, and I would have had to clean up. That was not the job I signed up for. I don't have a cape or wear tights, and I'm not a selfless superhero. However, if those were my instructions, than that's what I would have had to do. So it's quite possible that I revealed the plans for the "TRA 2000" program as much for the benefit of the company and my colleague as I did for myself. And for those poker players among us... *"I blinked".*

The introduction of the program to the larger group was entirely upbeat with a sufficient level of fanfare. My colleague emphasized that the purpose of the program was to help position the group to meet the demands of the new labelling law and to be able to meet the challenges of the future. The Director expressed his support as did the Sr. VP. The Sr. VP also added an incentive; he stated that once the group had completed the current challenge and converted all the company's packaging to the new format, he would sponsor a night of celebration in Manhattan. He would take the group, along with their spouses or significant others, into the city for dinner and a Broadway show. There were smiles and excitement all around with a little uncertainty as to what the "TRA 2000" program would mean to them on a personal level. As for me, two things really stood out. There seemed to be a real disconnect between the work the regulatory staff was doing and their awareness as to its importance to the company; they seemed to be complacent, and while they knew of the deadline for compliance, I couldn't detect any sense of ownership, urgency, or commitment on their part to meeting it. To me, that was exactly what I would have expected to find whenever there is poor communications and leadership. They saw others at risk, but not themselves. When I looked around the room I saw 11 staff members, 3 managers, 1 director, 2 VPs, the Sr. VP's secretary, and 3 outside consultants. I tried to guesstimate how much these 3 to 4 hour meetings were costing the company, and it was plenty. Yet, remarkably, my colleague's staff couldn't see that this was a *really big deal*. The other thing that stood out was the presentation put on by the consultants for the first 2 hours, prior to the introduction of the new program. I asked myself, *"What was their purpose, and why were they even there?"* From my prospective, I couldn't see any value in their work. They were presenting a *"canned"*, off the shelf, general *"stock presentation"* on skills training and teamwork, trust, collaboration, communications, and other topics that they could have presented to any generic audience anywhere. They never made a direct connection between what they were presenting to the actual shortcomings and deficiencies of the people in the department and in the room. And, because they didn't target their message to their audience, none of what they were saying was being internalized by the staff, and people were just not paying attention. In my personal assessment, these meetings were a colossal waste of time, money and human resources.

Let's fast-forward a few months. By this time the manager and the director are working together and the staff had been made aware of what was expected of them. New job descriptions, with measurable objectives, had been developed, and everyone had gotten additional training. There was some initial pushback from some of the staff, but the Director was unable to provide any relief[15]. Two of the three staffers who had been assigned to the group due to nepotism decided to move on, one because he found a position in information technology with another company, and it was more in line with his training, and the other decided that it was time for her and her husband to start their family. Unfortunately, she was poorly equipped to do the job and was never able to make the transition from Office Assistant to Regulatory Affairs Officer. A third employee was also lost. The subject employee was not adding much to the overall productivity of the group anyway. She was working on her Master's Degree and was spending the majority of her time at work reading and doing school assignments. Now that everyone was put under closer supervision, she decided to leave the company and pursue her degree fulltime. My colleague was able to recruit at least 2 top-notch Regulatory Affairs officers from the outside. When they joined the group they helped to increase productivity over 100%. The original employees had to play catch-up and they did, they all made significant improvements in both productivity and accuracy. It was

---

[15] The Director's operating style was such that he wanted to be liked at any cost; but as a manager, he wanted his people to do what was expected of them, though he lacked the courage to insist upon it. Therefore he was only able to refuse their request for relief when he could point to someone else as being the bad guy; in this case, it was the Sr. VP who was the cause of their discomfort, not him.

a challenge for my colleague to begin to back away from being a micromanager and to stop being her own departmental bottle-neck. Now she had at least 5 others that were competent enough to proof the final copy, checking for accuracy, before the graphics and labelling were sent to the printer; and her manager was among them. After 2 or 3 months, the contract with the outside consultants was terminated. But because so much time had been wasted on the front-end, she and her manager decided that it would be necessary to farm-out some of the lesser known labels and those intended for wholesale and institutional sales to a private consultant that they had worked with in the past. The Sr. VP of R&D concurred and in the end, they completed the entire labelling project on time having at least 2 months to spare.

The Sr. VP took us all into Manhattan for a night on the town and we were all given plaques and key chains commemorating the project. I don't think my colleague or her manager gave it much thought, and if they did, they didn't let on. But I was waiting for the blood bath to come, there had to be blood. I was an observer and saw the level of dysfunction, poor leadership and lack of professionalism in the department, and so did the Sr. VP. The Regulatory Affairs department reported through his office and were it not for the "TRA 2000" program; the department would have stumbled and failed to deliver to the new law, which would have put the company as well as the Sr. VP's position at risk. No leader could allow a repeat of that. So I waited for the letting of the blood, because I knew it was coming...and it did. After about 6 months the Sr. VP realigned his organization so that the Regulatory group reported in to one of his VPs and its Director was reassigned to a temporary position where he would have sufficient time in his day to look for another employment opportunity, and my colleague was then promoted to his position.

There is a tremendous amount of valuable information contained in this case study, but at this point in our discussion, very little of it should be new to you. The only thing that I would consider new was the way in which we had planned to make the program public. After all else had failed and she was committed to going forward with the program; regardless of the outcome. Our original plan was to give the Director an opportunity to hear about the program and come on-board early. If he had resisted or tried to supress it going forward, he would have been circumvented and we would have gone to his mentor. Our last and final option was to present it to the Sr. VP directly, and due to the circumstances, that became option one. This was clearly one of those times when it would have been easier to beg for forgiveness than to ask for permission; particularly when you already knew permission would never come. Remember, my colleague had no other options. You might find yourself in a similar situation at some point in your career, and if you do, you will have to determine how best to move forward; weigh the pros and cons and the potential outcomes of each before making your move. The risk you face for doing nothing could be far more damaging and destructive to your organization and your career than the risk you would face for just taking some form of appropriate action. You'll have to be in tune with your environment and the current situation. To a large extent, the tangible and intangible problems we found in the first case study and in the widget scenario were (with some small variations) the same as the ones we found it this case study. And in each case, immediate and forceful corrective action was required in order to avert failure and to turn things around. However in this case, the Director was incapable of such actions and became an obstacle to success and had to be overcome. But we also have to look at the company, the company's culture, and the environment that we were in. You'll find that in large companies change occurs slowly, at a glacial pace, and this was a large company. The smaller the company, the more likely it is for all levels of the leadership to be receptive to new ideas and innovations. But when companies grow large, every level of the leadership resists bold new ideas like the TRA 2,000 program. Instead, and in most cases, they are intent on maintaining the status quo; protecting their place within the company's hierarchy and risking nothing. Change will always be resisted and if it ever comes, it will come agonizingly slow. That's why, we decided on the three distinct options in order to publicize the program. We knew we would have to get through several levels of resistance before the proposal would see the light of day... and time was not on our side.

The Six "Cs" Standards of Persuasion and Innovation:

There is some value in flushing this case study out a little more, and to do that I want to recall a leadership forum I attended some years back. The CEO of a large corporation spoke directly to the middle managers. He stated how appreciative he was for middle management's contributions to the overall success of the company and how he was well aware of some of the difficulties they faced with respect to moving their creative ideas and innovations forward. Then he asked that they not lose faith, but keep pushing their ideas in order to get their innovations heard. He told the group that a company's culture can usually be categorised as being either evolutionary or revolutionary. And small companies tend to be revolutionary and more receptive to new ideas and new thinking which makes them much more nimble and quick to innovate, as compared to larger firms. However, he noted, that as a company grows in size and complexity it starts developing levels of bureaucracy that restricts flexibility and change and everything becomes an evolutionary process. He stated that the evolutionary culture that was systemic in his company and many other large enterprises cost those companies tens of millions of dollars each year due to lost and missed opportunities; a failure to innovate, streamline and modernize. He also told the group that he was painfully aware that his organization, like most others, was organized in such a way as to assure that new and innovative ideas and methods would be choked off and suppressed long before they could get a fair and open hearing and be judged on their merits. So in appealing to the middle managers to continue their creativity and innovations, he asked that they keep their work underground in the early stages. He encouraged them to work out all the flaws and anything that might discredit their new approach. Then, he told them that they had to generate momentum for their ideas at the grassroots level while still keeping the major components underground. In that way, when they publicize their bold new innovation, it would already have so much support and acceptance that once it broke the surface and became public, most reasonable managers would find it irresistible and would be unable to stand against it. He concluded by telling the group that before they publicise their innovations, they needed to be certain that their work would stand the test of *The Six "Cs" Standards of Persuasion and Innovation:* That it was Clear, Concise, Compelling, Connected, Contrasted and Credible.

- Clear: Your idea, approach or solution has to be clear and intuitive to a 6th grader so everyone can understand what it is.

- Concise: It has to be tightly packaged and encapsulated so people will know what to expect. There should be no drawn-out details associated; it needs to be elegant and simplistic.

- Compelling: Your approach or solution should be irresistible. It should add value and be free of flaws, and if possible require less time, money and human resources to implement. This is what's called the *adrenalizer*.

- Connected: You won't find an audience willing to entertain solutions for orphan problems. If the problem is minimal and off in the weeds, no one really cares. Your solution or innovation has to be connected to something that is of current relevance to the organization and it has to be important enough to be on other people's radar screens.

- Contrasted: There should be a clear contrast between the benefits of what you propose to everything else, up to and including, doing nothing at all.

- Credible: There should be no doubt that what you propose will work.

We will be returning to the 6 Cs when we get to the section on Communications, specifically the sections on the Influential Presentation and the Persuasive or Argumentative Essay. But for right now, just take a quick review of the TRA 2000 Program and the way it was presented...was it clear, concise, compelling (with an adrenalizer), connected, contrasted, and was it credible?

The Responsibilities of the Manager - Continued:

Returning to the broader topic: Man is inherently xenophobic and will resist any new ideas, innovations or solutions simply because they are foreign and a potential threat or a disruption to the harmony within his world. But, in general, man is more of a follower than a leader and is less likely to stand against you when your innovations or solutions has garnered wide ranging appeal from the masses, political support at higher levels and has developed its own self-sustaining momentum. Think about the Director in this case, and other situations where you have seen those that were diametrically opposed to something, then once it has gathered support, they ran to get out in-front, leading the parade and in total support of whatever it happened to be...can you say "hypocrisy"...why sure you can.

I recognize that we have covered a number of important but wide-ranging topics in this section. But even then, you should be mindful that we have only pricked the surface of the dynamic world of the manager as they navigate their way through the nuances of man's self-serving nature. You can expect your interactions with your staff, your peers, your managers and the daily challenges of the work will be complicated and diverse and they won't present themselves to you as discrete, compartmentalize units that can be worked separately in isolation; they are all individual threads that make up a tightly woven tapestry that is the manager's job. You should expect to find that one interaction will reverberate and play on to another; it's all connected. You can't afford to become distracted by hidden agendas, infighting and backbiting, or needy or disillusioned staffers. Your job is clear; manage the people to get the work done. And from my perspective, if you try to manage with an open kind hand, you fail. And if you manage with an iron fist, you also fail. You need balance. My approach has been to treat everyone with a genuine level of respect and human dignity. I recognize that people are highly intelligent sophisticated individuals that are in their jobs by their own choice and that they are being compensated for what they do. My expectation is that they will work with me and each other in order to move the work forward to a satisfactory completion; that was their agreement. I don't look to garner their admiration or affection; but I do give and demand a basic level of respect toward myself and everyone on my staff. My expectation is that we will operate as professionals regardless of environmental turmoil. This is not too much to ask. There will be time to work through and resolve intangible emotional issues. But the time I invest in them is targeted at resolving them and putting them to rest; not for it to be the first of many dances. They say that the squeaky wheel is the one that gets the most grease, and if that is your thinking, then once again, you have failed. Grease is a short-term fix, a patch over a much larger problem; one that deserves your attention. If you have a squeaky wheel in your department, get it fixed, or get it replaced. To do otherwise would only jeopardize your success going forward. You don't have time to pander and prattle to disgruntle employees or Prima Donnas. Therefore, you should expect to lose some people either because they are unable or unwilling to meet the requirements of their jobs or they just can't find it within themselves to become professional actors. And while the loss of an employee is a serious matter, more likely than not, it would be to the betterment of the entire group. When I noted the differences between the manager and the boss, I stated that the manager should provide leadership in an unencumbered, non-threatening environment, that they should allow their staff to share power and responsibility for the work so that they take ownership in what they do. And I believe that all managers should operate in this fashion. But I also know that man's commitment to you, their work, and even their family is tenuous and not to be relied upon. Man's true allegiance is to himself and that should never be forgotten. Additionally, I believe that it is in your best interest, as well as theirs, that you hold them to the same level of accountability for their work as your management has established for you. I also believe that a manager should prepare their people and clear the way in order to facilitate easy access to the work, and encourage their staff to grow as individuals. They should provide them a sufficient level of incentives so they can decide for themselves if it is to their advantage to follow their lead, or to opt out. A manager has no right or authority to mistreat anyone on their staff, but the staff should also know that push-back, resistance and rebellion are serious performance issues and won't have a place in your organization, though professional dialog will. When you take a fair, balanced and unbiased professional approach to your work, your people, and to your areas of responsibility, you begin a process that will ultimately result in a fundamental change from one culture to another; one that is preferred as opposed to one that is not.

Now, let's go back to that iron fist. You have to maintain ultimate control of your area of responsibility, but you don't have to act like a tyrant. You should trust your people but verify that your trust is not misplaced. You should learn to identify with your people on a one-on-one level and show an interest in them and their work. This will help you improve your interpersonal skills and become more charismatic in your everyday human interactions. These human interactions help you to develop a velvet touch, and an easy way with people without compromising professionalism. Now you can turn that velvet touch into a velvet glove in order to conceal the iron fist. There is just no way to get around it; you have to maintain control of your department and your staff. If you become a good manager, everyone will know where the power resides and there will be no need to flaunt it. Most prudent managers keep their powers concealed. People begrudge overt displays of power and control over them because they are interpreted as forms of intimidation and veiled threats that they find offensive, obscene, and demoralizing. So, in view of how power and authority are perceived by the powerless, you should be discreet and measured in how you exercise them. But you should never hesitate in using them when the need arises.

A Note to the Female Reader:

You will forfeit your success and your careers if you try to avoid being labelled a *bitch.* To be called a bitch is both unfortunate and unavoidable. But for me to tell you about name-calling, the fact that you're constantly being maligned and discriminated against, and that the professional playing field is tilted against you would be a waste of time and space in this book; no one has to tell you what is immensely apparent. My words here are just that, words. I don't know what effect they will have because they don't provide you any solutions or new information. But I am compelled to say something, so this will be a talk about the other elephant in the room that no one wants to talk about; *"The Pink Elephant"*. I don't know if any man could ever get this right, but this will be my third rewrite and attempt at it.

Everyone knows, but few *men* will admit, that you have to work a lot harder than a man and be much more effective in order for your contributions to be considered adequate and acceptable. No matter where you go in the world, even in the most sophisticated first world countries, glass ceilings and institutional sexism are realities and are ubiquitous in the workplace. When you apply yourself and become the most effective and successful manager in the organization, you should be lauded, rewarded and applauded, but you seldom ever are, you're merely tokenized, patronized and tolerated. In a male dominated society, the vast majority of men will never be able to bring themselves to accept you or your contributions as being equal. It's just another one of man's weaknesses and insecurities that continues to pit men against women. Its man's bias, competitive sexism, and his desire for unquestioned hierarchical dominance that is all but monolithic in the world's cultures. Man is vain, arrogant, and has a sense of divine superiority that, collectively, prevents him from accepting you as their professional or intellectual equals. Despite the fact that you have already proven yourselves to be man's intellectual equal, he will never acknowledge it. What he will do, is to continue to work to restrict your access to professional and financial equality. Yes, there is *"a war against women"*, and for those of you reading this, you see it as restrictive bias, patronization, and discrimination; for you, while they are barriers to social, professional, and financial equality, your war is also a war where only small arms are being used. What about your sisters around the world? In their war, there is no mercy, men are using the big guns of oppression; and their war is both bloody and inhumane. Many live in cultures where they cannot own property, where education is forbidden, where they are, in effect, slaves and the property of men. They live in cultures where they can be raped, and while their attackers are sent for *rehabilitation,* they are sent to be *stoned*. This war is a real war, and all in your gender are affected by it. Man has done everything in his power to establish and solidify the sexual hierarchy since the creation of Eve, and he is reluctant to see things change. Whether you believe the mythology of the first people or not is unimportant, man appears to believe it, and has reacted to you as if it had been a point of fact! History has shown that because of *this* and other *contrived reasons*, man has institutionalized a doctrine that assured that Eve, and all women thereafter, would never have a claim to equality. The doctrine contends that she, and consequently, they were *deliberately* made, by the Creator *from lesser stuff – Adam's rib*. Therefore, hers and their subordinate positions were forever fixed in the human hierarchy by the Divine. It really doesn't matter what your position is on the validity of this historic, religious, or mythological doctrine, the fact is, that man is currently in the position of dominance and he just can't deal with the notion of having to face another Lilith...*an equal*. Therefore, in his attempts to keep you subordinate to him, man has maligned and persecuted you from the very beginning. In man's mind, you stand duly accused as the sole cause of his every misfortune: It was you that was tempted and committed original sin, resulting in the loss of the garden and our only chance for immortality. It was you that seduced, corrupted, and mated with the Angels, giving birth to the Nephilim[16] (the Mighty Men, the Tyrannical Giants). It was Pandora that opened the box and unleashed war and pestilence upon the world. It was because of Helen that war came to Troy. And it was Delilah and Cleopatra that led to the downfall of Sampson and Mark Antony. Just pick up a book, all this stuff has been written down...and if it's written in a book, it must be true...*right?* I'm not being facetious here, this slanderous and pervasive taint is infused into many of the cultures around the world, and it is believed. It's not just believed by the dirt poor and the illiterate, it is an accepted truism in the minds of the *right-wing* political extremists, the religious zealots, and our social bigots. And because it is believed, on either a conscious or unconscious level, in the minds of those *intellectual midgets*, they've become comfortable with the notion, and the justification of your institutionalized discrimination and outright suppression.

We have to take a break here, to allow some of our male readers to catch-up; particularly those that are in denial, and can't see the war that's in front of them. I will talk more about this when we get to the next chapter entitled *"Morality and Ethics"*, but for now, you just need to know that I believe that institutional evil exist and has, among other ways, manifested itself as sexism and institutionalized discrimination. The political elite has poisoned the ground around women with a constant flow of negative propaganda, and baseless accusations that are intended to subordinate, debase, and dehumanize them. The notations above are just a sampling of some of what has been disseminated over the millennium. The political elite's intent is to subjugate, dominate, and thereby rule over women; it's all about acquiring and holding power. The politically powerful feed

---

[16] See the Book of *Genesis 6. 1-4*. While the actual meaning of this passage is still a point of active debate among scholars and theologians, it states that the Nephilim were the offspring of Angels (sons of God) and the daughters of men (women). In addition, some writings point to this passage as being an abomination to God's law and is the reason women, in many cultures, have to keep themselves vailed and/or completely covered so as not to tempt the Angels or the much weaker men.

their malicious propaganda to the impoverished, the illiterate, and the mouth breathers of society and they become the foot soldiers of bigotry. *Do you see the war yet…*no matter, I'm not done yet.

When the political powers are aligned against you and the masses follow, your position is all but impossible. But this is only malicious bigotry; the worst is yet to come. Let's stay on the subject of power in order to flush this out a bit further. Because women have historically been denied **political power**, few were ever able to achieve any **position power**; therefore, they have had no voice in hierarchical affairs (social policies, practices, and norms). And when we look at financial power and physical force; where women have also been impoverished, we'll begin to understand some of the drivers of infanticide in female children. Yes, *"infanticide"*. Infanticide is still a major social and cultural problem around the world, and its levels get to be remarkable when you consider their rates in India and China. And, while it targets both male and female children, why is it that female children are targeted at 2 to 3 times the rate as male children? In my view, and I clearly don't have all the answers, it appears to be directly attributable to their perceived value and worth within the society. Physical strength for tribal protection and a reliable labor force are valued higher **(physical force)**. They increase the prospects for clan, tribal, and family survival during times of conflict and economic hardship. They also help to insure financial security and the retention of wealth. It all comes down to *"value and worth"*; the value that those in high positions and those with political power assigns to the contributions of females and males to the benefit of the greater society. And because of competitive sexism and institutional discrimination (in addition to other reasons), the contributions made by males are given a higher value and overall worth to that society than those made by females. For example, in this particular instance I am talking about the acquisition and the retention of limited resources (security and wealth). Because of the physical differences between men and women, the traditional male role has been that of a hunter, warrior, provider and protector of the family and tribe. And, the female role was that of a gatherer, nurturer and caregiver, as well as keeper of the household. As a consequence, the contributions made by men to the overall security and viability of the tribe has, and continues to be, valued at a much higher worth than the contributions made by women. Additionally, males have long been the ones that have been given the right of inheritance, so as to preserve the families or tribal wealth **(financial power)**. And, with that accumulated wealth, they are expected to provide a safety net for their parents in old age. Daughters are considered temporary members of the family unit and will marry and move into a different family or clan.[17] So to sum up, society (*both men and women*) have put a higher value on the contributions made by men than women. And because of that, and the existing universal anti-female bias, during difficult times and social hardships, females are made the victims of infanticide at much higher rates than males. And tragically, women, mothers, and sisters are as complicit in the act of infanticide against their own gender as their male relatives. They are just considered to have far less worth than males[18] . Consider this; in today's China, there are 17% fewer females in the general population than males (about 22.5 million less) and in India, there is 9% less (about 11.4 million less). *Is the war becoming any clear to you now?* Let's move on.

I am going to move away from infanticide and go back to discrimination and subordination; we have to circle back and pick up our religious zealots. When we look at the religions of Judaism, Christianity, and Islam sharing a similar theology and that the theology teaches that a woman's position, within the sexual hierarchy, was fixed by the Divine; for the religious zealots, the matter is closed. And while religious scholars and theologians continue to interpret the meanings within their Holy Books and Scriptures, the religious zealots only accept their literal interpretations (as written). So as a consequence, they truly believe that a woman's position is subordinate, relative to a man's, and that their subordination has been ordained by God. How are women supposed to combat that type of thinking?

I won't ask you a third time if you are able to see the war against women, but I will apologise if I was not able to demonstrate it for you. You either see it or you don't. But if you do, what are you going to do as a manager or as a human being to help put an end to it? The war is against your mothers, your wives, your daughters, your sisters, as well as all your nieces. What are you willing to do to help them? Or will you just sit there, doing nothing, clutching your own fears and insecurities and finding justification for the discrimination in the rhetoric and propaganda of the political extremist, the social bigots, and the religious zealots?

---

[17] In many cultures, a dowry is expected, and even demanded by the family before your daughter will be accepted. In some other cultures, women are sold into marriage for so many goats or heads of cattle. In either case, the women have become essentially the property of the man and his family.

[18] When the Chinese Government introduced its One Child per Family Policy in 1979, there was an unintended and unexpected increase in female infanticide across the nation. The rates increased in urban areas but skyrocketed in rule China. The female children were reportedly being killed for financial reasons. Males in China have greater earning power than females and males provide additional income for their elderly parents.

Let me get back to the word "bitch". When you bring together all of man's justifications and all of his fears and insecurities, those of us that are challenged and intimidated by you and those of us that can't compete with you; *in this society*, the most we can do is to call you a bitch. But, believe me, if man could subjugate you even more, he would. But bias, patronization, discrimination, and bitch is all that he has available to him in this society, and he uses them all in a vain attempt to disarm, discredit, diminish, and try to control and dominate you. And some of you let us...you let it happen. You give up your control and let us run all over you and do what we want while you just pretend to be in charge (a lot like what happened with the Maestro). On those occasions, we relish in our victory over you and have no sympathy for your loss; *finally, a woman that knows her place*. Now, get your ass on back there and make me a cup of coffee and a fish sandwich *"girl"*. Demeaning isn't it? Ladies, what's your thinking; is this the life you want for yourselves? Do you think that just by acquiescing to us is somehow going to help advance your careers or help you avoid being called a bitch...well it won't! How did things work out for the Maestro? He surrendered his control, and when he did, everything went south, including his career. You can't let that happen to you. You'll have to step up and take control and continually fight to maintain and advance your position within the hierarchy. But man will continue to discriminate against you and call you a bitch; "no" it isn't right or fair, but few things are in our society, it's just inescapable and unavoidable. Every time you prove yourself to be man's equal you actually earn his respect, but along with his respect, you also earn his fear, and because of his own insecurity and fear, you become a bitch. Don't let that deter you. Try to remember that you are not at your place of work to be liked or loved, but to do a job. Conversely, when you try to make yourself liked, useful, and one of the guys, you end up earning neither man's fear nor his respect. At the first sign of displeasure with you, the very first descriptor is "bitch". This time it's not due to insecurity and fear, it's due to sexism and his lack of respect for you. Ladies, do your jobs and become the best managers that you know how to be, but recognize that the playing field is tilted against you and you will never, never, ever escape this singular belligerent verbal attack; irrespective of how you approach your job. It's already clear to us that, with the exceptions of our shear bulk and physical strength, you are equal to us in every other respect, and the word "bitch" is the only piece of artillery we have left in order to try to keep you from pulling even with us, or overtaking us altogether. The war against women is a real one and is being fought on many different battlefields all over the world. If you elect to ignore it, that's your choice, but that won't make it go away. This struggle for dominance is an unfortunate point of fact in male and female interactions and I don't see any changes on the horizon. You just have to deal with it if you hope to be successful, or you can just turn away. It really makes no difference which path you choose because bigotry and sexism will still follow you wherever you go and whatever you do.

In writing this book, I made a conscious effort to make every word, every strategy, tactic, and tool presented here to be as applicable to women as to men. I have a wife, 3 daughters, a goddaughter, 4 granddaughters, a sister, 2 sisters-in-law, and a multitude of nieces. I wish them, as well as all of you, the very best in your careers, and the best of luck and success in the war. I hope that what I have provided will help to level out the playing field for you. So, take what you need from this book, and *actually use what you take.* It's your career and your choice. Lastly, and just as important; because you have to deal with the added burden of discrimination and bigotry, **it doesn't give you an excuse or the permission to fall short of your goals or to fail**. Those that preceded you didn't. Each of the achievements that you make and the successes that you have *"today"* will, in time, breed achievements and successes for the daughters and granddaughters of your sisters *here*, and in distant lands and in different cultures. Even those that have yet to be born are depending on you.

Man will never give you equality just by your asking...*if you want it, you'll have to take it!*

Chapter # 16:

Morality and Ethics

Ethical and Moral Behavior – Scenario # 2; Group Think, Power & Acceptable Morality; The Life or Death Decision; The Rise of the Conscience; The Line in the Sand; Our Ever Evolving Value System; Independent Financial Power and Personal Autonomy; Unintended Consequences – Example # 3 & 4; My Weighted Value System; Moral and Ethical Guidance - Example # 5 & Scenario # 3; Evil

By any measure, Morality and Ethics are two of the most important character traits that should be apparent in any manager of people. But it goes much further and it is far more important than just managing others, morality and ethics are personal and unique to the individual. And how you performed, on this job or that, is really irrelevant if it came at a cost to your personal value system. When you move from one job to the next, everything changes, your responsibilities, your staff, your status within the organization; everything is fresh and new. But any and every action you took (or didn't take) in your personal and professional lives that created an internal conflict between what you believed to be *right* and what you believed to be *wrong* will follow and gnaw at you until you're able to rationalize your decisions or until you're able to accept your actions and grant yourself dispensation. The point that I'm trying to make (and possibly making it very badly) is that all of us have a conscience and a moral compass, and when we follow them, they don't always lead to success and prosperity but in the larger scheme of things you'll find that you're psychologically better off for it. I can't tell you what is moral and ethical for you, that's something each of you will have to work out on your own or with the help of a guide. Morality and ethics differ from one society to the next and between different people within a society, and even over time. But within those societies and among the people at any given time, morality and ethics appear to be fixed and unchanging, though they are constantly being adjusted and modified. Every society and group within the society tries to refine their definitions of what it means to be moral and ethical in a relentless search for perfection. But In doing so, they've established rigorous utopian definitions that are impossible to attain in the world in which we all live. The standards are too high and too rigid, and though we are aspirational and want to become better human beings, we are also chained to our Ids and our Egos, and they are far too primitive and controlling to allow us to get anywhere close to the *Godlike* state that would be required to meet the moral and ethical standards of the society. Therefore, in view of the standards, you would have to conclude that we all (as human beings), by our own standards, are immoral and unethical; full stop! And while some groups have accepted that interpretation and go through life on their knees with a closed mind and cast-down eyes, following the dictates of some demigod preaching about their sinfulness and demanding that they repent because *the end is nigh*, most of us are unable and unwilling to accept that interpretation. We are human beings, not angelic beings. And while we may someday evolve to a higher state of being, for now, we are what we are. And we invite emotional and psychological conflicts when we set unrealistic expectations that are completely outside the realm of possibility. For example, you can't expect the greatest chef in the world to prepare a 5 course gourmet banquet from a single can of tuna fish; it's just not going to happen regardless of your expectations. Likewise, you can't expect human beings to be angelic…if you only have lemons to work with, then the best you can hope for is lemonade, and you have to find a way to get comfortable with that. You have to recognize and accept actual human limitations and move on. They are human limitations, not human failings, if you consider them failings, it would create an internal battle between good and evil that you can't possibly win. We could never hope to approach a state where the purest form of morality was attainable and all our actions were above reproach and ethical. Not in this world. A world in which the societies we've constructed requires us to compete for everything; a world in which every day is a constant battle for our very survival. So, *no*, we won't measure-up to the purest moralistic and ethical standards, but we can't accept the notion that we are immoral and unethical either. We have chosen to believe that because we are human and aspirational, that we are entitled to claim, at least, the human measure of ethical and moral consideration for ourselves; the purest forms will have to wait until we evolve before we can claim them. We will never accept the verdict of the purest because we can never accept that level of human failing. Therefore, as a consequence, we've chosen (for better or worse) to view our world and our morality through the prism of *situational rationalization*. Situational rationalization is nothing more than situational ethics and morality. In our world and in the lives we live, we don't allow our morality or ethics to be fixed, independent, and objective variables. If we did, we would fail utterly. Now let's be clear, I am no different than any of you, and I use situational rationalization in the same ways as you. But when viewed from the position of an outside observer its apparent that our values constantly float, shift, adjust and change dependent upon the given situation at hand and how that situation might impact our survival, our place within a given hierarchy, and/or our level of depravity when we are confronted with an opportunity for self-gain or aggrandizement, or when we submit to our baser desires and find ourselves compelled to take revenge. Though we inherently know the difference between right and wrong (morality and immorality, and ethical and unethical), dependent upon the situation, we frequently find ourselves practicing situational morality and ethics. Based upon our own subjective assessments, we often move forward selecting the most expedient path of least resistance; frequently turning a blind eye to what we know to be right and correct. And this is where our problems get their start. If we go back to our psychological nature and consider our baser being, our competitive being, and our aspirational being, we find that our baser and competitive beings are our drivers for survival and prosperity, and they are aligned and far stronger than our aspirational being. And while they will insure our survival and competitiveness, our aspirational being, though far weaker, is not just sitting there impotent and silent. It is that distant and persistent voice that keeps reminding us of our humanity and our desire to do the right thing and it is the shame that we feel when we look in the mirror and know we've taken the wrong path. It is our conscience, our moral compass that has been put into conflict because of an overt action on our part. By nature, we want to be moral and ethical but habitually the forces on the other side are much stronger and as a consequence we frequently cower and turn away; choosing to pick a different battle or a different hill where we can take the moral high ground. The problem with this delusional and self-pacifying thinking is that (realistically) the high ground will always be out of reach so long as we remain aspirationally weak. And you will always be aspirationally weak so long as the baser being and the competitive being within stay aligned. Your aspirational self has nothing, absolutely nothing of value to say to your baser self that would cause it to change or modify its primary mission of protecting and preserving the survival of the self...they just don't talk to each other. Therefore, your only option is to build an alliance between the competitive self and the aspirational self so that the aspirational self can tap into the competitive self's powerbase. Then, as long as what you attempt "aspirationally" doesn't threaten the survival of the whole being, the baser self will ignore your attempts at ethics and morality. So now, your aspirational challenge is to get your competitive self to (within reason) follow your moral guidance. But if your competitive being sees itself in a pitched battle for dominance or needing to carve out a new place within the hierarchy, it would consider itself in a position of disadvantage (weakness) and will have no time to indulge in anything aspirational. Though there is a constant dialog between the aspirational and the competitive, everything aspirational is given a lower priority and takes a back seat. It's only when the competitive self has established and fortified its position within the hierarchy and feels that it is no longer under immediate attack, will it be willing to listen to the voices coming from the aspirational self. The competitive self has to feel secure and in a position of strength before it will take on any additional risk; any ethical and moral considerations that would be considered within reason. Therefore, as humans, we cannot move in the direction of morality and ethics unless and until we are in a position or in a situation where our survival is not being threatened and our position within the hierarchy is assured and not under attack. There is no profit for being ethical or moral, and in our society, they both come at a cost. No one in our society will allow any of your good, ethical, or moral deeds to go unpunished.

Ethical and Moral Behavior:

Now I would like to clarify a misconception around *good deeds* and *ethical and moral deeds*. Good deeds are altruistic and philanthropic acts that you choose to do because they give you pleasure or, provide you with some level of self-fulfilment, superior control, pride, etc. You benefit from them because you decided to incur the cost of making something happen that may not have been possible without your generosity. So, from your personal perspective, it puts you in touch with your higher being; you ring your little bell to signal your accomplishment and all will feel right in your world. But, because your good deeds or good works were actually selfish in nature (for your own aggrandizement), your deeds were neither ethical nor moral. And just so you'll know, a few of us that are directly benefiting from your generosity resent you for it. We are small-minded, ungrateful little cretins, that can't appreciate your gifts for what they are, we are grasping and gluttonous and can only see that what you've provided was not enough and, in our minds, you only did what you did to make yourself look good and to make us look bad, inferior, and dependent. Sad, isn't it. I'd like to take this a step further...we live in a society that's governed by certain moral and ethical codes of conduct. And by-in-large, we all stay within these established codes and meet the standards outlined by the society; we don't disturb the peace or violate the laws, we pay our taxes, and nurture and educate our children. We consider ourselves fine, upstanding members of a moral and ethical society. And if you're comfortable with that assertion, I won't argue the point. The results of your actions may well be considered moral and ethical, but they were not initiated for moral or ethical reasons. Morality and ethics are determined by the intent of the action, not the results or outcome of an action. Therefore I would suggest that while your conduct was exemplary and there may be room to argue that the results of your actions were ethical and moral...you were not acting ethically or morally when you were following some arbitrary societal code of conduct. Your compliance with the rules was dictated more by your desire to avoid reprisals and societal sanctions than anything else. In addition, your choice to nurture and educate your children was done out of your love for them and your desire to protect and preserve your genetic strain. So in both instances your actions were self-directed and self-rewarding. *There are **no tangible rewards** for being ethical or moral, just the knowledge that you did what was right as you understood right.* Morality and ethics are driven by your aspirational being, your internal guide, your conscious mind that is forever looking for balance, fairness, and intellectual purity; your desire to do what's right, because it's right. It points your way to a higher level of human existence without regard to the forces working in opposition. It has allowed us to evolve this far and has separated us from the other animals on the planet (without regard to our big brains), and if we are to grow further, as a species, that growth will be driven by our aspirations; they are our only hope and promise of ever becoming higher functioning beings.

Now, for illustrative purposes, let's try to put the requirements for morality and ethics into some kind of contexts. And, we should start by recognizing that while our aspirational being is forever vigilant, it doesn't necessarily translate into a condition that requires us to be in a constant struggle trying to decide good over evil; it's just not a fulltime job. Because we, for the most part, instinctively follow the rules and codes of conduct within our society, the *results* of our actions can be considered both moral and ethical *behaviors*. It doesn't matter if we do it to avoid punishment and pain. And, because I don't want to put too fine a point on it, we can also call your good deeds, your acts of generosity and actions out of love, moral and ethical *behaviors* as well. Though you acted for selfish reasons, you did no harm. This is how we live our lives and go about our human activities. We spend about 99.99% of our lives servicing our own personal interests, seeking gratification and rewards while avoiding difficulty and pain, and so long as we don't infringe upon the wellbeing of others, we cannot be considered immoral or unethical[19]. But it's that other 0.01% that will determine if we will be honorable and aspirational, thereby deciding to do what is right, or will we find another reason to use situational rationalization to again justify our avarice, cruelty, and/or our craven cowardliness. This is where you initiate an act that is either moral or ethical, or both, or neither; the decision is yours. I can't help you, and neither can theologians or an ethical guide. The majority, maybe 75% of the 0.01%, of what you will have to decide will be internal to you and in direct opposition to your competitive nature. You will have to find ways to climb above the everyday battles and unrelenting backbiting and set yourself apart from the masses. You will have to learn to recognize your weaknesses, your fears, your biases, and vices and listen to your voices of fairness and reason. It is vitally important to make the right decisions here, regardless of the cost to you, because these decisions; those that are internal to you and under your control will follow you for a lifetime…did you act honestly or with favoritism and bias, did you make right and fair decisions at the time or was your decisions clouded by greed or anger, was your decisions injurious to someone, even if they were not aware of your act; how injurious were they, can you live with your crime, and so on. In the general scheme of things, these are usually one-off moral or ethical challenges. For example, you find a wallet that is full of cash but clearly with sufficient identification to locate its owner; you find yourself being a witness for the prosecution against a defendant that you dislike; or, you serve as the only judge in a rhubarb pie contest where your Grandmother had entered a pie using her *God-awful* family recipe. Will you be able to return the wallet to its rightful owner or give in to your greed? Will you be able to be balanced and objective in your testimony even when you want that jerk to go away for a long time? And will you be able to judge the pies based solely on the criterion set forth and not be swayed by Grandma and the other 50 family members in attendance? Remember, there are no tangible rewards for being ethical or moral, just the knowledge that *at this time* and *at this place*, you did what was right. Suppose you decided to keep the money, how might that have affected the rightful owner, would he/she have been able to feed their family, keep their home, get that operation…better yet, how would it have affected you? With respect to the trial, suppose you keep to the truth but slanted and embellished your account just a little and an innocent

---

[19] Any and all approximations of time that I am making and denoting with the use of percentages are, in my view, reasonable assessments of the time we use to actually decide ethical and moral issues. Aside from being directional, they hold no relevance in fact.

person was falsely convicted on the weight of your testimony. How evil and damaging was your action and your crime? And if you can't recuse yourself from judging Grandma's pie, you still have a choice to make. You can decide to act unethically and immorally and grant Grandma the blue ribbon or you can choose to be ethical, balanced and fair in your judgment. Regardless of your choice, someone will come away injured; there's no easy way out. Let's make this our next scenario.

Scenario # 2:

Grandma and the family have every expectation that you will lie, cheat, and steal, if that's what it takes, to make Grandma the winner; even though, the crime they expect you to commit is in total opposition to everything they have taught you to this point (your family values). In their minds, fairness, balance, honesty, morality and ethics applies to other people and other situations, not to Grandma. For her, it's ok to be dishonest, unethical, and immoral if that's what it will take for her to be the winner. If you reject what is expected of you and judge fairly, you'll have to deal with Grandma and the rest of the family; and it will likely be a long ride home. But let's just suppose you let Grandma win...what damage have you done to the other Grandmas competing in the contest. They put in long hours over a hot stove (or oven) tweaking their recipes to give their entry just the right mix of flavor notes and texture; what about them? They have been competing with your Grandmother for years and they know that the swill she bakes up every year doesn't even deserve to be on the same stage as their pies, let alone win the competition. If you announce your Grandmother the winner, they would know they had been cheated, treated unfairly and were discriminated against. And, as a judge in a pie baking contest, you would have lost any and all credibility and any hope of ever being considered an even-handed honest broker. And, if you were to show that level of bias and partiality as a manager, you would have put yourself into dangerous waters and would have lost the trust and respect of your staff. Let's move on and try this turn of events...suppose Grandma's pies were some of the best in the county, and made it into the finals. If there was only a slight difference between your Grandmother's pie (though it was the best) and Grandma Mildred's and Grandma's Sadie's pies, would you discriminate against your own Grandma and choose Grandma Mildred's or Sadie's pie as the winner so as not to give the appearance of partiality... would that be ethical and fair to your Grandmother, or was this another time where you chose to use situational rationalization to worm-out of doing what was right? Or conversely, if based upon all the criterion, your Grandmother was the clear winner, are you naive enough to think that Grandma Mildred and Grandma Sadie will let you escape being called a liar and a cheat. You would have made enemies of these old battle-axes and they will never forgive you. Even as they descend into the fog of Alzheimer's and lose sight of who they are, their memory of you and your decision will always remain crystal clear. You will never be able to think your way through moral or ethical issues trying to find a middle ground because, there is none. Your actions are either moral or ethical or they're not. But when faced with a moral dilemma, you have to assess how best to proceed and that's when we turn to situational rationalization; you can't fix the world and you can't fight every moral and ethical battle. But in order to quiet the nagging voices of our conscience and avoid a confrontation with our aspirational selves and our desire to become more than what we are, we have to do something. We have to pick and choose when and where we'll plant our moral flag and fight that battle. It's unavoidable, we will find ourselves compelled to take a position on some moral or ethical issue (even ones we couldn't possibly win) because *at that time* and *in that place*, it was the right thing to do. If we resist these impulses, these opportunities to take a stand, they will begin to collect and start to weigh us down like so much excess and unresolved psychological baggage. The voices will grow louder and we'll begin to dislike the person we're allowing ourselves to become. On the outside, people will see little change in us, but when we look into our mirrors we might catch a glimpse of *our own* Portrait of Dorian Gray.

Group Think, Power & Acceptable Morality:

Up to this point we have been talking the 75% of the 0.01% of the time where you have to decide if you are going to act morally and ethically or in opposition to them. And as you have seen, your decisions were not easy. But on a graduated scale, those decisions would be ranked among the lower of the hurdles you will have to negotiate while you are on your path of becoming a better manager and human being. Your decisions become far more difficult and your use of situational rationalization becomes much more frequent when there is resistance and pressure from your peers, your superiors, and the whole of the hierarchy. Staying with my approximation of percentages, in about 20% of the 0.01% of our moral and ethical decisions, we might feel compelled to take an unpopular position on an issue, because in our mind, it's the right and moral thing to do. But when we take such a position it puts us in direct opposition to forces that can easily destroy our reputation and cripple us financially, politically, professionally, and possibly even deprive us of our freedom. To put this in proper perspective, I'll need you to walk a little ways with me. And as you do, I want you to stay mindful of how our morality and ethics were influenced by our politics, religions, and economics. In a previous discussion of the four powers, I didn't spell out the obvious at the time but I'll do it now; *"might makes right"*. If you have the power, you make the rules. And the rules, whatever they happen to be, normally receives broad based acceptance because few, if any, will sacrifice themselves in opposition. And because a rule is accepted broadly, we don't challenge it because to do so would put us in opposition to the prevailing powers as well as the masses. We tend to accept them for what they are, and over time, they become part of our cultural experience and are rarely ever questioned, a lot like the societal laws and rules we live within 99.99% of the time. Few, except the suicidal and those with a moral imperative ever challenge the morality of the rules; and collectively, we avoid that question all together. We let them float in the ether of our minds, forever unquestioned and unclassified. I am about to walk a bit further afield in order to make my point, but I will bring us back full circle and you should have a better sense of the forces that will be working against any moral or ethical decisions you might make and why everyone expected you to name Grandma the winner of the contest. When we talk about power and rule-making we should start by looking at what (according to legend) happened with Adam and Lilith. They were evenly matched so as a consequence, accept for divine dictates; there were no agreements on anything, just confusion and chaos. But after their separation and Adam was given Eve, the powerful Adam established a set of rules that until today has served to suppress and marginalize all women in almost every society on the planet. Those rules went on to be codified in our politics and in our religions, and have been widely accepted and were considered both ethical and moral. Ladies, without using obscenities, how would you classify those written and unwritten codes that were established by men and have discriminated against you for millennium? Further to our blind acceptance of unethical and immoral rules and practices...let's look at graft and how it was widely accepted in the Roman Catholic Church. This was during a time when people were fleeing Europe to avoid religious persecution and to escape the tyranny of the Inquisitions and at a time when Martin Luther was leading the Protestant Reformation; at considerable risk to his life. In his view the Church had become corrupt and immoral for its well established and widely accepted practice of selling *indulgences* to its wealthy and sinful parishioners so they could buy their way out of sin and buy their dead out of Purgatory. Selling these indulgences was one of the many ways the Church used in order to generate the vast amounts of monies that were needed for the construction of St. Peters Basilica, in Rome. The question then becomes, was the Church's behavior of selling indulgences, moral and ethical, or was Martin Luther just another heretic? And with respect to the Inquisitions, if you had any thoughts that were inconsistent to the Church's Cannon Law you could be subjected to the Panel's questioning (for example, if you were Jewish, Muslim, or a follower of Luther). And just think of those faithful and God-fearing souls that were able to flee the tyranny of the European Church, and were able to settle in the New World, they saw no reason not to bring with them what they had learned in Europe to the New World. Therefore they saw nothing at all wrong with torturing those that were different, to the point of confession, then burning them at the stake for being witches, or seeing nothing of moral consequence in slaughtering the native people and pushing them from their lands when there was the possibility of economic gains. After all, they were depicted as savages and didn't have the same God as the immigrants, so I guess that made it okay. Throughout the making and breaking of treaties, one widely accepted view was constant; *the only good Indian was a dead Indian.* And while this disenfranchisement and genocide was moving from the east to the west, these same good people chose to ignore morality and ethics and enslaved a whole people for over 200 years because there was profit to be made from their labor. Again, this is *"group-think"*, societal norms that are self-directed, and because they were also self-rewarding, they gained broad acceptance. The powerful have a vested interest in maintaining the status quo and change would not have been possible without someone, somewhere taking a moral stand. Unless you're a genuine sociopath, you'll find yourself compelled to take an unpopular moral decision at some point in your career and during your life; good luck with that. I need to wrap this up and bring us back to Grandma, but before I do, I would like for you to think about how a nation became so morally and ethically disconnected that group-think allowed them to accept the slaughter of over 12 million people and the intentional genocide of the Jews, the Gypsies, and those that were considered inferior. Some have said...well, it was a different time...something like that couldn't possibly happen today. When I hear that, I usually just stand there, *gap-mouth*, convinced that they, and people like them, are those in society that accommodate and enable these evils by letting them go unchallenged and ignoring what's going on around them. They deliberately choose to take a moral stand on nothing. Immorality starts small but grows quickly and wherever it goes unchallenged, it becomes acceptable and a part of the social fabric. Even today, look at the genocide that's occurring in the Middle East and Africa...is this another one of those different times?

Now to the situation with Granny; Grandma is part of a click, a clan, a syndicate, a tribe, a family and a hierarchy in which you are a member. Your mistake, in addition to accepting the role as judge, was to use that occasion to exercise honesty and fairness (morality and ethics) in an environment where they had no audience. You are part of the group, and the group-think was that there could only be one outcome. As far as they were concerned, *the fix was in*, and Grandma would be the winner...*What Happened*, you're part of the group now!? In the early years when you were running around the forest, in isolation, you could rape, rob and pillage as you chose. But you quickly recognized that there were some serious drawbacks to being a solo night raider, particularly when your role changed from predator and you became prey. That was when you started to band together into small, then larger and larger groups, because you learned that there was security in numbers. The group afforded you significantly more security and protection, but it came at a price. You could no longer rape, rob, and pillage as you chose; that would be a group decision now. You had to adjust to the group's rules and codes of conduct, and you had to give-up a considerable amount of individualism and take on the doctrine or persona of the group. Ethics and morals are very important concepts within any group so long as they favor and benefit the group and its interests. But when they are adversarial to the group or any of its members, then they are subordinated, bastardized, re-evaluated, twisted, ignored or outright rejected in order to benefit the group; and you knew that going in, so what happened? Now there are 2 realities here, the first is that everyone in the family, with possibly the exception of Grandma, knows her rhubarb pies taste horrible. This is real and universally accepted. And the second is that no one in the family can under-stand why you didn't announce Granny the winner when you had the chance. You can spend the next 6 months trying to explain your decision using crystal clear logic, but no one in the family will ever be able to consider that logic because no one would be able to get beyond your act of clan betrayal. You risked being excommunicated from the family, *and this is not an exaggeration!* People will ask you, "What did our sweet little old Grandma ever do to you to deserve this"? And if there were any psychologists anywhere in the family, their questions would be a bit more probing. For example, "At what period in your life did you come to realize that you had a deep seeded hatred for your Grandmother"?

This, and similar situations are where you will face your greatest moral and ethical chal-lenges. You'll have to choose between doing what you know to be right, or demonstrate your allegiance to the group by being a **"Team Player".** Any family, organization, religion, political party, team, social group and workplace you join or are a member has a clear and unwavering expectation that all of your actions will be for the betterment of the group. You are expected to join them in their group-think and to like what they like, hate what they hate, and conspire as they conspire. The more groups in which you are a member, the less there is of you to contemplate the rights and the wrongs of anything in society. The various groups make you commit to one side or the other and regardless of your choice, you will lose a piece of you. Managers and leaders, like I said, no one can help you with this or any other moral dilemma. Theologians and moral guides will insist that you stay independent and always take the highest moral and most ethical positions possible; that's their job. But if your positions were reversed, they would actually do neither. In preserving their public images, they are programed to give you the purest moralistic advice; the advice that reinforces and sustains their lofty position within the hierarchy. They don't have a stake in your battle or any skin in the game so they're not exposed to any of your downside risk. And if you have been paying attention to the news lately, you've seen how many of the most revered and respected theologians and moral-ist have stumbled, both morally and ethically, in their private and public lives and have fallen into disgrace. No one can help you, all of the choices that you make "here" must be your own, and not be influenced by the dictates of a demigod. I can only hope that your decisions will preserve your safety and independence and be ones that are easy for you to live with when you sit alone in isolation.

The Life or Death Decision:

I won't spend any time on the 5% of the 0.01% because there is no learning to be had here. These are life and death decisions that can be assessed as being right or wrong by an impartial outside observer. But when the decision is yours, the baser being takes over and preserves the self; aspirations don't even come in to play. We can play as many little lifeboat survival morality games as we'd like and impress others by being altruistic and give up our seat in favor of someone more talented or needed to insure the survival of the entire group. But if the scenario was real, we would insure our own place in that lifeboat or else, there would be bloodshed. In my assessment, there's no need for further discussion here, though if you want to debate it further, you're always free to do so.

The Rise of the Conscience:

I recognize that the picture I've painted may make you wonder why anyone would ever want to expose themselves to the negative forces and personal risks associated with acts of morality; just doing the right thing. And while I have no clinical explanation, I will say it's quite possible that we are compelled to do good things. Our aspirational being may well be the weakest of the three, but it is also likely to be the most persistent. It keeps giving us feedback (a report card) on our actions and/or inactions and compares and contrasts them to the images of the person we aspire to be (*the ideal self*) to the individual we actually are (*the phenomenal self*). And even with the knowledge that the ideal self is unattainable, when the gulf between the two gets too wide, it arouses our other beast; our moral compass, *our conscience*. And though the survival instinct in our baser being is hardwired, the power of the conscience should never be underestimated because, in rare cases, it can override the baser being and result in one's own suicide. But let's just step back from the brink and take a closer look at the shortcomings of the phenomenal self. This is the self that is forever running and trying to catch up with its ideal image. The further back it falls, the louder the voices of the conscience becomes. So, how is this possible if the aspirational self is as weak as I had assumed? Remember, I don't have any professional qualifications in these areas; I'm just another observer trying to figure out what drives our morality in spite of everything that opposes it. I believe that we were saved from ourselves when we adopted situational rationalization because we could never approach the standards of morality that are attainable by higher beings. But I also believe that situational rationalization has its limitations and the phenomenal self knows what they are. And when we fall short of what we knew was possible, reasonable, and moral, our conscience responds. Further, I believe that our morality is also hardwired and though it appears to stand alone and be weak and feeble, I can't help but think that it is somehow connected to our baser being and is essential to our survival. It's the only thing that stands between our *warlike* competitive beings and total anarchy and mutual destruction. It's the only thing that I can see that has provided balance and civility so we would have the time in which to evolve. Therefore, I believe that at some point in our evolution, morality gave rise to the conscience and the two became forever linked in the psyche of the phenomenal self. And if our morality is actually weak, our conscience is anything but. Our conscience serves at the direction of our morality and acts as the nemesis to our immorality. Therefore, when we strive to be better, to do what's right and good works, it may be because of our hardwiring that has programed us to be moral. But in addition, we also have to recognize that we might be equally incentivized to do good works and to do what's right because of our inability to endure the pain of retribution inflicted on us by our conscience.

The Line in the Sand:

Now, from a moral perspective, this is where you start to get in to trouble. It's a well-established truism that everyone has his price. We use any available facts around a given situation to rationalize our behavior and to justify decisions that we make based primarily upon how those actions will impact our stability or security. Dependent upon the level of risk or rewards, we can often find ourselves compromising our values in order to realize some benefit, or to avoid some form of danger. We all have a price, and more often than not, once that price is reached, we sell-out. However, what is far less known, but equally true is that each of us has drawn a moral line, *at some point*, in sand that we will approach but would be loathed to cross; morally, we will go **that far and no further!** What seems to be surprising to most people is that they never realized the line was there, but when they get to it, it's unmistakable and they take ownership of it. And while we've taken little pride in how we've compromised our values, we were always able to hide behind situational rationalization to justify our actions. And on those occasions when we've heard the voices of the conscience begin to grow louder, we would try to atone for our actions by doing good deeds and moral and ethical acts in areas that were less controversial and threatening to us personally. This is how we go about trying to balance our moral books. But beyond this line in the sand, there is nothing to protect us, and we know it. Short of a life or death scenario, we can't rationalize this violation; it is a step too far. So it is *"here"* where we have to make our stand; regardless of the opposition. This fight has now become immensely personal; you are fighting for your honor, your dignity, your integrity, your ethics and moral codes as well as your entire value system. It will make no difference how the line gets crossed, but if and when it is, it's your violation and your crime. These are the ethical and moral failings that will follow you throughout your lives and the ones that put you in direct conflict with your conscience. You only have three choices; you can avoid crossing the line by taking a stand and doing what's right; at considerable cost to you personally. You can avoid crossing the line by doing nothing, by refusing to engage in an immoral act; this also comes at a cost. Or, you can be seduced by selfish gain, enraged by hatred and a lust for revenge, or yield to the pressures of intimidation and allow external forces to override your values. In either event, you would have crossed the line and violated your own moral code…the price that you pay here could be devastating. There will be no reward for taking your moral stance or for refusing to act immorally, but at least you retained your honor and dignity. But if, in an instant of greed, passion or fear you acted immorally and crossed your own line, you will have created a crisis of conscience that may not be immediately apparent, but when all the dust clears and thing settle back, you'll find yourself locked in a cage with a monster of your own creation; and your monster will beat you and wear you down. Personally speaking, I've usually found the size of my monsters to be proportional to the size of my crimes. Your monster is your conscience and it's inescapable, it's always there and goes where you go. Sometimes, it even creeps into your unconscious dreams…it is omnipresent and the punitive companion of your own morality. It works to deflate the image of the phenomenal self, putting it even further away from its ideal. We sense this deflation as psychological pain and discomfort. It can take the form of disappointment, shame, guilt; despair, apathy, self-hatred, and it can even lead to depression and in rare cases, has led to self-destructive behavior and even suicide. The pain inflicted by the conscience should always be expected for anything you consider a moral infraction, but it should never be underestimated; it is real and persistent. Only time and some form of atonement can quiet your monster and reduce it in size; but if you've crossed your own line, your monster will eventually grow smaller and quieter, but it will likely never go away. It will become that moral baggage that we drag around with us through life; the residue of the memories of our crimes. So, as you struggle with morality, it's important to stay mindful that what you decide today will have a direct impact on the reflection you see in the mirror tomorrow. You will have to be able to live with what you see, so you need to make decisions today that you can live with tomorrow.

Our Ever Evolving Value System:

As we move on, I think it is important that you come to recognize that human morality is not, and never will be a fixed point in the ether of the mind; forever unchanging. It is dynamic within you and everyone else in your society. If there was some way to measure morality for everyone in a given society, I would predict that 95-98% of the results would cluster around some predetermined norm; except for a few outliers (the moral zealots and the sociopaths).

But if you could statistically pars the data and isolate the populations based upon age, gender, race, religion, political affiliation, economic status and educational background, I would expect you would find much tighter clusters within the groups proportionate to their level of similarities. And I would suggest that this could be attributed to *group indoctrination* or *group cultural values*. I would expect that each identifiable group would have a statistically significant different position on morality when compared to the next, but that difference becomes obscured when the greater population is considered. And I would also suggest that this is due to the levelling effect of the universality of the *"Golden Rule."* My last hypothesis; I would expect that if you went back to the original data from the larger population and bracket the population into two groups based on age (for example, ages 20-25 and 50-55), I would expect that you would see two separate and unique clusters of how morality is defined by these two groups. My point here is that your current perceptions of morality are likely to change over time as you mature, as your place within the hierarchy changes and as you grow and learn more about a given situation and about the nature of mankind. The perception of morality and ethics that you hold today will be different from how you will view them next year or even next decade, your position on these values won't be any better or worse in the future than they are today, they will just be different. As I noted earlier, our values constantly float, shift, adjust and change dependent upon the given situation at hand and how that situation might impact our survival. I would like for you to consider my assertion about changing morality, but before you do, I want everyone to be clear about what I am saying. I postulated that, for the most part, we (our particular society) are all in the same ballpark when it comes to morality and ethics. But because of a multitude of situational variables (age, gender, race, religion, political affiliation, economic status and educational background) we are all at slightly different places in that ballpark. Moreover, as our situations change, we mature, and acquire new information and our positions and views of morality and ethics will also change. Some of you have already determined where I'm going with this; and you would be right. In any group or gathering, it's almost next to impossible to find anyone that holds the same moral and ethical views as you on a given situation or at any given time. Some may be close, but not the same. Now, what's your thinking...is this reasonable or am I too far off base? Well, regardless as to whether I'm right or wrong, the reality is that every time you take a moral or ethical stance, *__you're standing alone__*. And it's not because everyone around you is immoral or unethical, it's just that they are not in the same place as you are and not viewing the particular situation through the same set of lenses. You have to make your moral statement based upon your own value system. You're hardwired to do what's right as you understand right *'today'* (not at some distant time and place in the future), if you choose otherwise, it will be left to you and your conscience to sort-out. As you move through life and at work, you have to be vigilant and not become bias because we are all judgemental and opinionated, and because we don't see your moral imperative in the same light as you, don't be so quick to label us evil or immoral; because, we are neither.

Independent Financial Power and Personal Autonomy:

If you recall, when I defined my objectives, I opted for financial security over everything else. And while I am not now, or ever have been rich, I knew that some degree of financial freedom was a requirement for anyone wanting to maintain at least some small remnant of independence and balance while living in a capitalistic society. Your position power and political powers are dependent upon the particular hierarchical setting you happened to be affiliated with at any given time; they are non-transferable and the powers you enjoyed in one hierarchy buys you nothing in another. But personal financial power goes with you wherever you go and affords you a level of independence and autonomy that you don't get from position and political powers. And having that extra bit of independence and freedom allows you to clear away more of the fog you've created to justify some of the situational rationalization that you've used to protect yourself from negative consequences and financial hardships. Financial dependency colors the way we think and leaves us open and susceptible to the forces that would have us compromise, or even violate, our values in order to be allowed to continue to suckle at the corporate tit. How many of you would be where you are now, and putting up with what you're putting up with, if it wasn't for the need of money? How many of you have had to stand-down and compromise your moral or ethical positions because the financial risk to you was too great, and those that were standing in opposition to you were too strong? How many of you have made an effort to squirrel away at least a little financial power and believe that you have some small degree of personal autonomy? When I chose financial security as my primary objective, it was because I knew what it felt like to be bullied (in my childhood), and I also knew what it felt like to be poor (as an adult). And I knew that if I didn't have some independent personal financial power while working in the corporate environment, some unscrupulous people would try to bully me in order to get me to violate my own value system, and commit an unethical act because I was financially dependent on the company for my job and livelihood. I also knew that if I had refused, they could have taken my job, leaving me poor and destitute had I not prepared and insulated myself beforehand.

We will get to a section called Image Projection later, but for now, how many of you look the part of the manager or the person you aspire to be. I don't mean the individual primping and prepping and posturing and the like, I mean how many of you are living the role, living large and beyond your means, projecting an image of high social, professional, and financial status; showing everyone that you have arrived. Now, what is it costing you? Do you drive a domestic or an import; is your house the biggest on the block, do you have the boat, the ATV, and all the other trappings and toys that are supposed to communicate your status? And lastly, do you have any personal financial power, or are you so completely leveraged that you have no other choice than to compromise your own sense of values, and what's right and wrong, just to be able to stay employed and be able to pay your bills? How is that working for you...do you sleep well at night... what do you see in the mirror...have you crossed your own line in the sand...what is the size of your monster...etc.?

My point is that without self-confidence, self-esteem, self-worth and some personal financial independence, morality and ethics will always be things you will aspire to, but you will never possess them. When you compromise your values for toys and status, you widen the gap between the ideal and the phenomenal self, and that creates internal conflict and stress. You also indenture yourself to your benefactor and forfeit any independence and personal autonomy that you might have had. You have capitulated and have been seduced by the dark side. Your values are now determined by others, and you dare not resist any of their suggestions or dictates for fear of redundancy. But that won't save you, because, at some point, the company might decide that you are no longer needed. And if that happens, they will take everything from you; your position power, your political power (in that hierarchy), and your financial power along with all your toys...you'll be left with nothing but self-hatred. But if you would **stop,** and take this time at this moment to review your current position, you could avoid this trap. You need only realize that if you had moderated your vanity and tried to live within your means and stock-piled a little financial security you could maintain your self-worth and esteem, maintained your system of values, not violated your line in the sand, been able to sleep at night, and could have actually started to like the person you saw in the mirror. And if you should lose your job, while you would have been stripped of your position power and you would no longer have access to your political powers, you would still have some independent financial powers that would sustain you until you found another position. You would have lost two powers but you would still have one. And during our discussion on power, I mentioned that if you already had one of the four real powers, it would be easier for you to acquire them all. But if you had none of the powers, your ability to acquire them would be far more challenging, and your road to recovery would be much longer and harder.

Unintended Consequences:

During my own career, I did my very best to avoid the moral and ethical traps that were laid out by a few to allow them to reap some advantage or to cut corners to make their world less complicated and their jobs a lot easier. It should be clear, that these were not bad people and in 9 out of 10 times their intent was to streamline a process, sidestep what they saw as an unnecessary or nuisance regulation or procedure, and/or to improve productivity and throughput. No one gave any real thought to what they were doing was wrong because they only made a very small change to the standard procedures. And while it is true that the changes they made were small, imperceptibly the deviations from the standard grew wider and wider until they simultaneously became illegal and unethical. You see it almost every day in the construction and manufacturing industries when there has been a loss of life because official procedures and practices were not followed. It also appears in the news when companies issue massive recalls of their products that have the potential to cause injury or death to their targeted populations. And it became most apparent during the recent foreclosure crisis, where banks and mortgage companies were breaking the law for the sake of expediency and their own financial preservation by robo-signing foreclosure documents on millions of homes; depriving people of their rights to due process under the law. Some of you are scratching your heads wondering, just how does any of this relate to me and my job. Well it has to do with your contractual agreement with your company. When you joined the company you agreed to follow all of its official rules and procedures in fulfilling the responsibilities of your job. When you sidestep procedures and cut corners, you violate that agreement and your actions become dishonest and unethical. I would bet money that after a thorough investigation of the root causes of the incidents above, there was somebody on the other end that tried to explain that they *just* did this or that, and they were *only* trying to improve or expedite this or that, and *they intended no harm*. This is exactly what you're going to find in your workplace; procedures that have been compromised and bastardized with good intentions. Now if you cut corners and sidestep the rules and procedures, what about your staff; they're not blind, they can see what you're doing, if it's ok for you, then why not them? Here are two real life examples:

Example # 3:

I was a corporate compliance officer housed at one of my company's manufacturing facilities in a Midwestern state. The manufacturing process required tremendous amounts of corn and other cereal grains in order to produce the finished products. There were over 24 massive silos on site to store the grains. The wind is always blowing in the Midwest so grain dust was always flying about in the air. The company had designated 2 areas within the grounds where it was safe for smokers to smoke, but all other areas were smoke and flame free. I quickly learned that the prohibition against smoking except in designated areas was, at best, loosely enforced, when I happened upon one of the senior employees smoking in a restricted area directly proximal to the silos and all their dust. He cupped the cigarette in his hand when I approached and he engaged me in conversation; but he didn't put the cigarette out until I told him to. He didn't see his infraction of the safety rules as a big deal because the Management would often turn a blind eye to it, particularly if it involved such a valued employee. Well needless to say, I made it a big deal. I didn't write that safety rule, but it was put in place for a reason. And if you go up to the internet and do a search of grain dust explosions and look at the damages in the blast area and consider the death toll you will see why the rule was put in place and why I made it such a big deal. After meeting with the facility's manager and his staff, the facility's safety program was dusted off and brought to the attention of all the employees at the facility so they would know that, going forward, the program would be strictly enforced; including punitive actions, up to and including termination. I can't say I made many friends doing what I saw to be ethical and right. But then, if you give it a little thought, if my actions prevented a future explosion, then I probably save myself from having to attend a number of funerals...maybe even my own.

Example # 4:

This incident occurred very early in my career when a highly trained employee took it upon himself to circumvent a *cardinal safety protocol* at great personal cost. This happened when I was with my first employer when I was fresh out of school. As I had already mentioned, this particular employer attached great valued to educating and properly training all its employees. Human safety was of paramount importance and a safety officer was in place that would provide safety instructions on a regular basis. But, when an employee becomes too familiar and confident in his job, he can become a danger to himself and others around him. The employee in question was scheduled to work overtime on the weekend to do cleaning and sanitation on some of the processing equipment. He stopped by my office that Friday evening to ask if there were any areas that I thought might requires special attention. I checked my sanitation reports and those of my colleagues and couldn't find anything other than routine cleaning and sanitation. The company had established a strict procedure intended to provide rapid support and aid to any employee in the event of an accident…it was called the *Buddy System*. The Buddy System required that at least two employees be at the facility, and working in the same area, whenever any work was being done. In that way, no single employee would be alone in the facility without having a safety companion. In addition, there was a strict *Lock-Out* procedure that was to be followed before any maintenance or cleaning could be performed on any of the equipment. The lock-out procedure required the employee performing the maintenance or cleaning to *"personally"* de-energize that piece of equipment and put their own unique padlock on the main power source preventing it from being inadvertently turned back on. The employee doing the work was to keep the key to that lock with them at all times. That didn't happen in this case. The eye witness to this tragedy was the second employee working with him in that area. He stated that the employee was standing inside of one of the 3,000 pound mixers when he questioned him to ask if he was sure the mixer was locked out. He stated that the other employee said ***yes***, then reached to the outside of the mixer to toggle the power button to prove it to him. He had assumed that the main power was in the off position but he didn't follow the cardinal rule in order to be certain, by locking out the main power circuit and putting his own personal lock on the control box. The machine was energized; it cycled once and seized. He was killed instantly. I, along with the rest of the management team got a call and we went in to the facility. It took Fire and Rescue over 6 hours to get him out of the machine. Even when procedures are in place and well documented, people tend to go on automatic and begin to cut corners and violate the rules because they become too familiar with the work and begin to take chances. I have no doubt that he was convinced that the machine was de-energized, but he violated the procedure and was late to find out that he was wrong. He was a great guy, and I can still see him standing in my doorway wanting to be helpful.

I am not proposing that every rule infraction or bit of unethical behavior is going to lead to some great tragedy down the road; I am merely cautioning you so you can be aware and take appropriate actions if you discover any shortcutting in your organization that might be putting you or your staff at risk. Small infractions can have major ramifications.

My Weighted Value System:

All along we have been talking about morality, immorality, and ethical and unethical acts and behaviors. And we often use the terms interchangeably and we shouldn't. Let's take a break here, because I want you to get a pen or pencil and a piece of paper and write down your definitions of what you believe morality and ethics mean to you, because in my mind there's a difference. Ok, short break, let's get back at it. As I moved through life I came to realize that I needed a set of reasonable and honorable ground rules to live by. When I got to morality and ethics, the definitions got confusing and to me, they seemed to overlap. After some time, I was able to separate their meanings to my own satisfaction and was able to prioritize them in my value system. But having done so, I found that they didn't cover all the areas where I needed guidance and direction. Therefore, I had to come up with 2 more guidelines to live by and that would help me to keep the monster that is my conscience at bay. In the end, I decided on *honesty and legality*. In doing so, I found that these 4 value system guidelines were sufficient to help guide me through my personal and corporate jungles. My recommendation is that you should use what you wrote down, or come up with something else that works for you. Consider my rationale, in my mind, I don't see morality and ethics as being equal because, something could be ethical but it might not be considered honest, and something might be legal but it could still be immoral and unethical, and something could be ethical but also immoral, and so on. So I set a personal standard that I wouldn't do anything that was, *by my judgement*, immoral, unethical, dishonest, or illegal. It was my goal that everything would have to pass all four litmus tests before I could move forward, if not; I would reassess the outlier before deciding how, or whether, I should move at all. I arranged the standards in a hierarchy base upon my value system; with morality at the top, followed by ethics, then honesty, and legal. The definitions and the rationale I used are as follows:

Morality: Conduct that is to the benefit of people or other living things.

Ethics: Behavior that is in accordance with social standards and codes of conduct and acceptable established procedures.

Honesty: A commitment to the truth and fairness as I understood it.

Legal: A set of civil requirements that have been adjudicated, established and codified by an authorized governing body.

Note that in my world, morality and immorality impacts people and other living things, while ethics relates to behaviors and adherence to procedures. In using these definitions I was always able to know what was being asked of me. And over my thirty year career I have been asked to do something unethical on 3 occasions and to do something immoral only once. And because my definitions were clear in my head, I was able to define the request for the requester so they knew that I knew exactly what they were asking, as I declined their request. You have to arm yourself with this or a similar set of definitions for when you are ask to violate your values; that day will come and you'll have to be prepared for it.

Just to expand upon the point above, in my value system, morality trumps everything. Sometimes there is a battle between ethics and honesty because ethics deals with codes of conduct and social norms. Sometimes those codes and social norms are wrong and need to be re-written, in those cases, honesty wins out. With respect to legality, some of the laws that are still on the books are being challenged in our courts this very day, and some others have already been judged unconstitutional, while others may be considered immoral and unjust. So when it comes to laws and regulations I have chosen to focus only on that part of the law that is the subject of the investigation at hand; but morality, ethics, and honesty always trumps legal. Go back and take another look at the section on Group Think, Power & Acceptable Morality. Note how, in every case, the powerful codified the laws and because laws went unchallenged by the masses, they became acceptable, though some were immoral and unethical. They became the norm – *"group think"*.

Of course, you should all understand that there is *risk* associated whenever societal values and your own personal values collide. And by using my own personal value system, we can determine my level of societal and personal risk. And in doing so, let's take a look at *"Standing"*. Believe it or not, morality and honesty don't have any legal or ethical standing in a society if they are contrary to established ethics or laws. We can begin by taking a look at ethics. Ethics are like mini laws or honorable practices and codes of conduct that are generally limited to a small segment of the population. The sanctions that can be imposed for a violation of the group's ethics are localized and only affect the group's members. So in the greater society you should expect to find many different shades and definitions of what it means to be ethical dependent upon the principles of a given group; religious and political affiliations, professional and social organizations, and even in criminal enterprises'. They all have established ethical codes of conduct complete with ethical sanctions; there ethics have localized standing...morality and honesty don't. When we consider morality and honesty on a global level we will find slight differences between one population and the next and smaller differences within a given population. But on a global scale, what it means to be moral and what it means to be honest is (with some small differences) universal. But again, they don't have standing if they conflict with legal or ethical norms. For demonstrative purposes, let's take a look at the Catholic clergy and the United States legal system. In both cases morality and honesty has to take a backseat to professional ethics. Here I am referring to the sanctity of the confession and attorney client privilege. These two professionals are bound by their organizational ethics to keep any, and all, their learned information confidential, even if it could prevent a future crime or free someone that had been falsely convicted. In honouring their ethical codes, they have to violate human morality. There is always a cost, and they will always lose. If these moral and honest people violate their oath, they will be sanctioned by their organizations and if they don't, then they will be sanctioned by their ever vigilant conscious minds.

When we turn to the law, laws are far more wide-ranging than ethics and affect a much larger segment of the population. They are generally derived from common law (social preferences, practices and norms) and by the prevailing powers in a society. Laws are generally bias and favor the religious, financial, and political positions of those that are in power and to a lesser extent the populist. The legal sanctions for violating the law cuts across the entire population and the sanctions are usually severe. Morality and honesty, and what's right and what's wrong are often not considered during law making and once a law is made, they have no standing in the courts, only the law as written. Consider the work of Oskar Schindler during World War II and the abolitionists John Brown. Both violated the law for noble, honest and moral reasons; though one could question the merits of Brown's approach. And if Schindler's morality had been discovered, he would have suffered a similar fate as did Brown.

Therefore, when you look at my value system (and maybe even yours) you will find that had I put the law and ethics at the top and weighted them accordingly I would have a very low risk of suffering societal sanctions. But I put myself at risk by putting a higher weighting on morality and honesty and far less on the law. I am in no way advocating that you violate any existing laws or regulations, I am just saying that in my world, my values are not all weighted equally. In your world, you might have a different set of standards and have them equally weighted or weighted in accordance with how you interpret the world and their importance in your life. As long as they makes sense to you and provide you guidance, it should be ok. But you should expect to receive harsh judgement regardless of how you choose or weight your values; you should expect that there will always be those in opposition to you, and that will put you at some increased level of risk. None of us will get a pass when it comes to our personal values, and some of us will suffer more than others. The strongest among us; those that have self-worth, self-esteem, self-confidence, and personal pride will inevitably find ourselves at odds with some of the societal norms and practices. And on those occasions when we just can't justify situational rationalization, we will be forced to take a stand. And when we do, we will subject ourselves to the defined sanctions within that society. And for the rest of us; those of us that are weak pusillanimous pretenders, we will go along to get along and try to rationalize our every retreat from honest and moral conduct, fearing societal sanctions. We will turn away from our values and will instead construct a world in which we will *"forever"* suffer the unrelenting sanctions of our own conscious minds. And, as I mentioned earlier, I can't help you with your moral, ethical, honest or legal decisions, and I also noted that neither can a theologian or a moral guide. And to demonstrate that reality, I will use it as my final example in the following section. I hope that it will serve to clarify my meaning with respect to soliciting outside moral council.

Moral and Ethical Guidance:

There is a segment of people in all the world's societies that holds themselves above the masses and proclaims themselves to be the most righteous, religious, and moral of all earthly creations, including all of mankind. And they see their life's mission is to convert the unconverted and get the disbelievers to see the light and the error of their ways. While many of us try to find ways to deal with these intrusions on our own personal faith in a polite, but discouraging fashion, we've soon come to recognize that dissuasion doesn't work and these demigods persist and insist upon having you discard your beliefs and replace yours with their own. So for me, I decided long ago that as a personal policy, I would always avoid any discussions of religion, politics, or abortion. To me, it would be a waste of time and energy. Each are highly charged topics and everyone has their own limited, but very passionate view on each. Therefore, short of having a fistfight or going to all-out war, it's not likely that I would be persuaded to change my views or be able to convert anyone to my way of thinking. So, this was a place I just didn't go. But about 20 years ago I worked alongside one of those people. And regardless of how clearly I explained my reluctance and refusal to discuss any of the three topics; my co-worker would constantly pick other discussion topics and try to bend them back to some religious or political theme. So one day we were having a philosophical discussion about morality (right and wrong) and I posed him the following scenario:

Example # 5 & Scenario #3:

I asked that he supposed that he, his wife, and their two small children were destitute and starving. And because they had no money, they were squatting in an old abandon farmhouse somewhere in Nebraska. The farmhouse was surrounded by a 50,000 acre industrial farm that happened to be brimming with a mature bumper crop of corn. My question to him was…if this scenario were real, would you take a few ears of that corn to nourish your family to avert their deaths from starvation? He didn't hesitate in his response; his answer to me was clear, and I felt, almost scripted. He said *"NO*… that would be stealing and stealing is a violation of The Ten Commandments and a violation of The Ten Commandments is a violation of God's Law". He went on to say, that he would rather his family died in grace then to have their souls condemned with tainted corn on their lips. Now that was his actual response, and you can make of it what you will. But in my world, that kind of reasoning is alien, because when I look at all ten of the commandments I can point to numerous events and circumstances where man, through his own reasoning and justification, has found ways of violating every single one of them. And if you glance back to see how I've weighted my value system, you would see that I have defined morality as being a benefit to humans and other living things; and have weighted my values accordingly. I positioned morality at the top and gave it the most value; laws are listed at the very bottom. So if you were to assume that I would have stolen the corn to preserve the lives of my family, you would be right. There is a commandment that states *"Thou shall not steal"*, but there is also another that states *"Thou shall not kill"*. I didn't question his logic and just let it drop. I don't want to slander him because I have no way of knowing his true beliefs, but when I find myself talking with a person that I believe won't admit that *water is wet* or, that on a clear day, *the sky is blue*, I simply just let it be. I don't persist because it only leads to frustration. In my world, and in this scenario, he would have had to violate at least one of the commandments; either to *steal* or to *kill*. My reasoning may be different than either yours or his, but as I see it, it's equally possible to kill someone by failing to act, as it is, by taking the actual murderous action directly. His type of reasoning was alien to me; and if what he said was truly what he believed, than I'm certain that my rationale was just as alien to him. But for you, neither of us would be of service to you as a moral guide, because if you chose him, you would have starved to death, but at least you would have died in grace. And there would be no way for you to have chosen me because, I became a thief. Everything that you decide in your life will ultimately be decided based upon the *aspirational* and/or the *pragmatic*. Therefore, you'll have to develop your own value system to allow you to be comfortable with whatever you decide. But before I conclude, I'd like to stay with my value system for just another moment, recognizing that yours might be different. But in this example, he chose to obey the law and he remained ethical and honest by refusing to steal the corn. I violated the law and committed a dishonest and unethical act by my theft. Based upon our individual decisions, his family would have perished while mine would have survived. Consistent with my thinking, and in my world, the highest expression of humanity is manifested in morality, and morality supersedes all other human virtues; including ethics. In my mind, I would have acted morally, aspirationally and pragmatically. He, on the other hand and by my thinking, gave no consideration to the pragmatic and may have thought he was acting aspirationally, but in my assessment, his actions were immoral; they were harmful to other human beings. You are always free to argue the merits of either decision; but in the end you'll find that no one can truly guide you when it comes to moral or ethical decisions. The choices you make, in deciding these issues, must be yours *and yours alone*.

Evil:

One final thought…I didn't want to leave this section without saying at least a word about evil. In my experience and through observations, historical accounts and news reports, there is clear and unmistakable evidence that evil is living among us. And though it exists, there are 2 things that I would like for you to take with you. The first is that, as individuals, we have a considerable capacity to do evil. But because of societal restraints and our personal value systems the number of incidents of evil that actually occur is extremely rare. And it's important to note that evil always has a human face, it is never some natural phenomenon like an earthquake, drought, flood, or tornado, or the like... it's a product of intelligence, man's intelligence. It will show up as a deliberate act that is committed in the heat of passion, greed, or great fear or it can be a manifestation of cold and careful deliberate planning. In either case, the actions of evil were deliberate (in the 1st degree) and were intended to harm a person or a people. The savagery and severity of an evil act goes well beyond what would be considered unethical or immoral; it is in a category unto itself. My second point is that, in any specific individual, evil is almost always unexpected and we're usually surprised by it. And the evil actor often turns out to be an individual that, until he acted, was thought to be *predictable* and a person of good moral and ethical character that was in good standing within the community. One of the problems we face when it comes to dealing with individual evil is that evil is not an on-going activity, and evil people don't put out a sign when they are at work. In individuals, evil is usually a singular expression of passion, rage, fear or self-preservation from someone that, up until that point, had been considered normal. Therefore you can't just look around society and identify a person or a group of people and label them evil simply because you think they are bad people or you don't approve of what they happen to be doing at any given moment. So, this puts us all at a disadvantage because this means that the real face of evil is only apparent either during or after the act has been committed and the actor has been exposed; rarely before. My assertion that individual evil is rare is predicated on my understanding of our competitive nature and some knowledge of our built-in safeguards. While none of us would want to admit it, we have all experienced those private thoughts and baser desires to reach out and take what we want or to luxuriate in some act of revenge. And though those thoughts continue to bubble up and even trouble us, we don't act on them. The vast majority of us (excluding sociopaths) have sufficient controls in place to help curb those thoughts and emotions before they get us in to trouble. But in some extreme situations, our emotional controls can get overridden and we start to act out. And, for the most part, we usually regain control before the damage we cause becomes irreversible. And in my assessment, while acting-out can readily explain unethical and immoral behavior, in my mind, it can't and doesn't explain evil. There must be some other mechanism at work, because evil appears to be a deeply personal and destructive act that most of us would not be able to reconcile. Nevertheless, individual evil appears to be the unpredictable actions of a lone and well-disguised wolf. And because it's rare and nearly invisible before it acts, it would be a waste of our limited resources and energy for any of us to spend any time trying to ferret it out, we can only react to it, and punish the offender.

Here's a thought, maybe we should try to turn the job of ferreting out individual evil over to the practitioners of institutional evil. They would know where to look and they wouldn't have to look far. I am referring to those fringe groups in every society whose sole purpose is to divide one people from another. Their evil is far more pervasive, systemic, and dangerous to the population than any lone wolf. They are always vigilant and always ready to stamp out evil wherever it exist. Although the problem with that is that, in their minds, evil is anything and anybody that is not a part of their group and any thinking that is contrary to their own political, religious or moral doctrine. They see themselves as the redeemers of mankind (or at least those within their group) and they label those that disagree with their views unpatriotic, traitors, heretics, or disbelievers. Their objectives are clear in the minds of their leaders, though they keep them concealed and hidden from their followers. The leaders are focused on gaining and maintaining power, wealth, and influence over large segments of the masses, while the followers are fed a constant diet of propaganda designed to make them believe that they are superior and more deserving than other groups in the society, thus deserving a higher position within the hierarchy and more of its riches. These fringe groups will normally be found hiding under one of two umbrellas; the right-wing political extremists or the religious fundamentalist (*the zealots*). And usually they establish some form of restrictive initiation criterion for potential members (for example, political affiliation, religion and religious denomination or sect, tribe, race, sex or sexual orientation, nation of origin, etc.) anything that will make them unique and distinct from those they intend to victimize and subjugate. And without walking down through their entire indoctrination process, suffice it to say, they use their strict interpretation of their morality and twisted doctrine to reach their penultimate goal; to dehumanize the group or the people that they have targeted in order to make them appear unworthy of basic human considerations or human rights. Then, as their final act, they move to marginalize, dehumanize, and discriminate against that group. And unless there are elements in the greater society to stop their act of evil, it will become self-perpetuating and can quickly move from marginalization, discrimination, victimization, up to and including genocide in the blink of an eye. Just take a look at the schism within Islam and the rise of The Islamic State in Iraq and Syria, or look back at the Crusades, the Salem Witch Trials, the Indian Wars, Human Slavery, and the Holocaust. These are but a few of many examples of institutional evil. And as far as I can see, when considering the incidences of civil unrest, the suppression of human rights and the disenfranchisement of the weak by the powerful around the world, I am not hopeful that we are likely to see an end to institutional evil in my lifetime, or yours. So I will repeat, in my world morality is a benefit to people and other living things. Therefore it is my position that it is always possible that a person or a people can be immoral and still escape being considered evil. And likewise, it is very possible for a person to be unethical and yet not be immoral. But when I consider evil, I have to conclude that it lies well beyond any infractions of morality and ethics, and because it is a deliberate act, intended to harm and inflict great pain on another human being which could accidently, or intentionally, result in that person's death, evil has to be set apart and put into a class all its own. So, when you look for evil in the eyes of the lone wolf, you won't find it there. Evil is extremely rare in individuals, and even then, it's sporadic, it will only be apparent when the evil doer is in the act or after the fact. But institutional evil is an on-going process among many extremist political and religious fringe groups. They all appear to be indifferent to their own evil, possibly as a result of their righteous indignation of other people and groups. They may also be finding justification for their cruelty in their beliefs in their own propaganda; they see themselves as morally, politically and/or genetically superior to other groups and deserving a higher place and a larger role in society's hierarchy. So, for anyone still looking for evil, just take a moment to consider these people, and take a good hard look into their eyes, you'll see the self-righteous evil and hatred they deny, but cannot hide.

Now, let's talk *Communications*.

Chapter # 17:

Communications
Prelude to Communication; Listening; Incomplete or Bad Information; Image Projection & The Avatar; False Pride, Humiliation, Retribution and Satisfaction – a warning

Meetings

Presentations
The Informative Presentation; The Influential Presentation – Examples # 6 & 7; The Strategic Review Presentation

Writing
The Narrative Essay; The Persuasive Essay also called The Argumentative Essay; The Persuasive Essay Guide; The Descriptive Essay

The Communication Observation Circus

The ability to communicate is the most important asset or tool that you could ever have in your professional and personal toolboxes. Having the ability to communicate affords you an access to the world around you that is far beyond the *observer status* that you get with just your 5 senses. Communication allows you to make contact with others in the immediate environment, those that are at great distances and even with people across large expanses of time. With the ability to communicate we are able to transfer abstract thoughts, messages, and ideas in real time or in the form of physical and electronic records and signage that are valid today or accessible in the form of time capsules so the information would be available to those that might benefit from such knowledge at some distant place and time in the future. And while we take our ability to communicate for granted, it is arguably the most valuable and least developed of all our interpersonal skills. And because of that, this will be a difficult topic for me to cover. I actually put this topic off for months, trying to decide how best to approach it. Even now, I'm not certain how it will turn out, but I know it will be challenging. One of the challenges I face is how can I talk about communications in such a way that you will come away with a greater appreciation of the differences between communications and *effective communications*, how both are done, how others might be interpreting what you communicate, and how you can refine, control, and direct your communications so they benefit you and not become a personal or professional liability. Another challenge, and this one is twofold; on the one hand, how can I get you to recognize that communication is far more involved and complicated than most of us realize. And on the other, how can I convey an effective message when it's nearly impossible for me or anyone else to teach anything to anyone where the students are confident that they have already mastered all the relevant subject material? I will do my best to provide as much support and direction as I can, but because there are so many nuances and facets associated with what and how we communicate, I would strongly recommend that you consult other resource materials because clear, concise, and effective communications will be essential to your success as a private individual as well as a manager.

Prelude to Communication:

As we move through this, largest of the book's sections, it is important for you to try to appreciate the fact that communication is far more than the words you speak or write down, you communicate both intentional and unintentional messages with every action or inaction you take or don't take. In order to help you get a better feel for where I'm going with this, I'm going to run down here and jump into the deep end of the pool and work my way back to give you a clearer understanding of what I mean when I say you are always sending out messages and constantly communicating. Supposed there was a corpse lying before you, it could still tell you a few things, one of which would be that, by its persistent lack of animation and silence; it would be telling you that it's dead. And another would be that though it's dead, it still has the ability to communicate that fact to you, but you can't communicate anything to it, it's no longer listening. Now, I recognize that this may not have been the best possible example but if you were to consider that even a dead person can have something to say, then you might realize that by your very existence, just standing or sitting there, you are constantly speaking to some audience on some level at all times. The question becomes, what are you saying to them? One of our biggest mistakes is to think that we only communicate when we open our mouths or put pen to paper, and for legal purposes, that would hold true. But you don't need to say anything to let others know what you're thinking; often, they can sense it. In addition, people only believe about 15% of what you say anyway. They listen more closely to your word selection, the tone of your voice, the intonation of your words and their cadence and give it a *truth weighting* of about 35%. Then lastly, they give the heaviest weighting (about 50%) to their interpretation of your body language; your facial expressions, your neutral, defensive or offensive body posture and/or any subtle or overt gestures that you make[20]. But then none of this should come as new news to you because these are the same observations you make when trying to decipher the exact meaning of someone else's statements. What you say provides little weight to your degree of believability. Try to recall some recent court verdict; you likely had liars on both sides of the case (the plaintiff and the defendant), but one side was successful and the other was not; why? If you were to interview the jury, they would tell you that they just didn't believe the testimony of one side. For example; if people only went by what you said, then why is the defendant going down for 16 to 20... after all, they said *they didn't do it!* Another example; when someone tries to sell you something and you begin to feel the hairs on the back of your neck begin to stand up, you stop listening to the words and start listening to what they are *not saying.* Next, you begin watching their body language to detect when they start to exaggerate or flat-out-lie. You begin to get uncomfortable and start to ask specific probing questions, if they give you straightforward satisfactory answers and their body language supports their words, your comfort level returns. But, if you perceive their answers to be evasive and you detect an increase in their stress levels, you begin to distrust and reject their entire presentation. In each of these instances, it's not what someone said, it was what you read and perceived from their voice and body language that made you decide the way you did. So, unless you are a skilled and effective communicator, it's all together possible that you could be saying one thing, but be conveying something that's entirely different and unintended.

---

[20] When you research these percentages you'll find that there is some minor difference in the numbers, but directionally the above percentages are right on target.

Another mistake we make is to believe that once we've made our statement, everyone understood exactly what we said and fully understood our meaning...but, most often they didn't, and they don't. This is a primary cause of missed or failed communications; we mistakenly believe that others see and interpret the world the same way as we do. If we said something was *blue* we just simply assume that everybody would get the same picture of our meaning; *Robin's egg blue*. But that's not the picture they get, and your message starts to get distorted and corrupted. We don't have the ability to communicate telepathically; we can't transfer an abstract image or concept from our conscious mind, intact to someone else's. We have to use words, and words are wholly unsuited for communicating abstract or complex concepts or ideas. And, when we try to be precise in our language we usually end up with something that is tantamount to *legal speak*; something that no one can really understand. That's one of the reasons engineers, architects, rocket scientist, physicians and others that require precision in their work use pictures, diagrams, and measured drawings in their attempts to leave nothing open to interpretation. Their work requires their communications to be clean, crisp, and exacting. But we can't make a drawing, a diagram, take a picture, or get bogged down in legal speak every time we want to convey information, our world is too dynamic and we just don't have the time or the inclination to do so. So we bundle our thoughts, put them in an information packet and throw that packet over the transom thinking that when it hits the floor, on the other side, all the pieces will magically come together and convey our intended meaning, and it doesn't. We also assume that if our meaning was unclear, someone would ask for clarification or just say *"I don't understand"*. Some might, but there's a very large percentage of people that, for whatever reason, won't. And this opens the door for a second opportunity for our communications to breakdown. In order to become an effective communicator, we have to stay aware that both these opportunities for missed or failed communications are always present. Oh by the way, with respect to blue, some small percentage of you may have pictured Robin's egg blue, but the majority were all over the blue spectrum, from navy blue, sky blue, royal blue, indigo and some may have even envisioned teal and everything in between. Whenever we have a thought we want to transmit to others, we have to translate that thought into words and that translation always distorts and degrades the message. Then, the message is further distorted and degraded when the receiver of the message attempts to reassemble our words into an image that will help them to understand our meaning. Therefore, the only way that you can be sure that the majority of your message was received and understood is to ask for feedback; ask the receiver to play the message back to you. Don't just ask if they understood, ask them to paraphrase what you said in their own words. And when they do, you'll be shocked at the number of times you get feedback that bears absolutely no resemblance to your original meaning or verbal message. We will be talking about the **Three Tells** later on but I will say a word about them now...in order for you to become an effective communicator you'll have to know something about your audience (something else we will talk to later) and whenever possible, and especially for important communiques; **Tell#1**, you should tell them what you are about to tell them (this gets their attention, brackets your message and puts it in proper prospective). **Tell #2**, you tell them (transfer the information). Then, **Tell#3**, you need to tell them what you just told them in order to reinforce the message. Then you need to follow up after you told them what you told them. You still have to get feedback; they need to tell you what you told them. You have to close the communication loop in order to be an effective communicator; *message transmitted, message received and translated, then conformational feedback*. Closing the loop is essential.

Listening:

Now let's move to the other side of the ledger; *listening*. In order to be an effective communicator you'll also have to be an effective and insightful listener; you have to be able to receive and translate the transmissions of others in your environment; listen to what they say and compare or contrast that to what they are conveying, e.g. what do they really mean? We are all guilty to differing degrees of shutting people out and not listening to what they have to say. Or if we do listen, dependent on their status relative to our own, we tend to minimize the value of anything spoken by a person of lesser rank and prioritize anything coming from someone of higher rank; even if they used the same words to say the same things. Has this ever happened to you; someone says exactly the same thing you said last week and because they are of superior rank everyone can now see the wisdom of their approach and the genius of their thinking, though only a week earlier they had rejected yours? How did that make you feel? Was this when you began to discover that the message was far less important than the status of the messenger? Again, how did that make you feel...what message did it communicate to you about your status in the organization and their personal character? Did their actions cause you to gain respect for them or did you lose some? This is just another example of non-verbal communication, there will be many others. But the question for you is; have you done this to someone else, someone in your own group. And if so, what message do you think you communicated to them? Throughout the ages, people at all levels demanded and expected to be heard, even the peasants and serfs expected to get an audience with the Landlord, the Governor, or even the King so they could air their views or complaints. And, as we talked earlier, when the people are ignored by their leaders they lose faith in those leaders, and that often leads to civil unrest, revolt and revolution. As a manager, you have to learn to be as attentive a listener to the lowest ranking member of your staff as you are to the CEO of the company; it's just that important. Furthermore, I can't point to a single instance where I was able to learn anything when I was talking; you learn when you pay attention and listen. You listen to their words, their word selection, tone and tenor of their voice, the cadence of their words, and their gestures and body language then you try to distil the essence of their message in order to understand their meaning. And if necessary, you paraphrase what they said and repeat it back to them in order to assure accuracy and clarity in understanding. When you take this approach, you'll begin to build individual profiles of your people and learn how best to respond to their communications. Different people communicate information in different ways, while the majority of them will communicate in a predictable fashion there are a few at the extremes. You might have people in your organization that are *hyper communicators,* they'll come running into your office with their hair on fire to report an extremely minor issue that they themselves could have and should have corrected without making it such a big deal. This person could be telling you that they feel inferior to everyone else and they have to keep drawing attention to themselves in order to feel adequate[21]. At the other end of the spectrum is *the reluctant or under stated communicator:* the employee that casually tells you that while you were away, the dog died. Naturally you would have a few follow up questions (how and when). But this is one of those employees where getting information out of them is like pulling teeth; your own teeth. So after an agonizingly slow extraction process you learn that an asteroid fell from the sky, blew-up the neighbour's house and burned down your house. The tree outside of your dining room window caught fire and toppled over on the dog house, the dog panicked and ran into the street and was hit by a car...so, the dog died. This employee is telling you that they don't understand the importance and value of relevant and timely information. They may not even know the difference between what's

---

[21] This person may be lacking in confidence and as their manager you should provide them the necessary training and support they need to grow their skill levels so that they could become more confident in themselves and their work. But special handling has its limits and if the need for attention persists, this could very easily become an employee performance issue and will have to be addressed accordingly.

important and what's not. As their manager you have to provide them with the necessary training so they can learn to identify and report relevant information in a clear, concise package in a timely manner. Most relevant information comes with a *freshness date* or a *best before date*; stale and outdated information is of no value to anyone. Communication from both these employees could create problems in your organization because one would yell *"FIRE"* in a crowded theatre as an overreaction to seeing someone lighting a candle, and they could set off a human stampede. And the other would just stand there, doing nothing, as they saw a dam failing; the thought of notifying the people downstream that are directly in the path of the oncoming flood never occurs to them, in their mind, the people downstream would find out about the dam failure for themselves, sooner or later. Had you not developed your own individual communication profiles for these employees, one may have caused you to overreact to a minor situation and the other to under react, or not act at all to a life or death event. But in either case, you and others could be put at significant risk because of their problems with communications.

While we are still listening to information coming in to us, we often overlook the fact that deliberate verbal and nonverbal communications are designed and calculated to further the agenda of the overt communicator, not necessarily yours. The communicator decides beforehand what you should know and what you shouldn't. If the information is vital to your operation, you should be listening to everything that is being said, but also for holes in the information (information that you would have expected to be relayed but wasn't); and if you find them, you might need to follow up with questions or find a different source for the information in order to get the complete picture. Trust is an essential part of an informational exchange, and if you don't trust the messenger, it's hard to believe the message. As a manager, the vast majority of the communications you'll encounter will be in the form of progress and status reports, and usually, the information is generally accurate and up to date; and it's normally easily verifiable. But from time to time and for a variety of reasons, information will be withheld. When you find that information is being withheld within your own group, it could put the entire group at risk, and it's something you have to correct. More often than not you'll find that someone just dropped the ball and benignly failed to pass along the needed information. Though, in some cases you might find that a disgruntle employee deliberately withheld information in order to do damage to you and/or the group, or to make a personal statement. Then there is the employee that will withhold information to gain some edge or to take some personal advantage; this type of behavior is more correlated to what you would expect from a competing peer or colleague, not a subordinate. However, regardless of the cause, you'll have to take some form of appropriate corrective action; you can't afford to fail because you didn't know what you should have known.

We also get a fair share of bias information that is intended to influence our views or thinking about one thing or one person or another. You have to recognize that in these instances the communicator is deliberately attempting to take control of you and to have you do their bidding. They want you to see the world through their distorted lenses. Whatever they present might be factually truthful but tilted to advance their particular agendas. What truth there is in their presentation will be just enough to make their presentation plausible. But, if the whole truth were known, their positions would fall apart and their story would take on a completely different complexion. In the work setting, these persuasive informational exchanges come in the form of project proposals or sales presentations; some of which you may have done yourself. But it also occurs within the ranks of your staff...you'll find one employee who will always be touting their skills, experience, and value to you and to the company over their fellow co-workers. They don't directly attack their fellow workers but use every available opportunity to blow their own horn and elevate themselves above the others. This is just egotism, vanity and self-promotion, and is generally harmless. But at the other extreme you'll find those that I consider to be the *sowers of discord,* and there's nothing harmless about them or what they do. They use half-truths and negative innuendos to deliberately sabotage the character and capabilities of others by planting little toxic seeds of doubt, suspicion, and notions that your other staffers are incompetent, disloyal, and cannot be relied upon. They try to convince you of their loyalty by acting as your unsolicited *departmental spy.* Their intent is to poison the ground around anyone they see as their competition or they just don't like so they can position themselves on the right-hand of power; your power. When you allow this to happen, you communicate to your entire group that you've chosen a lackey and a spy, and that tells them that you are not the fair and even-handed honest broker you purported to be, and that will cause you to lose their trust. A loss of trust might be extremely costly for you down the road. On occasion, when I have seen this playing out, I've brought it to the attention of the manager in question. And almost to a person they've told me that they didn't realize that was happening...that they didn't know a particular employee was acting as their lackey. And each time I've heard that, I felt it was my obligation to tell them that *"they were a liar"*...I didn't just fall off the turnip truck...I was a supervisor, a manager, and a director, and I know that if you've ever had someone kissing your ass, for even a half a day, you'd know it. So if any of you have a lackey and a departmental spy, go back and re-read the section on the Tyrannical Boss and consider the calibre of person you are working with. These people are opportunist and their loyalty is to themselves, not to you. They are as likely to betray you as readily as they've betrayed their peers; for them, there only has to be the potential for gain and they'll sell out. But the more important consideration is how much damage would you have already done to your credibility if you chose to let a *rat* loose in your organization; how would it have impacted the image you've been trying to cultivate, what effect has it had on departmental cohesiveness and morale?

Incomplete or Bad Information:

Let's move on to the information. Because of your position in the organization you should expect to be an information hub. Information should flow in, it should be sorted and analysed and you should transmit relevant information out in order to inform and/or to direct the work. There will always be problems with the information you receive, partially due to the issues noted above or the issues I have yet to mention, we're just not very good at transmitting clear, concise information. You will usually be able to manage your way around minor communication glitches but there are some, and one in particular, that could cost you everything. That one would be the time where you took some inappropriate action that was based upon inadequate, spotty, and even faulty information. During the course of your career, it will be a rare occasion when you would have all the information you needed laid out before you so you could make an informed decision. You'll often have to decide forward actions base upon what little information is available to you. The pitfall here is that over time you can delude yourself into thinking you've gotten good at teasing-out the facts from bits of incomplete information, and that's when you start to get confident and careless. You start to make assumptions and start connecting dots where there are none. You begin to stop questioning the accuracy or validity of the precious little information you do have and begin constructing your own images of reality without the benefit of facts or proof; as a consequence, you begin jumping to conclusions and filling informational voids with unsupported imaginings. We have all done it, we've all gone off half-cocked, with bad information and often blinded by emotion, with absolutely nothing to support our position. And as fate would have it, we don't discover our error until after we have taken some extreme position or action and/or have made some very serious and unfortunate accusations, and made an ass of ourselves. Once the damage has been done, and now the Genie is out of the bottle and there's no way to get it back in. It's only now that you realize that you've stepped in it, simply because *you knew it all* and didn't take the time to verify the little information you had or didn't bother to gather additional relevant facts that would have helped you avoid this professional blunder. Now what do you do? You have already communicated to everyone involved that you've exercised poor judgement by your overt and misguided actions, and people may have already been injured. People that had once held a positive perception of you are now reassessing their views. You feel naked and vulnerable and the adults among us realize that it's time to cut our losses and admit our mistake. Regardless of what our egos are telling us, we know we can't save face. We have to suck it up and demonstrate a level of genuine contrition that is appropriate to our offense. We have to give a full and complete apology with no half measures. But many among us lack that level of maturity and are so arrogant, narcissistic, and socially deficient that we just can't bring ourselves to admitting that we had been wrong. We try to justify our actions and try to persuade others that, though the information might have been wrong, had it been accurate, then we would have been right in taking the actions that we did. We can't bring ourselves to take responsibility for our own misguided actions. We don't take ownership or apologize but blame the information or the messenger, never ourselves. We fail to recognize that when we try to justify, obfuscate, deny, or minimize our responsibility we create an even deeper wound; one that might never heal, only fester. The message we are communicating here is that we are a very small and insecure person that is not yet, and possibly never will be, ready for a leadership role in this or any other organization. And, that you will do whatever is necessary to shift the blame to avoid accountability for your own actions. Wonder what that says about your character and credibility? But when we step forward and take full responsibility for our actions, it will start the healing process. While it still puts a black mark on our record, over time the mark should fade to a lighter and lighter shade of grey and eventually it might disappear altogether. But in the end, it will come down to the size of the blunder and the magnitude of the unfortunate reaction that determines the outcome. There will always be some damage when we jump the gun, it's unavoidable, but in most cases we can survive and recover from it. However, there may be a time when your offense was so great and remarkable that only the submission of your resignation and your departure will be sufficient to resolve it. Many careers have already been brought to an unfortunate end by an inappropriate kneejerk reaction. You'll have to learn to be patient and be sure you have the facts before you act. Don't be misled and undone by *what you thought you knew*; find out *what actually is,* and always look *twice* before you leap.

Image Projection & the Avatar:

As a species, we rely heavily on sight and visual cues to tell us about our immediate environment and the greater world around us. Much of what we know and perceive about our world comes to us through observations, signs, signals and events that unfold before us. And while we are endowed with other senses, none of the others are able to compete with the sheer weight and wealth of information we get through our sense of sight. Therefore, it should come as no surprise that we've chosen a variety of visual mediums as our primary means for human communications and interactions. Visual communications are easy and relatively inexpensive to exhibit and/or demonstrate, they can be broadcasted to a wide audience in a short period of time and they generally provide much more information, allowing for a higher level of clarity and accuracy when attempting to convey the abstract or an intangible (as compared to the verbal or the written word). So it should also come as no surprise that the tools we use to project positive images of ourselves to the world are visual. For example, when we want to communicate a specific, or a variety, of personal qualities or character traits we create suitable *Avatars* (ultra-egos) whose purpose is to project and demonstrate those attributes openly. We become our own Avatars and carry forward the qualities we want others to believe are our own. Thereby, we are able to visually communicate our desired message while, at the same time, avoiding any attempts at verbalizing a quality or pontificating on a particular character trait in such a way that would be considered crass and indiscreet. We deliberately communicate our status, or desired status, whenever and wherever we are a part of a random group setting or within an established hierarchy. And subject to the specific environment and the emotional temperature within the group, we modify our projections so as to maximize the impact of the images we want communicated while minimizing the risk that any of our exaggerations or personal flaws will be discovered. Plainly speaking, this is nothing more than posturing, and to varying degrees we all do it; even those of us that will never admit to it and are the most confident and self-assured in our own value and worth; no one is immune. Group dynamics seems to have a way of bringing out the competitor in us all. But let's be clear, when we project these images and act out through our Avatars, we know exactly what we are doing, and what we are doing is self-aggrandizing. We either want to establish our place, re-affirm our place, or elevate our place within the hierarchy; or some combination of all three.

Before going much further into image projections and moving on to you and the images you project in the workplace, I think it might be beneficial if I were to digress for a moment to do a bit of housekeeping and clarify a few things. The first thing I want to do is go back to what I said about your ability to be believed and the way your audience weighs the truth in your message. Everything is connected, and the rationale here is that if you are going to deliberately project an image, you'll want that image to be believable. Earlier I said that people weigh the truth of your message by your words, the word selection, the tone of your voice, the intonation of the words and their cadence and your body gestures and language. And if you are addressing a new an unbiased audience, that's what they'll use to assess the truth in your message. But if you have a history with that audience, the criterion changes; they'll put more credence into your character (their interpretations of the images you have already projected, their assessment of those images and what they've determined to be an honest reflection of who you really are, as compared and contrasted with the images you have projected). The success of your Avatar is directly depended on a reasonable correlation between your actions and the images you try to project. Another point that should be made is that I've found that words don't always carry the same meaning or impact when interpreted by one person and then the next. So when I use the terms communicate or communicated when talking about your image projections (or anything else for that matter), I don't want you to come away thinking of some benign and passive informational conveyance because, it is not; it's far more impactful than that. When you project an image, any image (either deliberately or inadvertently), your actions are overt, therefore, what you are actually doing is *acting and talking out loud,* albeit without using words. And in your overt actions you communicate that message or that image, with equal clarity, to your targeted audience as well as any unintended audiences and casual observers. So, if it helps you to understand what you're really doing with your Avatar and your image, every time you see the word "communicate", just substitute it for *"acting and talking out loud"* because that's what's really happening. Another bit of housekeeping is for you to recognize and understand where you fit in the grand scheme of things, it's *not all about you*; you're not the star of every production. While you are judged on how capable you are to step-in and play the leading role, your ability to play a supporting role, or even a bit part, is also being scrutinized. The members of the hierarchy recognizes your competitive nature and expects you to demonstrate it, but they are also looking to see how well you play with others; are you a team player, or do you think it's all just about you? Just keep in mind that every hierarchy is a political affiliation and they have the power to relegate you to the margins or to banish you altogether, so don't overplay your hand. The last bit of housekeeping I want to do before moving on is to remind you that, in life, we're required to play many roles (parent, child, sibling, team leader, team member, manager, subordinate, etc.,.) and the images that we project should be standardized in nature and in character and generally consistent with where we hope to be aspirationally. For example, we would want to be perceived as being knowledgeable, talented, assertive, kind, generous, patriotic, faithful, trustworthy, reliable, altruistic, honorable, moral, sympathetic, and the list goes on. These are some of the general character traits that society is looking to find in its respected members and in their leaders. Everyone reading this has the capacity for each of those personal qualities and attributes, but without a sense of self-worth and confidence and security in our own selves, our basic humanity will continue to take a backseat to our competitiveness. We have to change as individuals if we are to grow, and it's going to take strength and determination to be able to project and possess those positive character traits. And the images we project and our overt actions will have to be seen as being consistent or convergent over the long-term before they will be seen as being genuine.

Now let's turn our attention to your position in your current organization along with the messages you'd likely want to communicate. If you are already a manager, you'd want to communicate to your staff that you are knowledgeable, fair and even-handed, professional, and in charge. To peers, you communicate your independence and competence to assure them that you are their equal in every respect. You project an image of cooperation and collaboration so you're not seen as a threat to them, therefore, they'll be less likely to compete with you head-to-head or try to sabotage your work and/or your reputation. To your manager, you'd communicate an air of confidence, assertiveness, commitment, loyalty and trust. You would want your management to see you as *a leader* and *a partner*, not just *an employee,* and you'd want them to see you as a reliable resource and *a person for all seasons*. These are all non-verbal signals and character attributes and traits that you'll find ways to demonstrate to your targeted audience through your Avatar. But you should be aware that there is a downside to projecting an image that you have yet to master. People are smart and observant, and are always on the lookout for the pretenders and the frauds. Therefore, if you have any personal or professional weaknesses and vulnerabilities, don't let people get too close; they could discover and expose them. Maintain a respectful professional relationship and a professional distance between you and your subordinates, your peers, and your management. This is what would be expected and it will afford you the time and distance you need to correct your weaknesses and shore up any vulnerabilities. Another potential downside to image projection is that you really don't have a reliable mechanism to gather feedback. You might think that you are transmitting all the right signals and character traits but your message could be getting garbled and distorted and your intended audience might be receiving something entirely different, unintended and unflattering. You have to study your audience, watch their body language, listen to what they say and are not saying, monitor the interaction between you and them, and feel the temperature and level of energy in the interactions. Vanity tends to blind us to reality and we often filter out negative but valuable feedback. We should stay mindful that we are never as good as we think we are. But, we still need some way to discover how we are measuring up to target. There may come a time when it might be worthwhile to consider getting a Needs Analysis Profile done; actually, I would personally recommend it. It would allow your subordinates and peers an opportunity to evaluate you (your Avatar) freely and anonymously and for you to learn exactly how your manager sees you and what he might think. But don't expect to be showered with accolades here, because by definition a Needs Analysis Profile focuses on areas of weakness and where you still have opportunity for growth. I took advantage of the program at two different points in my career. The second time was much better than the first. After going through the program the first time, and once I was able to recover from the results, and was finally able to put aside my suspicions that the entire corporation was conspiring to discredit me and hold me back, I started to begin to see some of the value in the program; and it wasn't because my wife and family had been pointing out many of the same shortcomings to me for years. The second time was a lot better because I knew what to expect and prior to getting the results, I gave my ego the week off. A Needs Analysis Profile and/or generous unbiased feedback provides you an unvarnished baseline as to where you are, as compared to where you thought you were, and where you want to be. It gives you the feedback you need so you can make adjustments in your management and interpersonal styles and to the images you project. You need feedback, and if you can't decipher the feedback you're getting on your own, A Needs Analysis Profile and/or generous unbiased feedback will do it for you. You'll have to fold up your ego and put it away, because unbiased feedback is vital to your development and career advancement. It's going to be really unpleasant and hard to swallow, but then, you could always choose to opt out and fly blind with no guidance or meaningful direction. Choosing ignorance over enlightenment will undoubtedly help to stifle your career and prevent your growing professionally as well as an individual. Just look around...is this who and where you want to be 10 years from now? You can't fake your way through your career or your life. At some point you'll have to develop the skills you need and become self-assured and confident in your own abilities and become secure in your own place in the hierarchy... or...you could wait until your personal and professional shortcomings begin to limit your career growth or see your exaggerated images get exposed and you see everything around you begin to unravel and start to come down like a house of cards. It's your choice.

So far, we have been talking about aspirationally positive images that we purposely project in our never ending quest for acceptance, superiority, then dominance and ultimately adoration within the group. Now we should take a look at some of the inadvertent images we broadcast and communicate that contradicts our Avatar and becomes our greatest nemesis. We have already talked at some length about the primitive, competitive, and darker drivers of our nature (pride, anger, envy, greed, etc.), and how we gave up some freedoms and controls and came together in larger and larger groups to build civilizations for our own prosperity and protections. And over the thousands of years of being social and civil, we all should realize that we are still only a heartbeat away from disaster, mob rule, societal breakdown and chaos that could be brought about by some environmental, political or financial calamity or some national or global pandemic. It's happened before, and it will happen again; and no one knows when or where the tipping point would be...but there is one. Think about the number of times the end of the world has been predicted, and think about all those *Dooms Day Preppers* preparing for Armageddon. The point that I am attempting to make is in reference to our own tipping points. Throughout the millennia, while we have suppressed our primitive and competitive instincts to comply with the dictates of society, nothing has really changed about us; we are as predatory now as we were then. If we have evolved at all, the evolution has been incremental and it defies measurement. Aspirationally, we had hoped to evolve into a higher level of human being with a higher level of intellect and morality through introspection, our philosophies, and our chosen religions. I think we would all agree that we are not there yet. So when we put our little Avatars out front to project a more aspirational image of ourselves, we make the mistake of standing far too close behind them, which often allows some of the worst of our nature to bleed through. In a controlled environment we believe that we are largely in charge of our image. But control is ephemeral and elusive and in the end, it might even just be an illusion, and in reality, we might find we really never had actual control of anything, including our image. I say this because when our environment gets chaotic and becomes unpredictable, or if our image is threatened, we step from behind our projection and show our true colors; *our tipping point*. We communicate our anger, fear, avarice, hatred, lust, weakness, prejudices, immorality, selfishness, depravity, contempt, and other emotions and character traits that are hardwired in all of us but which we would have preferred to have kept concealed from public view. In reality, we are both beings. We are the Avatar when we are secure and have the confidence to be generous and altruistic. But we are also human and the darker characteristics help us to survive and are a fundamental part of our whole being. So as you move through life be mindful that the images you project are being widely broadcasted and communicated to a variety of observers and they are weighing everything you do and say; both your deliberate and inadvertent communications[22]. Eventually they will establish, for themselves, just who you really are. We all know that the Avatar is there, on stage and acting the part. Over time, and based upon our best performances, people just might even come to accept the Avatar as an actual reflection of ourselves, but again, that will take time for them to truly believe the Avatar. People know that it's hiding our true nature, and as observers, there'd really like to know what that nature is. And when our world becomes chaotic and we feel as if we're under threat, or when we think no one is looking, we show them. We revert back to our nature, even if only for a moment, yet it's still enough to allow them to see that not so perfect side of our beings. And while the Avatar has taken months and even years to be believed; these small glimpses into our innermost selves have instant credibility with onlookers and distorts the perception of our Avatar. My point here is that, you are always on stage and always communicating something to someone, even in your most private and sheltered moments; so you should just be aware of it. There is a lot you can change, the way you interact with people, the way you manage, the way you project your image and so on, but you can't change your basic and baser natures; you are what you are. All you can do is try to control what that is and how it is perceived. In addition, you should never lose sight of the fact that the people around you are also operating in a modified style...just like you. They are not really who they appear to be,

---

[22] It takes time, effort and dedication to craft a positive social or professional image. You have to work at it and your actions have to be consistent with the image being projected. But an inadvertent flash from your darker nature could nullify all your work and destroy your credibility.

you are seeing what they want you to see and what they aspire to be; you are almost always watching their Avatars.

False Pride, Humiliation, Retribution and Satisfaction – a warning:

I struggled with where to put this information because, while it will be important to you, it's not a neat fit anywhere in this book. Nonetheless, because false pride, humiliation, retribution and satisfaction are actually manifestations of communications and are powerful emotional drivers in all human beings, I've included it for your consideration. And after completing the above section on Image Projection, this seems to be the best place for it. I will admit that this may not be an easy read, and might even be somewhat controversial, due to the complexity of the subject matter and my lack of psychological and literary expertise. But at some point, and this is as good a point as any, we have to take a closer look at some of the emotional drivers in man's baser nature in order to know what they are, and to find ways to avoid being trapped by them in our own lives. I am referring to some of man's *narcissistic competitive drivers*; pride, status, respect, and honor. And if you didn't already know, we are all susceptible to their pressures and their traps because we are all vain and narcissistic. These vanities are our highest prized and most cherished drivers; they feed our egos and give greater confidence to our Avatars. But when they are threatened or lost, we suffer humiliation, shame, and the loss of face, and our reactions to the threats or loss is almost always disproportionate to the injury; our responses are animalistic, and often violent...why? What is the mechanism that triggers this response? Factually I don't know, so you shouldn't expect any answers from me. All I can do is speculate about what I have seen, and because I think it will be important to you in your careers as well as in your lives, I've forced this discussion of the topic and will talk it the best I know how...so, bear with me. Just remember that I'm not offering any of this as a psychological proof of anything, but just an opinion and a position based upon my own personal observations. I would like for it to serve as a warning to you and make you aware of this axiom of human nature; our overreactions to humiliation, embarrassment, and shame. My intent in putting it here is to help you recognize how easy it is to lose your way and get caught up in the daily battles for honor and respect, while chasing an illusion of something or someone you think you ought to be. Additionally, I hope to help you avoid the pitfalls of false pride and vanity that could destabilize your Avatar and lead to your humiliation and loss of face, which will cause most of us to want to take some form of revenge. And finally I wanted to restate, for those of you that are still not clear on the intent of my message; *you can't expect to humiliate, dominate, and demoralize people without there being some serious and very negative consequences.*

I will argue what to me appears apparent, and as I do, you should be forming your own perceptions of what you think is occurring in man's mind when he is subject to public humiliation, embarrassment, and shame. What we want to do is postulate what causes the negative emotional pain and when it occurs, why we act out so violently toward those we hold responsible for causing it. Let's start by taking a pedestrian look at man's psyche; we should be able to agree that man's survival instinct is hard-wired and essential to his longevity. We should also be able to agree that the primitive beast that resides within each of us (the Id) is tasked with the preservation of the self and doesn't get caught-up in the petty squabbling of our competitive being (our ego). And lastly, we should be able to agree that because they don't talk, and because I have not been able to find any evidence to the contrary, the Id doesn't even know that our aspirational self even exist (the Super Ego)[23]. I could very well be wrong in my supposition, and if I am, I don't think that there'll be a shortage of professionals willing to point that out for me. But for now, let's just go with what we have, the precision of the psychological mechanism is less important than the way it manifests itself as an acute over reaction in man to any form of humiliation or any potential for him to lose face. To me, humiliation means extreme embarrassment and the loss of face means extreme shame. Neither of which is life threatening, but frequently our reactions to them suggest otherwise...why? In all honesty, I don't have a clinical explanation and I really don't want to disturb the Psychological Gods and my intellectual betters, but I'm still going to give it a shot. I will argue that under abnormal conditions, it is very likely that the Ego (or Super Ego) could be under such an extreme level of stress from events occurring in the outside world that it bombards and excites the Id, stimulating it to such an extent as to cause it to believe that the body (the self) is under mortal threat. The Id, blind to the outside world, forces the Ego to preserve the self; which in these cases, causes it to respond disproportionately to the actual threat. At least,

---

[23] The Id does not have a direct window onto the outside world but communicates its needs for security, nourishment, rest, and sex to the Ego. The Ego is continually interacting with, and evaluating, everything it perceives of the world through the five senses to satisfy basic needs as well as many of the higher level activities of consciousness. But the Id, in large measure, ignores most everything that's occurring in the world of the Ego except threats to the survival of the being. When a threat is communicated from the Ego to the Id, the Id forces the Ego to eliminate the threat or to retreat from it in order to preserve the self.

that's what I believe I'm seeing when I observe man's inappropriate, and frequently unpredictable, response to these stresses. So, the question for me becomes, just what is it about humiliation, embarrassment, loss of face, and shame that causes us to have such a supersensitive reaction to them when they don't directly threaten our existence? In my mind, I can see how someone could perceive the possibility of real loss during these instances; the loss and discrediting of your projected image (your Avatar) and the loss of social status within the hierarchy. But again, these are not life threatening. So I think we'll have to look elsewhere in order to find why our reactions to those stresses are so far out of proportion to what we would normally have expected. We have to look to Pride, Self-esteem, and Honor; manifestations of the Super Ego (the higher conscious mind). And when we look at who we are (the phenomenal self) and who we aspire to be (the ideal self), and so long as the gap between them is not too great, we tend to be content with who we are and take pride in what we have accomplished so far. We look back at where we started and compare that to the progress we have made in our attempts to better ourselves and to get closer to the ideal. If we interpret the progress we've made as genuine, it reinforces our sense of personal value, self-worth, self-confidence and esteem; we feel good about who we are and what we are becoming. But in taking a closer look at pride, personal value, self-worth, self-confidence and esteem, it becomes clear that they are all personal characteristics and are internal to the individual and are not communicated openly. And because they are internal, I don't see how they can be subject to humiliation or the loss of face. Let's go back to Adam during the time when he was alone in the forest. He had pride in himself, personal value, self-worth, self-confidence and self-esteem. And during that period I really can't imagine any scenario where he would have experienced humiliation or the shame associated with losing face; not by himself and alone. If you recall, things only went downhill when Lilith showed-up...why? What is it about the introduction of another human being (a competitor) that is so destabilizing in our lives and to our world? And why is it that this introduction makes humiliation and the loss of face a real possibility? Let's just keep looking. Let's take a look at honor and status and their demanding little minion, *"respect"*. Honor, in my view, is not a personal or private thing, but is a deliberate public projection of our status, superiority, and virtue within a given hierarchy. If we are honest with ourselves, our perception of honor would be a direct reflection of how well we're able to comply with, or be seen to comply with, and adhere to the accepted codes of conduct in our immediate environment. Honor is not inborn like morality; it is a learned process, more akin to ethics, and ethics relies on a set of clearly defined standards. As a consequence you would expect to find a different set of honorable standards among prison inmates and street gangs then you would among law-abiding citizens in social or professional organizations. So I contend that when you comply with the standards (in whatever environment) you become recognized as a person of honor; an honorable person, regardless of your actual rank or status within the group. This causes your virtue to become public and your honorable status to be communicated broadly, whereas before your Avatar could have acted unilaterally and independently, but now, in order to retain your position of honor, you'll have to follow the dictates of the crowd and their code. As a result, you'll have something more than your hierarchical status to defend; now you have the added burden of defending your honorable reputation in addition to the perception of your Avatar – *your public face*. If any of this is beginning to hold water, then it suggests that your honor is more dependent upon how you *perceive you are being regarded by others* than how *you regard yourself*. And that's the danger. When you lose sight of your own personal integrity and self-worth and leave the verdict of who and what you are to the judgement of the masses, you instantly subject yourself to their dictates and increase your risk of humiliation, embarrassment, shame, and the loss of face. You become locked in a battle to defend your public honor and to get the level of public respect you believe is due you. You're always on defence trying to protect everything you are and pretend to be. And everything you are, and much of what you aspire to be is now on full display, just sitting out in the open, fully exposed in an unprotected glass case. You feel vulnerable and every competitive encounter even the smallest actual or perceived challenge to your honor, your status or to the level of respect you feel you're due only serves to increase your stress levels, before long, you enter the *General Adaptation Syndrome (GAS)* and never leave[24]. I would suggest that a couple of things are likely happening here, the first is misplaced values, you have lost sight of your personal values and are determining your value and worth by the feedback you get from the masses. You've become the puppet, instead of the puppeteer. And because you've put all your eggs in a single basket that is beyond your control (public honor, respect, aspirational status, your sense of pride, self-worth, self-esteem and your prized hierarchical rank), you treat a threat to any of them as a threat to them all. Yours are no longer personal virtues, character traits and strengths; they are now all public liabilities, vulnerabilities, and potential weaknesses. Again, collectively they don't threaten life but because the

---

[24] The Hungarian endocrinologist Hans Selye (1907 – 1982) first coined the phrase General Adaptation Syndrome (GAS) when describing how the body reacts both physically and psychologically to stress. In his explanation, he described 3 distinct stages of GAS; stage 1: Alarm, stage 2: Resistance, and stage 3: Exhaustion.

GAS makes it difficult to rationalize clearly, in your mind, you may-well see them as threats to the survival of the whole being. As a consequence we experience an overreaction that could turn something that was a minor issue into a major one, one that could actually become career ending or even life threatening. Let's take this simple and familiar example; how would you react to someone saying something negative about your mother? No, I'm not talking about if you were a kid playing on the playground; I'm talking to you, you 20, or 30, or 40 something year old people. How would you react? Your mother, if she is still with us, is in some distant place and is neither physically nor psychologically affected by their insults. Additionally, the insults don't affect you physically, but what effect do they have on you psychologically? If you were a person with self-confidence, self-worth, self-esteem and personal pride, the insults would have little to no effect. You would see that the individual making the insults is the individual with the problem and is crying out for some form of attention and recognition. But on the other hand, if you're not self-confident or self-assured, his insults become a threat to your honor, your status, your sense of pride (false pride, public pride, or even vanity), as well as to the entire essence of who you pretend to be. So in a real sense *peer pressure* forces you to take some form of action, ostensibly in defence of your mother's honor, but in reality, to preserve *your own sense of **public** honor* as well as *your own perceived level of **public** respect and standing* within the group. You've been manipulated, and your actions are not independent and voluntary, they are obligatory and predetermined. You've become a puppet, acting in someone else's play and following the *honorable* code of conduct established by those in that environment. You can rationalize it any way you'd like but in essence you've lost your individualism and have become a card-carrying combatant in the mob that is society. You've become indistinguishable from the masses and from here on out you're just another bit player in society's *Darwinian Plan*. There's nothing to be gained here, but everything to lose, you're not seen as a leader and/or being above the fray, you've become common and mundane. In my thinking, you can only blame yourself for this. You've availed yourself to the potential loss of face and humiliation because you've lost sight of your own identity and are acting in accordance with how you think society expects you to act[25]. In so doing, you acquiesce to the demands of honor, respect and peer pressure and accept them as your own public drivers and the masters you serve in order to avoid public disgrace,

---

[25] I never intended my explanation to be all encompassing because I know that there are other traumatic events that will be out of your control and through no fault of your own could have a similar devastating effect on even the most self-confident and assured individuals.

marginalization, and loss of status in that hierarchy. At least that's the way it appears to me. Further, I contend that the following is also true: When you blindly follow some artificial code of conduct, without questioning its validity or morality, you'll have to follow it wherever it leads. You stop thinking for yourself, and acting as an independent entity but instead rely on the code and society to tell you what you should think and how you should react. Now, I don't want to leave anyone with the impression that standing alone and being an independent thinker will somehow allow you to escape the pain of humiliation, shame, embarrassment, and the loss of face, because it won't; some things are just unavoidable. I am merely saying that by being independent and self-assured will allow you to freely choose how you respond to peer-pressure, attacks on your honor and open disrespect. I want to remind you of our discussion on morality and ethics where we took a look at a variety of practices (societal norms) that went unchallenged and unquestioned; I called it *group-think*. You should be able to see a similar parallel here. Everything has been decided for us, when I talk about false pride, honor, respect and social standing and how our overreactions to attacks on them have been preprogramed for us, it's true. Every hierarchy has a set of norms that dictates how we are expected to respond to a specific set of parameters, all we have to do is just fall into the trap. We, as a species, will do any and everything we can to protect our public image and standing, that's what all the competition and posturing is all about. But when we fail, we come away bitter, scarred, humiliated, and are not soon likely to forget those that served up our defeat. But when we fail badly, and our humiliation and loss is great, or we believe our undoing was unfair and unjust, we will seek revenge...*an eye for an eye*. I won't even attempt an explanation for this complex psychological response; suffice it to say that it's a part of your nature and should serve as a warning to you. Because, if it's part of your nature, it will surely be part of those you encounter. So when your actions, either deliberate or inadvertent, result in significant injury, humiliation, embarrassment and shame to another individual, you will have earned that person's hatred. And hatred will compel even the weakest among us to find ways to take deliberate actions against you in an attempt to *get even*. As a species we demand retribution and satisfaction...that's just the way we are...that's just the way you are. And in far too many cases, we won't stop our pursuit until our appetite for revenge has been sated. Public pride and hierarchical status with pride are powerful human drivers and you can choose to ignore them or choose to use them to your advantage in order to control your environment and the people in it; the choice is yours. But just give some thought to what has already happened and what continues to happen in a world where people perceive they have been dishonored, humiliated, shamed or disrespected. Consider how we are preprogramed to respond. Think about how Aaron Burr took Alexander Hamilton out to a field in Weehawken, NJ and shot him, because of their on-going feud that came to a head when Hamilton wrote an article about Burr that Burr took to be defaming and disrespectful. Consider the murder rates in some of our larger cities, how many young men do you think are being hurled into eternity everyday as others face a lifetime of imprisonment simply because someone thought they were being disrespected; they didn't get their *props* (their proper level of respect). Public pride and vanity drives us to extremes in order to save face. In some societies, nothing is more important than the honor of the family and preserving the family name. As a consequence, in several south eastern European countries (particularly Albania, Serbia & Montenegro, Bosnia & Herzegovina, and the Kurd's of south eastern Turkey) families still engage in blood feuds when they believe they have been wronged by someone from another family. They launch *vendettas* against the other family in order to preserve their family's honor and standing within the community; they have to save face. In the Middle East, as well as many south eastern European countries (Pakistan, Jordon, Israel, and in the greater Balkans), fathers, brothers and uncles seek out and murder female members of the family when they believe their actions brought disgrace or dishonor upon the family. They have come to be known as *honor killings*. And in the Far East, it was customary for those that bring dishonor or great shame to themselves, to their families, or to their village to do the honorable thing; *to commit suicide*... because they, independently or at the hands of others, have lost face. Again, false pride, peer pressure, and professional or social standing drives this preprogramed irrational behavior in man. And they will be your drivers too, if you buy-in to *group-think*. To be sure, these are examples where vanity, false pride, humiliation, embarrassment and great shame has driven man to act with extreme prejudice and malice toward those he saw as causing his pain; *retribution*! It's our way of balancing the books, levelling the score and getting an eye for an eye. We have to have a sense of satisfaction and justice before we can begin the healing process in earnest, and start to begin to be made whole. For better or worse, this is who we are. Though, retribution and satisfaction does nothing to undo the damage that we've suffered; Hamilton's death didn't un-write or erase his defaming and disrespectful article about Burr; one street tough killing another didn't undo the initial perceived disrespect, it only earn him a lifetime of imprisonment, A family's vendetta doesn't preserve the family status, it only opens the door for more killings until there's no one left in either family. And worst of all is the honor killings, is it so important to you to be looked upon favorably by neighbours that you will hunt down and kill a cherished love one in order for your family to save face? Have you ever given any thought to moving? In each of these cases, nothing was done to erase the shame or embarrassment, but everything was geared toward getting revenge. I won't pretend to know where the desire for revenge originates in the human being (in the Ego or Super Ego), but it seems far too complicated to have had arisen from the Id, and besides, the Id doesn't have a window onto the world. Revenge can be a kneejerk, heat of the moment reaction, or it could be something that is carefully thought through and considered, but in either event it is primitive and animalistic. And the drivers of vengeance are narcissistic (excessive pride, vanity, perceived self-worth, public image, etc.); all of which are higher functioning components of the Super Ego. And, I won't try to explain the subtlety of their collaboration and interactions either, because I simply don't know them. But I do know that we are all subject to them and no one is immune. Sigmund Freud did some work that attempted to explain how a *narcissistic injury* could drive a person to seek revenge (*narcissistic rage*). It's worth a read. I will say that through my observations and personal experiences, that the desire to lash-out and take revenge can rival a life or death experience; it can become a driving force in our psyche and becomes a must! And when revenge is delayed it can fester and become all-consuming. But when revenge comes, at the moment of retribution, every one of the actors above felt satisfaction and had a sense of rejuvenation and at that very moment they experienced a significant emotional release; almost sexually gratifying in nature. Then...it was only then; once the act was done and their appetite for revenge was satisfied that they were able to slowly return to normal (sanity).

Now, I'm not going to get off into the weeds here and burrow down into another rat hole, but I find myself in conflict. When you look at my value system, with a focus on morality and my assertion that evil is rare within an individual, how can I explain away our lust for revenge? Is retribution a moral and just imperative or is it an immoral and evil act of aggression that we conveniently hide under the guise of justice? And if it is a moral and just imperative, then why is it that when it comes, it's welcomed and is so emotionally rewarding; remember, there are no tangible rewards for acting morally or ethically. I have no explanation for what (to me) appears to be a contradiction of my earlier argument. If that contradiction holds, it would suggest that our capacity for immorality and to do evil is boundless, and I just don't see it in the world around me. Therefore, (to me) the issue is unresolved, and I'll leave any further debate on the subject to you, the psychologists, the moral philosophers, and the theologians.

Let's turn our attention to the suicides. In these cases there is not only a loss of face but also a loss of hope. When people believe their honor, their Avatar, their public face and their position within the hierarchy is being or has been lost or so severely diminished that they lose all hope of ever being able to recover, or that what it would take to recover was more than they could possibly endure, they turn to suicide. They develop tunnel vision and can only see what they've lost, not the world around them. They become consumed with emotional pain associated with public shame, dishonor, and emotional despair. As they struggle to find a way out, they eventually come to a fork in the road (the decision point). To the right; they can choose to endure the pain and suffering in an attempt to resurrect what has been lost. And to the left; they can choose relief from the psychological pain of humiliation and shame. They weigh both options, but because of the effects of the tremendous amount of stress they are under, their reasoning can hardly be considered rational. But once the decision to end their suffering has been made, and this is for me where it gets complicated and becomes paradoxical, they calm down becoming almost tranquil having made their choice and they begin to logically and systematically plan their own demise. However, if they have any reason to believe that their plight was caused by another, they will often proceed with rage to assure their destruction before seeing to their own. Now this is the part that I have difficulty in reconciling. How can we call suicide *the coward's way out* when we know that man will do whatever is necessary to preserve the self and to survive? What is it that ties us so tightly to the fabric of our hierarchy and our perceived place in it that its loss results in total desperation and despair? And what signals are being sent from the higher brain to the Id that would cause it to react so counter intuitively as to allow for the termination of the self? Are you beginning to see the power of man's vanity, his pride, his honor, his need for respect and status within the hierarchy? I can really only talk suicide from the outside looking in, though I have known suicides. And, I can't imagine the levels of confusion and pain they must have been experiencing prior to committing the act. Remember, and this is the paradox, they would have had to override the survival mechanism of the Id before they could take a deliberate action to stop their pain and shame. How much pain, grief, and self-loathing does there have to be in order to make suicide an attractive alternative? I have only questions here and no answers. So, if we go back to the top, I don't think you'll find that we've gotten any closer to a feasible explanation as to why we react so violently to perceived or actual challenges to our public pride and honor; but without question, we know they are powerful drivers; and, they seem to be primordial. According to Christian beliefs, it was pride, vanity, and the desire for higher and/or equal status that led to the rebellion of the Angels. Our innate drivers for higher status within the hierarchy and the prestige that comes with it seems to be no different than theirs.

None of this was intended to be instructional to you, just informative. It is my hope that you take away a greater appreciation of how jealously man protects, defends, and clings to the projection of his Avatar. In our world, our public pride, our sense of honor and respect and our public face are the things that sustain our status within the hierarchy, and they are our greatest weaknesses. Any threat to any of them becomes a threat to the Avatar. And a threat to the Avatar is often interpreted as a threat to the survival of the whole being. Just remember that man's ego is fragile and unstable. So, when you interact with him, avoid anything that might cause him embarrassment, shame, or to lose face. Even inadvertent slights can cause narcissistic injury without your knowledge. But even more importantly, don't allow yourself to get caught-up in the hierarchy's *Respect and Honor Games*. There are no winners in these games, just pawns and puppets. Resist the temptation to prove yourself and to affirm your status, so that you can maintain your own individualism and independence. Yes, I know it's a lot to ask, but try.

I recognized that I've used extreme examples to argue my position, and we're no closer to understanding why we react the way we do. Though we don't have any answers, it's important to keep in mind that in our competitive environment, similar but, less extreme dramas are being played out on a daily bases, and it's inevitable that someone's pride or vanity will be damaged. And when it is, they will want some form of retribution. It is my hope that at this point, you have developed your observational and managerial people skills to a level where they will allow you to recognize and avoid the majority of these unintentional slights and missteps.

With respect to your own desire to take revenge and get justice; those waters are too dark and deep for me, and I'm not an ethical or moral guide, so there is no way that I can advise you. The desire for revenge and justice appears to be another one of the hard wires in our nature, so I can't advise you to resist the natural urge to act on them. I can only suggest that you learn to be measured in your responses and free yourself from the trappings of group-think. You'll need to avoid the pitfalls and negative consequences that are associated with reactionary retribution...and be able to think things through.

As I had stated, there wasn't a good place to fit this section anywhere in the book, so I put it here because false pride, narcissistic rage, humiliation, shame and loss of face can all be considered manifestations of communications and are all a part of our world. And as a manager, as well as a private individual, they are things you have to be aware of. As you have seen, people can perceive an inadvertent slight as an assault to their honor and a sign of public disrespect. And in far too many cases, their reactions are totally disproportionate to the offense, and in many cases, they will want to take revenge against the offender. This can be true of anybody, there is no distinction among people, and it is as true for your staffers, your peers, your managers as it is true for you.

I will close by asking you to remember how public pride, honor, and respect can lead to confrontation, how confrontation can lead to psychological injury, how psychological injury can lead to aggression, how aggression can lead to a desire for retribution, and how a desire for retribution can lead to disaster in a bid for satisfaction...and, in the end, there are no winners, we all lose;...*just a warning.*

Now I want us to move on to some of the ways in which we formally communicate to a broader audience, specifically in meetings, presentations, and in our writings. Each time we use one of these vehicles to communicate we put ourselves on stage and dependent upon our level of professionalism and effectiveness, we subject ourselves to (both) acclaim and ridicule. Therefore, in the next few sections we will be studying what is likely happening around you and with your audience when you communicate using these mediums, and we'll also be exploring ways to make your communications as effective and impactful as possible.

Meetings:

Clearly, when we think of communications, one of the first things that come to mind is the meeting. The meeting has always been the preferred and most effective forum for the transfer of important information from man's earliest days, right on up to today. The meeting is intended to bring together stakeholders and interested parties in a single place and at a specified time in order to resolve conflicts or to solve common problems, provide updated or new information, and/or to decide important forward actions of relevance to them all. And though there are many similarities between professional or business meetings and social meetings, a professional meeting should always be kept tightly focused on the matter at hand and should be kept within its original scope and the time frame allotted. These meetings should have a defined purpose and an agenda; they are not social gatherings and should never be conducted that way. If it's your meeting you would be expected to facilitate the success of the meeting by determining the agenda, identifying the relevant stakeholders, and deciding the time and place where the meeting will be convened. But before scheduling your meeting there are a few things you should consider: the first would be to determine if the meeting was actually necessary, or is there another, less expensive but equally effective way, to communicate the information or decide the issue without tying-up time and valuable human resources. If decisions have to be made, are those with the authority to make the decisions going to be in attendance? If you are sharing information, is it new information and does it justify the cost of the meeting? And, have you done your homework so you are prepared to chair your own meeting? This last point is critically important; a meeting has to be controlled. While it's another opportunity for you to get on stage and promote your ultra-ego (your Avatar), you are likely bringing together people from different departments and at different levels in the organization who don't normally have an opportunity to interact with each other, and more often than not, they'll want to be able to share that stage with you. Its group dynamics, everyone is competing to establish their place within your meeting's hierarchy. Everyone wants to show everyone else that they run with the *big dogs* and their participation in your meeting is essential to its success. To be invited to a meeting is seen as a conformation of their status within that hierarchy; just ask anyone who didn't get an invite, what does that do to their perception of status? Just take yourself back to a meeting you've attended where the attendees were from different departments and organizations. If you had arrived early, you would have walked into a meeting room where there were as many as 5 to 15 separate one-on-one conversations going on at once. People would be circulating exchanging cards and contact information and boasting about their current role, involvement or reason for being there. We tend to call this networking, and it is, but what does that really mean; what's really happening here? Well, if you stripped away all the niceties, you would see that they are moving from person to person, *covertly and indirectly,* asking "are you somebody, are you anyone that I can impress, or someone I could benefit from knowing, or someone that could further my career or political standing?" The entire exchange will only take about 30 to 90 seconds and you'll generally know if they don't think you'll be any benefit to them when they move on without even giving you a card. But if they see you as a peer, they'll likely give you a card and maybe ask a few more questions before moving on; but this too will be fleeting, lasting maybe 2 minutes…3 at the most. But if they see you as a person with a certain amount of gravitas (or if they are insecure of themselves in the meeting) they'll give you a card, their contact information and spontaneously provide you and unsolicited informal verbal curriculum vitae. In addition, they will likely campout beside you during the meeting. Though on the other hand, if the senior people were already known, when you'd have walked into the room, you'd have only found a few subgroups clustered around those people and everyone would be, not so subtly, jostling and vying for attention and recognition. But then, this is your meeting, all of this networking, politicking, and posturing is just a part of the sideshow. You're the main event. Now, we've turned a lot of pages to get to this point, so I have little doubt that you have prepared and communicated the meeting's agenda prior to the meeting. That you are immensely knowledgeable and well versed about all the subject matter targeted for discussion and you have considered and prepared responses for anticipated first tier questions, as well as the likely follow-up ones (e.g., who, what, when, where, why, how). I am also sure that you have recognized that there might be people in your audience at all levels that, if given the opportunity, would hijack your meeting and divert a portion of its time to serve their own purposes. And I'm sure that by now you have picked up a book or some seminar materials that teaches you some of the finer points of controlling a meeting. If you haven't already, you might want to. They'll expose you to a variety of techniques that have proven effective in fending off meeting hijackers and sidestepping traps, tricks and other non-relevant questions that often emerge. While it might sound a bit cynical, it is no less a matter of fact, that there will be those in your audience who will do whatever they can to share your spotlight with you. Their questions might be directed to you, but you are really not their targeted audience. Their questions are designed to project their intellect or rational thought process to the greater group, not to you. And the purpose of their questions are to draw you into a dialog, just the two of you, so it will no longer be your meeting, it'll become theirs as well. They want to become the star of your meeting and demote you to a supporting role. This could be quite damaging to you and the image you have been trying to project; after all, how can you be considered a manager or a leader when you can't even control your own meeting? Just don't take the bait, follow your own script and sidestep the traps. Additionally, if your meeting is one where decisions or forward actions will be taken, do your homework and find out what those decisions are going to be before the meeting. You cannot afford to be surprised at your own meeting. Prior to your meeting, meet with the decision makers and give them the needed background information and a list of options. Let them give you their thinking and likely decisions early on. You can't afford to have the group believing they are moving in one direction, then have a decider cut your legs right out from under you. The group will blame you for that disconnect, and rightfully so; it was your meeting, you should have known.

Meetings don't have to be complicated; they should be simple and straight to the point. Everyone should have a copy of the agenda, or at least know what the agenda is, and you should tell the attendees what the purpose of the meeting is, what topics will be covered, and/or what issues will be decided. You, and/or the presenters should tell the audience what you're going to tell them, tell them, and, in closing, tell them what you told them. Be prepared to answer initial and follow-up questions, but don't get caught up in someone else's pursuit of recognition and glory. A meeting is not just a meeting; it's another arena and opportunity for you to contest status and garner political influence. And a successful meeting doesn't just happen, it takes planning and preparation. You have to know your subject matter, know your audience and their personalities; recognize and avoid obvious pitfalls, have a backup plan in place if one might be needed, be well rehearsed, and stay mindful of the competitive nature of your colleagues.

There is a difference between a meeting and a strategy session. If you've gathered people together to map out a particular strategy or to develop a solution to a particular issue, your role as leader or meeting's Chair changes. You still have to decide who should participate and inform them as to why they have been selected and the purpose of the strategy session. You still have to maintain control of the session and have to deal with many of the same sideshow issues. And you have to clearly define the problem and possible paths to resolution while staying in the realm of what is actually possible, with respect to budgetary restraints, return on investment, timing, etc. You have to separate the innovative and the bold from the ridiculous and impractical. In this role you are no longer a presenter, providing information, you are a facilitator, allowing others to contribute their genius to the resolution of the matter at hand. But yet again, this arena is thick with intellectual and hierarchical posturing and rivalries where everyone wants to be seen as having the best and most elegant solutions. Your challenge here is to keep the ideas flowing and focused on resolving the issue at hand. You can expect there to be a certain amount of bullying; where those with higher status will try to diminish the suggestions of those of lower rank. It will be your responsibility to control the flow of ideas and to prevent bullying from occurring or stop it when it appears; if you don't, those with lower rank will just shut down and stop contributing. And yes, they will blame both you and their tormentors because it was your meeting and you didn't protect them or afford them the level of respect and professional courtesy that they expected, and were due.

Your ability to successfully conduct a meeting and/or a strategy session speaks volumes about your leadership and management abilities, and senior people are watching. Back when we talked about those individuals who appeared to be born leaders, those charismatic people that made everything look so easy, we were talking about a *well-studied, well-rehearsed,* and *self-confident* you. Every meeting is another performance of your leadership and people skills. If you have a good performance you get good reviews, but if you trip, stumble, and fumble the reviews will reflect that as well. I said you had to control your meeting and keep it tightly focused to the agenda...and that's easy enough to do if you're having a staff meeting with your direct reports; you would have departmental authority and position power at your disposal. But at a cross functional meeting where there are attendees from other departments and at all levels (including senior management) you don't have position power. You have the responsibility for conducting the meeting and the authority to do so, but where does your power come from, the power to keep the competitive backbiting and personal sniping at bay? Based on the way I have already defined *"power",* you really don't have any. What you have is an illusion of power (Perceived Power) and it's held together by three, rather weak and ephemeral components. The first is twofold, and a little complicated. We humans tend to attach a great amount of importance to meetings, all types of meetings. There's a certain level of prestige and recognition of our status that feeds our egos when we are considered important enough to be in attendance. So we are driven to attend the meeting because we perceive it to be important and because the invitation plays to our *pride and vanity.* And the second is *fear.* We recognize that meetings are extremely expensive and time consuming, so if *the Gods on high* considered the subject matter important enough to have authorized your meeting, no one would want to be held accountable for the meeting's failure because they were a *"no show".* The next component is professional courtesy, everyone wants to demonstrate to everyone else that they are professional, and besides, one of the Gods that authorized your meeting might be in the room and no one would want to offend them. Professional courtesy will keep the attendees at bay so long as you can demonstrate your mastery of the relevant subject matter and are able to avoid the traps and pitfalls that will still be laid before you. If you trip, all bets are off and it's going to be a long meeting. The last essential component to exercising perceived power and control is dependent upon your own credibility and the confidence level of the image you project (your Avatar). We are predators and are always looking for any signs of weakness and vulnerability. If you don't show us any, we will be less likely to attack. Confidence is not something you can learn from this or any other book, it is a living thing that becomes a part of you and what you do throughout a lifetime. It has to be cultivated and nurtured and it will ebb and flow depended on a given situation, the level of risk confronting you and your mind-set at the time, you will either have it or you won't. In this instance, your confidence is a direct result of your planning, preparation and rehearsal. Therefore, you can't allow yourself to get knocked off point by some question from out of left field. And whatever you do, don't start tap-dancing, the instant you do, everyone will know it[26]. You will be successful if you take the necessary steps to succeed. No one is out to get you or bears any malice towards you, but it's your meeting and you have the spotlight and they want to share the stage with you; it's not personal, it's just human nature.

I think it would be appropriate for me to offer a few words of caution when it comes to using the meeting as your platform for communication. While it is undoubtedly a very effective vehicle for the purpose, it can be, and often is grossly over used. There are simply far too many meetings occurring in today's workplace. Meetings are expensive and they divert valuable resources that might be put to better use elsewhere. What's more, a large percentage of meetings, particularly informational meetings, are unnecessary and much, if not all, of their information could have been distributed through some other means (e.g., voice mail, email, newsletter, the company's website, etc.). Further, it has been my experience that, there was really not a compelling business reason that would justify the capital expense for many of the meetings we convene; we meet because that's what we are accustom to doing. And many meetings are just a waste of time. There is often no clearly defined agenda, no clearly defined scope, no agreement on forward actions and milestones or a time set for follow-up. And that's because we're not very good at communicating, and we're not very good at coordinating meetings either. If it's your meeting, you should know what outcomes you expect from your meeting *going-in,* and you need to communicate it to the attendees so they'll know what they should expect; this puts everyone on the same page. You have to establish

---

[26] Tap-dancing is a term use to describe some of the things a person does when they are in front of a group and finds themselves lost and out of their depth but they try to project an illusion that they are still in control.

and define clear roles and accountabilities so people will know who is going to do what, and by when. And there has to be a scheduled follow-up and a defined scope to avoid mission creep. And before the meeting is adjourned, you need to recap the meeting's proceedings so you'll know everyone got the same information and is clear on the objectives and their roles. If a meeting is required or expected, then have one. But take the time and make the effort to assure that your meeting will be effective, productive and worthwhile having.

Presentations:

When we communicate via a presentation we should bring everything we've learned from conducting meetings with us because much of what we will be doing is exactly the same. You can think of a presentation as just a different kind of meeting, a meeting within a meeting (a mini meeting). But when you do a presentation, in most cases you will be able to tailor your message and make it more impactful to your targeted audience then might have been possible in a meeting. My thinking here is that generally presentations tend to focus on a single issue or topic whereas meetings usually cover a range of subject matter and they are usually attended by a more divergent audience. That's not to say that you won't have multiple audiences at your presentation, just that those in attendance are more likely to have an interest in what you plan to present or at least some rudimentary knowledge of it. And while you'll still have a primary, secondary, and tertiary audience, it will be much easier for you to know which-is-which and how best to tailor your presentation so it will have the desired effect. Again, there are some excellent books and seminars available that are far more comprehensive and will help you to become a better, more impactful presenter, and you might want to pick one up. I will limit my coverage to some of the more basic, but still important, considerations when making a presentation that were not previously mentioned in the section on meetings.

Presentations come in all shapes and sizes, and the subject matter that can be presented is only limited by your imagination. But when we look at why we do presentations we find that they are done to inform, to influence, and to review (a strategic review). So whenever you undertake to do a presentation, you'll need to decide just what it is you're doing, what's its purpose, is it to inform, to influence, or to review the status of something? Your approach to each will be different as will the attentiveness and attention span of your audience. When your purpose is to inform, you should start big and end small. If you want to influence, you have to start big and end bigger. But when your presentation is designed to review and explain, you start small and expand the presentation to include the vital elements and end small with each of the elements. But in all instances, or wherever possible, leave enough time for a question and answer period (Q & A) in order to answer questions and to close the communication loop. And as was noted in the section on meetings, tell them what you're about to tell them, tell them; then tell them what you just told them. Before getting into the three different types of presentations, I just want to remind you that we are visually disposed. And your presentation would be far more impactful and will become much more relevant if we could see what you were presenting. A number of studies have been done that shows that our attentiveness and attention spans are substantially increased when a presenter uses visual aids. Visual aids gives us something *quasi*-tangible to look at that brings us closer to connecting with your intended message. Thereby, we're not left to wrestle with some abstract vision trying to make sense of your words. Visual aids helps you build trust and believability with the audience and enhances your credibility as well as the credibility of your presentation. Therefore, whenever possible, you should add simple (intuitive) visual components to every presentation you make (charts, graphs, drawings, pictures, etc.). Now I'd like to move to the informative presentation.

The Informative Presentation:

More than 90% of all presentations can be considered to be informative. They can announce the birth of a child, special events in a life, and up to and including a final eulogy. In business, it's what you did at your interview for the job, it can be a project status update report, a training activity, a public announcement, a citation, and any and everything that is considered of value or benefit to the organization and the attending audience. Most informational presentations should be, and are expected to be, an information dump of relatively short duration, very similar to a newspaper article or report. People have short attention spans and they need to know what you are presenting and how it might impact them on a personal or professional level. Therefore, you'll need to start your presentation with its most important components before moving down to some of the less important features. As before, announce your presentation (the topic and subject matter). Then tell the audience how you will be covering it. Give them the who's, the what's, the when's, the where's, the how's, and the why's so that those interested in your presentation will sit up and take notice, and so those that are not can go back to playing with their smart phones and tablets. A lot of work goes into preparing for and doing a good presentation; time, information gathering and distillation, and practice. So just between you and me, I know what it took to get your presentation to be impressive and impactful. Your audience doesn't know and they aren't interested, they really just don't care. So for those of you with the analytical or animated styles, stick to the presentation, not the prep work. If anyone is interested in the minutia or want to praise you for your presentation performance, they can do it at the post presentation session. Move on to the presentation. Your informational presentation should have three components: an introduction, the presentation itself (starting with the most impactful, descending to the complementary, but yet relevant). And it should end with a summation and a recap, and if possible a Q&A. Visually, it should look like the diagram below.

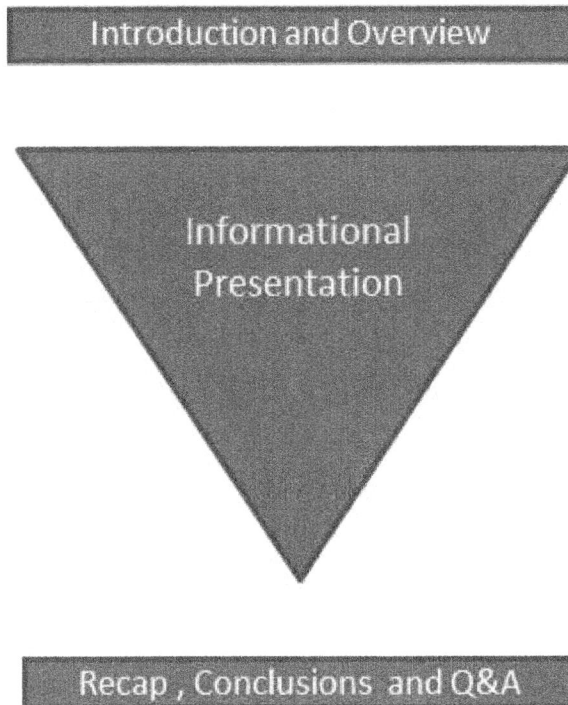

The Influential Presentation:

The influential presentation is a completely different animal as compared to the informative and the status review presentations. This is a promotional presentation; you want this presentation to be impactful and persuasive. It has to be done right because, in most cases, you only have one shot at it; so you should take the time in order to map out a strategy that will make the presentation as intellectually and/or emotionally compelling as possible. But before you can do that, you'll have to know a little something about your audience; and you already do. You already know a lot about human nature. You know that man is selfish and self-absorbed, and that he is driven by greed and hierarchical status and he avoids pain and ridicule. So when you put your presentation together, you'll have to do so in such a way as to tap into both these drivers in order to get and hold their attention. Your audience is listening for the *"WIFM"* in your presentation (*what's in it for me*), what are you offering that is of sufficient enough value that will get them to buy-in? Therefore, it follows that, your presentation will have to address a recognized need, desire, or demand that is deemed worthy of action and the expenditure of resources. If not, you'll have to influence your audience's thinking by getting them to see and recognize that the subject of your presentation is needed and worthwhile. And lastly, you'll have to be able to close the deal, otherwise this has all been a waste of everybody's time and you walk away a failure. You start the presentation big and end it even bigger with a deal closing adrenalizer. I'll give you two *real life* examples of how you might think about putting together an Influential Presentation. The first example, depending on your line of work, will seem to be over-the-top but I've included it for demonstrative purposes and it is often used by sales people to "at once" create a demand and seal the deal. The second example is one that we've covered earlier and you are already familiar with.

Example # 6 – *Creating a Demand:*

My wife and I spent most of our early married life poor; it was not something that we had planned, it was just the way things were. So, for us, a big night out was a drive-in movie where we brought our own boloney sandwiches and a thermos of Kool Aid. We lived in California at the time and would frequently get promotional flyers in the mail congratulating us on being selected to win one of 5 potential prizes; a marketing ploy. If I am remembering it correctly, the prizes were a new car, or $5,000 in cash, or a large color TV, and down to a very cheaply made and inexpensive kitchen wall clock. The only catch was that we would have to sit through their presentation before we could claim our prize. We were told that our inputs and comments were essential to their fact finding and to their market research so they would know how to position the products for retail sale in U.S. markets. On one occasion, I didn't have enough money to get us in to the drive-in, but I had enough gas to get us to their location to claim our prize, so that's where we went. However, before leaving our little apartment I explained to my wife that this was only a scam in order to get us to buy something and that we were going to be subjected to high pressure sales tactics, and we didn't have any money, so we couldn't and wouldn't be buying anything. Therefore, all we were doing was going to pick-up some cheap wall clock and then come back home. When we got to their location, it was in some rundown industrial park and they were set-up in one of the warehouses. When we got inside we saw that they had set the warehouse up to look like a luxurious showroom with a myriad of household products displayed all around. They had arranged it so different groups would arrive at different times so they could take every group through their presentation separately. They gave our group about a 15 minute presentation about how they were sourcing high quality products from around the world and making them available to discriminating consumers in the U.S. at less than wholesale prices. And we were told that we were selected to evaluate their products based upon population demographics and by our current zip codes. We were asked to walk around the displays and just form an opinion of the products and to pick 5 that we thought were of particular interest and that we would likely purchase if they became available in U.S. markets. Note, that nearly an hour had passed and there had not been any attempt to get us to buy anything; yet! Most of the group, including my wife, were like lambs going to slaughter. They thought that they were going to be rewarded with cars, cash and other prizes for helping the company with their market research. After all, they were all connoisseurs of finery and high quality; at least that's what they were told. And as you would expect, that played to everyone's ego. But let's move on...so when we'd completed our walk through and my wife had selected 5 products that she would one day like to own, we were taken into one of their cubicles by one of their people, ostensibly to be debriefed so they could record our impressions of the products and to determine which of the prizes we had won. My wife was thrilled, energized and very complementary of the products, while I on the other hand, knew where this was headed. The person listened to my wife's assessment of all their products and even though they had a legal pad in front of them, they didn't take down a single note, which told me that they weren't really interested in gathering market research. Then they asked about the 5 products she had selected as the products she'd likely purchase if they were ever available in the market. The person, I will call them the *sales person* now because that's where it went from there, opened a book that contained pictures of all the products on display and took out the pictures of the 5 products my wife had selected. He talked about the superior quality of the products and where they would be sourced from around the world and he asked my wife how much she would expect to pay for those products if she would choose to buy them at retail. Boy was she off! He explained that every one of the products she selected was to be positioned at retail for as much as 2 to 3 times as much as she had expected. He proved it by showing her their suggested retail prices on the back of the pictures; I guess if it was written on the back of the pictures, it must be true…*right?* Note, that we were a *quasi-captive* audience, in their facility listening to their presentation (their propaganda) with no other reliable point of reference. This should be considered the end of their initial presentation (the top of the diagram below). So I want to stop here to give you a minute to think about everything they had done to this point in order to set up the sale. They lured people in with a guarantee of winning one of 5 possible prizes. Then they catered to their egos by getting them to feel special, or in some way superior, for having been chosen to participate in their market research. They took us out of the real world and put us in a world of their own making by having their display set up in a warehouse where products were strategically placed and well lit in order to show them at their best. But we were left blind to any indication of their cost or actual value. Lastly, they asked people to select 5 items that they would like to purchase if they became available (their wish list), and when they did, they showed them a price that they could not possibly afford. The psychology here was to put the items financially out of reach which had the effect of making the *"mark"* (and that's what we were) want them even more. What they did, albeit by deceit and deception, was to set up the sale and cultivate the buyer by creating a need, a demand, or a desire for a product where none had previously existed… this is marketing.

Let's move on…the stage has been set and now it's time to move to the influential bottom half of the diagram, the actual selling part of the presentation. The salesperson continued to disarm us by playing to our egos, by complementing us (my wife in particular) on our selections and for having such a keen eye and appreciation of quality merchandise. He had a story to tell about each of our selections and oddly enough, and because he worked for the company, he had selected at least three of the same items for his own home and was more than impressed by them. Therefore he could give us his own personal recommendations. I think you can see where this was going. He went on to say that the company had decided, that because we were partnering with them on their market research, they would give us the opportunity to purchase the products we had selected and said we would likely buy if they were available at a steep discount. He immediately got my wife's full attention, and he knew it. He went through all 5 items discounting them around 30% but they were still way outside of our financial capabilities, and besides, I didn't come there to buy anything anyway, just to get a clock; we were poor remember. My wife recognized that the items were still out of our reach and he saw it. So pay close attention to what came next, *the hard-sell*. He took the picture of the most expensive item off the table (a set of 6 stainless steel pots and pans, and the very items he could see that my wife wanted the most) and put it in his desk draw, and then he ran the numbers for us again. He pulled out a financing contract where I could put down $100.00 and pay $ 10.00 a week for nearly a hundred years in order to pay them off. He saw some receptiveness in my wife but couldn't get a read on me because quite frankly, my mind was someplace else. I knew I wasn't going to buy anything, so that was a nonstarter for me. Although I was physically still sitting there, I had checked out and was actually wandering around in my mind, wondering if I read my gas gauge right and had a quarter tank of gas or was it an eighth of a tank. If I had a quarter tank, we could stop off on the way home to get a couple of hot pastrami sandwiches because I had $ 10.00 in my pocket. Lastly I was wondering how much longer did we have to be here before I could get my damn clock and get the hell out of here? While I was away, the salesman must have fallen in love with my wife because he really wanted her to get the 4 items which were still on his desk. He said he was going to do something that was completely against their corporate procedures, he was going to talk to his manager on our behalf. I think we all saw that coming too. I don't know if the cubical we were in was fitted with a microphone but if it was, anyone listening, would have known that my wife had been seduced by the *dark side* and was trying to get me to find ways to afford, what for us, was unaffordable. When my wife's champion returned, having done heroic battle with his manager, he told us that he was able to get us an additional 10% discount; in addition, our names would be included among the finalist to win the grand prize[27]. Then, here comes the adrenalizer, he sat back down at his desk and...wait for it...wait for it...now, just another moment more. Can you feel the tension building? He reached into his desk draw and pulled out the picture of the cookware, threw it in the center of his desk and told us that if we agreed to the 40% discount and purchased the products today, they would give us the cookware absolutely free; what a guy. My wife screamed, hit me on my thigh several times, then she jumped up and started dancing around as if we had just won the lottery. The salesman was ecstatic, in his mind it was an *affaire de complet*; he had her, hook, line and sinker. Under normal circumstances he would have closed the deal, but if you remember, when we walked in the door, we were severely financially challenged and nothing had changed over the preceding hour. And without getting too much further in the weeds, suffice it to say that we didn't buy anything, I got my cheap clock and we were finally able to get out of there; though I was made to feel that I wasn't going to get into heaven for not buying my wife her dream items. But for you, go back and take a look at how they lured people in with the promise of riches, catered

---

[27] This was another omission and a point of deliberate confusion. Most people thought they had already qualified to win the grand prize because the mailer said "Congratulations, you have already won 1 of 5 prizes". There was no mention of a multistage contest.

to their vanity, created a demand for a product where there had been none, drew in the mark by pricing the items just out of reach, taking the most desired item off the table, identifying with the mark and taking their side to fight for a better price (becoming their hero), then closing the deal with the unexpected adrenalizer. I don't expect that many of you will have reason to put together such an elaborate presentation but it's important for you to know how it's done and how it's put together. Every time you bring in a salesperson, buy a car, sit through a time-share presentation, and even interview a potential employee you're getting some variant of the influential presentation. So you should be able to know it when you see it and be able to predict what's coming next. You can't allow yourself to get caught up in the emotional heat of the moment and make a bad decision. As for me and my wife, needless to say it was a long drive home and she wasn't in the mood for a hot pastrami sandwich. Things around our apartment were quiet and icy for the next few weeks until I took her on a fantasy shopping trip. I was tired of being the bad guy so I took her out so she could identify and compare equivalent store items to those that were on her wish list. And while we still couldn't and didn't buy anything, she discovered that there were analogs for each of the items she wanted selling at retail for less than half the price they were asking; even after their 40% discount and throwing in the set of cookware. So, at long last, peace finally returned to our little realm.

Example #7 – Addressing a Recognized Need or Desire:

This is one that you are already familiar with and the example that is more in line with what you are likely to encounter over the course of your career. I am referring to the "TRA 2000" example. In this example the problems were overtly apparent to everyone on the leadership team, though the staff appeared to be oblivious to them. There was infighting between the group's manager and director brought about by mutual distrust and a lack of coordinated leadership. Nothing was working because nothing was designed to address the underlying issues; employee apathy and their sense of entitlement, their lack of ownership, responsibility and accountability for the work, their knowledge that any errors in their work would be corrected by their manager without any adverse repercussion to them, and so on. In addition, nothing was designed to address the root causes of the departmental dysfunction (the poor working relationship between the manager and the director, the desire of both the manager and the director to be liked by the staff, the conflicting messages being sent to the staff, their inability to confront and correct productivity and quality issues with the staff, and on and on...). So, the problems were clear, well at least they were clear to me. I never was able to understand what management was attempting to do with respect to the actions they had taken, bringing in a consultant group and having the director work with a mentor. How could they ever expect to correct the problems if they just danced around them and never got to their root causes? I was reminded of a time, back in high school, when one of my best friend's parents helped him get his first car. It was an old car, but it was beautiful. It was a 1957 Ford Fairlane 500. It was baby blue with a black convertible top. It had long sensuous lines and chrome spinners for hubcaps. You car guys, and some of you car women, know what I'm talking about. We spent hours washing and polishing it and got our pictures taken alongside it. We were in heaven, but there was just one problem...the car wouldn't run. It had three burnt valves and smoked like a poorly tuned diesel. The transmission was slipping and leaking fluid and the radiator was clogged, causing it to constantly overheat. We didn't have any money to get anything fixed but we continued to pamper it. But no matter how much we washed and polished it, we could never, ever get it to run. To me, the parallels between what we had done and what they were doing were remarkable and quite astonishing. My friend and I were hopeful and stupid; thinking that we could make things better by putting a little patch in here and a bandage over there and she would crank-up and purr like when she was new. It was not going to happen, the car needed a major mechanical overhaul and so did the Technical Regulatory Affairs Department. But, in my mind, bringing in consultants to conduct *generic* team-building exercises and to put on some *standardized productivity presentations* for the staff without addressing the real issues in the department, having the consultants work directly with the director on *"who knows what"*, providing the director a mentor, having my colleague to continually check all the staff's work and putting in long hours didn't approach the real problems. And because they never addressed the actual problems directly and head-on, they were just wasting time and resources. They were polishing a rotten apple as it was continuing to decay. When you put together your influential presentation, it will have to get into the meat of the problem at hand or provide the audience some tangible benefit above and beyond the status quo. Your proposal will have to be simple (if not eloquent) and intuitive because most people are blind when it comes to reconciling the abstract. You can't have any loose ends that a detractor could pull and try to get everything to unravel. Additionally, you have to take into account man's drivers (pleasure and pain). And you'll have to know who your target audience is and you'll have to show them what the upside benefits are to your proposed approach as well as any downside risk for taking another approach, or for doing nothing at all. This can be done by your effective use of the Six "Cs" Standards of Persuasion and Innovation. That it is clear, concise, compelling, connected, contrasted and credible.

Now let's take a look at how the "TRA 2000" presentation was put together and see how it fits the influential presentation diagram.

- **The introduction of the presentation:**

  My colleague told them what she was about to tell them, *the first tell*. Tell what the proposal is, why it was thought to be needed, what it is intended to do or fix, and why it is believed to be necessary.

- **The presentation:**

  The second tell...In this case everyone already knew what some of the problems were, and all the leadership was aware of the looming deadline to convert all the companies packaging materials and graphics. The Sr. VP was keenly aware of his responsibility to the company and that failure (for him) was not an option. At this point he needed to see a plan, any plan that was feasible and had a realistic chance of success. Go back and take another look at the 3 sets of bullet points showing the problems, the solutions to those problems, and the amount of time and resources that would be required to rollout the program. We listed the problems in the top half of the presentation and their solutions and resource requirements as well as important milestones in the bottom half. Note that the Sr. VP was the targeted audience and we knew that his *WIFM* and his *adrenalizers* were to meet the requirements and the timing of the labeling law and the expectations of his boss, the company's CEO.

- **The Recap and Q & A:**

  She recapped the presentation and told them what she told them, *the third tell*. Then she took questions. The presentation was clear, concise, compelling, connected, contrasted and credible and it got the green light. And as already noted, the Sr. VP was so *"juiced"* that he promised to take the entire group and their spouses (or significant others) for a night on the town in Manhattan once the project had been successfully completed.

You should take a bit of time and study these 2 examples for commonalities. Each played to man's natural drivers (pleasure (profit, gain, greed, etc.) and fear (potential loss, downside risk, possible failure, etc.)). Each was designed to satisfy a recognized need, desire, or demand (though the need or desire in the first example was created and contrived). From the prospective of the targeted audience they were both simplistic as well as intellectually and/or emotionally com-pelling. And while they each had plenty of *WIFM* for the targeted audience, they also had an adrenalizer right at the end to assure buy-in in order to close the deal; hook-line-and-sinker. Just a reminder to you, we are still talking about communications and the image you are projecting. And in these examples we're also talking about power; the power to influence...*political power.* When you finish this presentation you will walk away having either succeeded or failed, there is no middle ground, tries and best efforts, without success, are still failures.

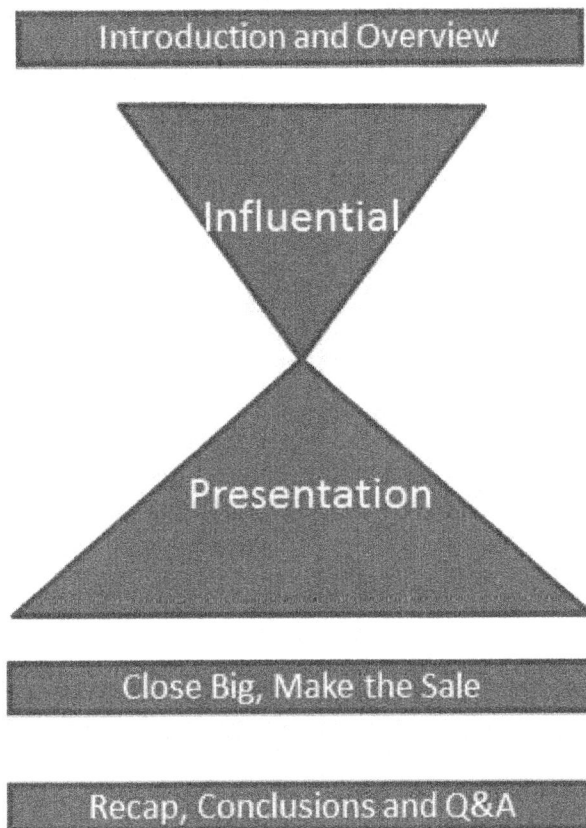

The Strategic Review Presentation:

The review presentation is just the name I have assigned to any number of specific detailed presentations where a vast amount of information is targeted for a comprehensive, in-depth, review and discussion. Presentations that would fall into this category would include Strategic Plans, Annual Financial Reviews or State of the Business Reviews, and Project Reviews as well as other very formal systematic broad topic reviews and/or progress status reports. These presentations are usually chaired by the senior leaders in the organization or the senior project leaders. There will generally be several presenters having expertise in each of the specific areas under discussion. Their presentations are really nothing more than informational presentations but they are all tied together and are essential to the whole (the topic under review). I won't spend any more time with this type of presentation because, frequently, individual organizations have their own particular approach to how they want the material presented. But, for the most part, the Chair introduces the presentation, gives a topical overview of what will be presented, and then introduces the first presenter. Each presenter follows the procedure already outlined above in the Informational Presentation leaving time to recap and for a Q & A. Along the way or between presenters, the Chair points to the relevance of one presentation to the next and to the overall relevance of each presentation to the greater topic under review. Finally, the Chair summarizes what has been presented and closes the review. The key for you is to become skilled in preparing and presenting the Informational and the Influential presentations. Once you've developed a level of confidence with both, the Review Presentation is nothing more than another logical, systematic distribution of information.

Introduction and Overview

Strategic Review
Presentation

Recap , Conclusions and Q&A

Writing:

There are any number of professional writing courses and seminars that are available to you if writing is important in your line of work and you believe you could benefit from participating in one. Most of the courses are designed to teach you techniques currently being used by some of our most successful writers and to help you learn how to organize your thoughts and format your information so that your writing will stand out and stand above the ordinary. Professional writing is beyond the scope of this work but writing as a form of communication is well within our bailiwick. Simply put, when we communicate in writing we try to capture our abstract thoughts in the form of words that are in a common language and we believe would have a similar meaning to the message recipient as they have with us (the transmitter). When we transmit that message, we never really know if the message was ever received, and if it was received, was it ever read and if it was read, was it understood; there's no automatic feedback loop. Therefore, in this section I will be focusing on helping you get your message read and understood. And to do that, I am going to assume that your communique will be formulated in a language that is consistent with the language of the intended recipient and the words you use will be standardized and consistent to the level of understanding of that recipient (the receiver). That leaves us with getting the message read. If your message is received but goes unread, you're not communicating, you're just wasting time and resources. When we communicate using the written word we lose a lot of the precision that we enjoyed with verbal interactions during one-on-one face-to-face communications or during conversations in meetings and during presentations. We are more restricted in what we can convey and we usually have no way of knowing if our intended message is being received as it was intended because there's no way to close the communication loop. During verbal communications the transmitter has the opportunity to color the content of the message using voice inflections, word cadence, tone, and they can get automatic feedback to determine how their message is being received just by asking questions and closing the communication loop. And when the verbal communication is done in person or by way of a video conference the transmitter can also communicate to their audience using facial expressions and body language. Very little of this is available to you when writing, you'll have to rely on the relevance of your subject matter, your word selection, your writing style and your limited ability to **_"SHOUT"_** in your document, using caps, italics, bold fonts, underscoring, and punctuations. And because you don't have the level of precision in writing as you do with verbal communications makes it all the more important that you vet every word in your documents so as to be certain they convey your message as effectively and clearly as you know how. You should avoid esoteric jargon and words that carry dual meanings. If you take the time to write it down, you should take the time to make it a free standing document. The entire who's, what's, when's, where's, how's, and why's should be part of what you put down. If it is a paper document, you can expect that it will be around for 100 years, and if it is electronic, you should expect it to proliferate and become immortal, and at some point, you might be asked to explain, expand upon, or defend what you wrote. And the only way you will be able to do that, particularly for an audience that was never intended to read what you wrote, and at some distant point in the future, is to include the background material in the document from the start. But we all need to use common sense when writing. There are some of you who write down everything, and you know who you are. This is a really bad practice and you should stop it. Most things are not noteworthy, and some things should never be written down...not because it would be wrong to do so, but because some things just don't look right or translate well on paper and could become the subject of deliberate misinterpretations which could ultimately put you and your company at a professional or legal disadvantage. So take care with what you write down because you might have to explain or defend it at some later date; once you put pen to paper or create an electronic document, it becomes judicable and can become a liability.

Most of what we write (excluding posted notes, squib notes, and text messages) are actually essays of one type or another. Some might be longer, some shorter but an essay none the less. And essays, very much like presentations, are purposeful documents that are designed to either inform, influence, or to describe, analyze, or review something of common interest. Therefore, your essay can be categorized as being narratives (in order to tell a story), they can be persuasive (in order to argue or influence a particular point of view), or they can be descriptive (providing an objective review and assessment of something). There is really little difference in the formatting of essays and the formatting of a similar type of presentation. For example, an Informational Presentation is really only telling a story, so it is a narrative. An Influential Presentation is intended to put forward or argue a particular point of view, exactly like a persuasive essay. And a Strategic

Review Presentation is intended to provide an objective description and assessment of some topic under review, so therefore it is like a descriptive essay. However, before I start losing some of you, let's not get too caught up in the word "essay", although that is exactly what we are writing. But the word, its self, is a bit misleading to most of us. When we think of an essay we thing about what we had to write in school and many of us still hold on to that particular meaning. We have to revamp our definition of what an essay is because today, we find ourselves writing reports, project updates, business proposals, operational or assembly instructions, performance reviews, audits, resumes, letters of recommendation and the like. And we just haven't thought of them as being essays...but they are. And the more you come to recognize that that's what they are, the better you'll become at writing them. As with presentations, the first thing you'll have to decide is what you hope to get accomplished by your writing; is it to inform, to describe, to persuade, or some combination of all three. Then you should determine what you know about your audience, how they are already predisposed and what words and phrases can you include in your document that will peak their interest. You may not be trying to sell anything but if you are going to take the time to write, it should at least be interesting enough to the intended audience to be read. But even then, most people never read a majority of the documents that cross their desk. They only scan them for relative importance and their own personal interest. So even before you start writing your document, you're already at a disadvantage. In order to get beyond a person's scan of your document to a read of it, it has to be impactful from the start and stay impactful until you have had your complete information dump, or you'll have to have some kind of hook (*a WIFM*) to keep them reading if you are actually trying to persuade and influence them. Holding an audience with a descriptive essay is a bit more challenging and we'll cover it a little farther down. But before I move on to the distinction between each type of essay, you should know that all written essays and essay topic materials are not created equal. You are not trying to be a literary master, that's not your role. You are an effective manager recording, in hardcopy, something that is of value to you and your company. Everything that you write is not your masterpiece and does not have to be powerful and impactful; some things just don't lend themselves to razzle-dazzle. So it's okay for some documents to be boring and humdrum so long as they are accurate, freestanding, and worthy of your signature.

I won't repeat what has already been provided in the Presentation Section but you might want to refer to it as a reasonable guide for your essay writing, it will be fully applicable here as well.

The Narrative Essay:

After the title, you might only have 10 - 20 seconds to grab the reader's attention and get them to read further. Therefore, all your strongest and most important who's, what's, when's, where's, how's, and why's have to be skillfully crafted in the title and in the first paragraph of your document. Other important information should at least make it into the second paragraph or it will likely be missed. If you have anything of value to relate, it has to be at the beginning of your document, otherwise you might lose the attention of the reader. Most of you probably do good work and write well, and I am sure you would like the reader to get to know how professionally skilled you are and how well you can master the written word. But this is not the place for it, your skill will likely be noticed during the read, but frankly, people are more interested in the contents of the document and its relevance to them, not how well you can string words together. Therefore, when you are providing information through a narrative essay, put everything of relevance in the title and the first 2 paragraphs. If the reader wants more, then they can read on. Keep your narrative focused and relatively short; only a few readers will get to page #2, and there is a better than even chance that no one will ever get to pages #3 & #4. If your narrative is offering a conclusion or a solution, you have to hint to it early on in order to prick the reader's curiosity and encourage them to read on. If not, your conclusions and solutions, along with your genius will remain unread and unnoticed. Like the informational presentation, it should start big and end small. Some informational documents won't fit the informational essay format or any of the other formats for that matter, and when they don't, don't try to force them. Just follow the guidelines as they have been established.

One final note; a contract is also a narrative, and there is a reason for them being long and laborious reading. The contract attorneys are counting on you not reading beyond the first or second pages, so they bury their disclaimers in the small print somewhere in the middle of the document, on pages 4 & 5. If you really want your hard work to go unnoticed and your contributions overlooked, just start your narrative off small and build upon it. And if you do, I can assure you that all your efforts and your best work will all be missed, because it will go unread.

The Persuasive Essay also called the Argumentative Essay:

In this essay you are trying to advance a position or you will be trying to argue a point of difference. It could be a new approach to solving a problem, a business proposal, a justification for a capital expense or additional human resources, a letter of recommendation or anything else you decide is worth the expenditure of your political and professional resources. With this essay, you either win or lose. Go back and take another look at the Influential Presentation and how it was presented. What was not very apparent at the time, but what I will speak to now is that in order to put forward a strong persuasive argument, you'll have to put forward a strong argument on both sides of the issue; not just supporting your own approach and discrediting the other. The difference between the two approaches has to be clear and compelling to the reader. The recipient of the essay should also be the decider, and you want them to decide in your favor. Now to the essay itself...there are some slight differences between how you structure this essay as compared to the way you constructed the Influential Presentation. In the essay you'll have to put everything of value in the title (what you expect to do (the WIFM and the adrenalizer)). You'll have to use your title or opening statement to set your hook to get the reader to read further. Put your thesis and major points in your first full paragraph (your rationale and approach). Put your sub points in the second paragraph and elaborate on your argument in the third and fourth paragraphs. Summarize your position in the fifth, and conclude your argument in the last paragraph. The success of your argument or ability to persuade will be dependent upon the relative importance and visibility of the subject matter, the cost benefit ratio and impact to the organization and its function, the simplicity and elegance of your compelling argument, proper timing, and getting your essay to the desk of the decider and getting it read. And as with the Influential Presentation, you have to start big and end even bigger.

Consider using the following outline as a guide:

The Persuasive Essay Guide:

Components	Contents	Purpose	The Six "Cs"
The Title and Opening Statement	An announcement of the topic and the intent of the document. The incentives for the reader, the WIFM and any adrenalizer you know of.	To spark the interest of the reader and set the hook to get them to read further.	**Clear:** Your idea, approach or solution has to be clear and intuitive to a 6th grader so everyone can understand what it is. **Connected:** Your solution or innovation has to be connected to something that is of current relevance to the organization and it has to be important so that it is on other people's radar.
The First Full Paragraph	Your thesis and the major points in your argument.	To present your rationale and approach to the argument.	**Credible:** There should be no doubt that what you propose will work.
The Second Paragraph	The sub-points that dovetail your argument.	To present a comprehensive consideration of all the relevant factors.	**Concise:** It has to be tightly packaged and encapsulated so people will know what to expect. There should be no drawn-out details associated; it needs to be elegant and simplistic.
Paragraphs Three and Four	A point-by-point unbiased elaboration and evaluation of the current situation or practice as compared to how it would change with your new approach.	To objectively and unbiasedly argue both sides and compare and contrast the old with the proposed new. To use facts, logic, and common sense to allow the reader to form their own opinion and buy in to your approach.*	**Contrasted:** There should be a clear contrast between the benefits of what you propose to everything else, up to and including, doing nothing at all.
The Fifth Paragraph	An objective summary of the argument you presented and of your overall thesis.	To provide a proof of the validity of your argument and to your approach.	**Clear** and **Credible**
Final Paragraph	A logical conclusion that is based upon the facts provided and points the way to the most effective and practical path forward.	To show the deciders the value and benefits of the new approach to them and their organization and to get them to buy-in (the WIFM).	**Credible** and **Compelling**: Your approach or solution should be irresistible and be intellectually and emotionally compelling. It should add value and be free of flaws, and if possible require less time, money and human resources to implement, and will work. This is what's call the adrenalizer.

* You will discredit your proposal and yourself if you present a subjective, unbalanced, partisan argument.

The Descriptive Essay:

From a business perspective, some of the most important essays we write are descriptive in nature. Some of the more familiar ones would include: Annual Reports, Project Reviews, Scientific Studies and Analysis, Sales Reports, Business Proposals, Operational Instructions, Audit Reports, Performance Appraisals, Resumes, and the list goes on and on. Some descriptors will fit neatly on a single page while some others can only be accommodated in rather large booklets and binders. Regardless of the size, your challenge remains the same, how to get your document read? With relatively short documents you can follow a similar format as you did with the Narrative Essay, though you will have less freedom to move back-and-forth between topics and ideas. In a Descriptive Essay, you'll have to introduce each topic, one at a time, and move through them in a systematic and logical manner until their conclusion before you can move to the next topic; to do otherwise would cause you to confuse and lose the reader. But if your document is not that long, say 3 to 5 pages, and has some relevance or provides some benefit to the recipient, it will likely get read. Voluminous documents are read selectively. They generally contain a vast amount of information and are divided into very different and distinct subsections. In addition, they will likely have been constructed and compiled by many different departments and disciplines. And, you can expect them to include a preamble, table of contents, an index, a reference page and addendums. This is not something that you will be authoring by yourself. This type of document is intended for widespread distribution to people of divergent backgrounds and interests. And with respect to readership, the total document will be read, but only in sections. The only people that will probably read the full document as compiled will likely be the people that compiled it; everyone else will probably only read those sections that have relevance to them and where they happen to be stakeholders. That leaves us with the medium length documents, documents between 5 to 25 pages in length. It has been my experience that most people don't read these documents either, at least not initially. When you publish such a document and you don't get any feedback, most likely, it's because no one has taken the time to read it. I can sympathize with anyone that's invested a lot of effort and much of themselves into doing all the groundwork and preparing a report or analyses of something that they believe is of great importance that provides new knowledge, or provides solutions and adds significant value to the company. Then, they find that no one knows or cares, because no one has read the document. This is an everyday occurrence in many medium to large scale corporations. People just don't have the time to consider anything that's off their radar screen (their "A" list of priorities). If your document is not on that list, it might get scanned, but not read. But at least a scan is something, it's a start. Therefore, when you have completed the construction of your document, attach a one or two page Executive Summary (a preamble) to it before you distribute it. The Executive Summary should be modeled on the Persuasive Essay format and put everything of value in the title and opening statements to set your hook to get the reader to read the majority of the summary. There are no guarantees, but in that way the reader will be able to at least form a mental note of your document's existents and that might cause them to recall it and refer to it at some later date when it becomes more relevant to them. The challenge for you is to put together a descriptive document that is up to the standard that is reflective of your professional expertise even when you realize it will likely go unread, be filed away, or will just lay around collecting dust until such time as someone considers it relevant. It will be a challenge, but you have to recognize that whenever it gets read (a month from now, a year, two years) the reader will not only be evaluating the document and its contents, but the credibility and competence of the author as well. You will be judged on the work you did years ago as if you just wrote the document yesterday. So stay mindful that whenever you put pen to paper, in either type of essay, you invite both acclaim and criticism, regardless of the passage of time. Let your work be representative of who you are and how you would like to be seen, now and in the future.

The Communication Observation Circus:

By now most of you are beginning to realize that your nature is no different than the nature of other human beings. Your drivers are the same as well as many of your preferences and biases. And because your emotional drivers change from day to day, they color and distort the way you see and interpret the world around you. That's just a matter of fact! So when it comes to talking the various forms of communication, I would hope that this section has provided you some level of guidance with respect to your verbal and nonverbal communications, listening and deciphering messages, conducting meetings, writing, giving presentations, and avoiding the traps of the Ego and false pride. But realistically, we have only been talking about our deliberate actions with respect to communications; learned tactics and strategies, tactics and strategies that we become skilled at and use to protect ourselves and project positive images of ourselves to the masses, while conveying our desired message. But communication is much broader than what we've covered, and there's no way that I could ever hope to cover all its various forms and nuances in this or any other book...so I'll have to leave it here. But just keep in mind that we've only been talking about ourselves, the message and image transmitters. We have no way of knowing, with any degree of certainty, how our messages and images are being received...are they being received as intended? A particular drawback, when transmitting any message, is that those that receive our messages are just like us, they like us, are subject to the same intellectual biases and emotional temperament. And as a consequence, they tend to be inconsistent in their interpretations of what they see and hear; and this is in large measure, determined by how they are *already predisposed*. Today they might accept what they see and hear at face value, tomorrow they might question the very same thing, and the next day they might overthink what was communicated and start imagining interpretations that were never intended. And when that happens, your image and your message starts to get distorted and garbled...just something for you to keep in mind.

I stated in the beginning that it would be a challenge (for me) to get through this section and it has been. Controlling your message and image will be critical to your success and effectiveness as a manager as well as in any social or professional hierarchy you join. And, because we are always transmitting some form of message (on some level) and it is being received and interpreted independently and subjectively, we're always running the risk of being misunderstood or even unmasked and discovered[28]. Both of which are real dangers and could very easily destroy the credibility of our Avatars.

Take some time and express your opinions and give your own personal assessments of the messages and images being transmitted below. What are your thoughts and how would you interpret these observations and communiques. What messages do you get about the character, credibility, and integrity of the person sending the message? I won't have any input here so you can call it the way you see it. Just take a minute and consider what you would think about that person and, if you were the one sending the message, what would people be thinking about you?

- What message is a person sending when they appear to have to be right about everything? When they seem compelled to callout and correct people in an open forum.

---

[28] Unmasking would reveal the hidden and private faces of both our Baser and Competitive Beings.

What are they communicating about themselves if they always need to be right on even the most obscure issues? Their need to be right seems far more important than being cooperative, supportive, and collaborative. How do you really feel about a *know-it-all*?

- What does a person convey about themselves from their conversational preferences, if they prefer to discuss ideas, if they prefer to discuss events, or if they prefer to discuss people?

- What message does a person send by the selection of their business attire? What could be the downside for getting it wrong?

- What message does a person send with their body language when listing to a presentation that they question or don't agree with? What does transmitting negative and bias signals to the group and to the presenter say about that person, do you think it's fair and respectful to the presenter or to the audience?

- What impressions do you get from people that attempt to defend themselves when they come up short, fail to deliver, or don't follow through when they were expected to. When they offer excuses like; I overslept, I didn't know that was my responsibility, something unexpectedly came up; it slipped my mind, etc. What does that tell you about their level of professionalism and priority setting? How much damage do their shortcomings do to the organization or how injurious are their actions to the project? And when they say "I'm sorry" or "I'll do better next time", do you really accept their apologies if you're one of those injured by them? Or, have they lost a degree of credibility and trust in your eyes?

- What message is sent when a person makes it clear that you and your interests are a low priority to them and are not even on their radar screen?

- What message is sent when a person sees that you are in need and voluntarily offers you support?

- What message is sent when a person sees that you are in need and refuses to offer you support?

- What message is sent when someone takes the time to listen to what you have to say and takes an interest in who you are and what you would like to do or become?

- What message is sent to you by the way one person approaches another when their approach is confrontational, sharp and short, or indifferent? What do you gather from their word selection and the tone of their interaction?

- What message is sent to you by the way one person approaches another when their approach is receptive, non-threatening and engaging? What do you gather from their word selection and the tone of their interaction?

- What message is sent when you find out that a member of your group has been withholding valuable information that would have benefited the group but was withheld in order to further their own private agendas'?

- What message is sent when the people on your team are all working toward the same ends without anyone having a hidden agenda?

- What message is sent when a manager uses their power and authority to suppress, silence and disempower their staff?

- What message is sent when a manager uses their power and authority to empower others?

- What message is sent when a manager micromanages their entire department?

- What message is sent when a manager is aloof and appears to be indifferent to their departmental responsibilities and their staff?

- What message is sent when a manager fails to support a subordinate and leaves them out in the cold, just twisting in the wind?

- What message is sent when a manager puts themselves at risk to defend and protect a subordinate when that subordinate is at a political or professional disadvantage?

- What message is sent when someone always wants to lead and will only reluctantly follow?

- What message is sent when someone demonstrates that they are equally capable of leading and supporting?

- What message is sent when a person honors their commitments?

- What message is sent when a person violates their commitments?

- What message is sent when a person honors the truth?

- What message is sent when a person becomes known as a liar?

- What message is sent when someone deviates from and agreed upon plan and does not communicate that fact to the other stakeholders?

- What message is sent when someone keeps the lines of communication open and active in order to prevent confusion and missteps?

- What message is sent when the manager takes full and total responsibility for the success of a project without any acknowledgement of the contributions of their staff?

- What message is sent when a manager acknowledges the contributions and support of their staff for the success of a project?

- What message is sent when the manager throws their staff under the bus and distances themselves from a departmental failure?

- What message is sent when a person makes themselves trusted?

- What message is sent when a person cannot be trusted?

- What message is sent when a manager steps up and accepts full responsibility for a departmental shortcoming or failure?

- What message is sent when a person demonstrates that they lack a moral compass and will pledge their allegiance to the highest bidder or for any personal gain?

- What message is sent when a person takes the moral high ground and holds their position because it is the right thing to do?

- What message is sent when a manager violates a confidence or a trust?

This list could go on forever but what's important to notice is that none of the messages were communicated verbally or by using the written word, they were all communicated by their actions and deeds. What messages are you communicating? Vanity and pride will cause us to want to associate our actions with the more positive and noble communiques. And in my opinion, if you are this deep in the book, that's where you deserve to be, so keep moving in that direction. But when we take a close-up look at reality, many of us are still inadvertently sending out a lot of the wrong messages. If you are actually a selfish, unscrupulous craven little urchin, then you're doing okay; you don't have to change a thing. But if you're sending the wrong messages, ones that you never intended, then you have to make changes and clarify who you are and what your intentions are. You are always telling a story and building a picture of who you are by every one of your words and actions. And just like the words in your documents and essays, your actions have to be clear, free standing, and unambiguous. If something is unclear or omitted in one of your essays, the reader will take it upon themselves to anticipate your meaning and fill-in any missing pieces. After all, it's not a dialog and you're most likely nowhere around to explain your intended meaning. Problems occur when people intentionally or benignly misconstrued your intended message. The same is true with respect to your overt actions. People observe your actions and interpret them as best they know how, and take away the message they believe you were sending. They don't ask you to clarify your actions; they just add that piece to the growing mosaic of who they believe you really are; it goes to your character and integrity, and someone is always watching. The images you project (either deliberate or inadvertent) provide us with a constant supply of relevant information so that we can continue to build our picture of who we really think you are behind the mask of your Avatar. Each time you chair a meeting, make a presentation, write a document, make a decision, or become stressed, you communicate some-thing about yourself to the society at large. You have to be sure that what you communicate is consistent with your intent and develop ways to determine how your message is being received. Whenever you find yourself explaining what you said, what you wrote, or what you meant, you can be certain that your first attempt at communication had failed.

We will end this section on communications the way we started...with a corpse. The corpse could still communicate a couple of things to you even though it lacked animation. Now it's getting a bit ripe so I think it's telling you that it's time to get it buried or cremated. Otherwise, it will continue to communicate something as long as it can be perceived by the senses. And just to follow along on that same theme, when we consider the many ways in which we communicate, the only time where we can be confident that we are not sending out any messages is when we are in seclusion, hidden from the world, and beyond anyone else's senses.

Chapter # 18:

A Review of your Management Tools, Strategies, and Techniques

When many of you started this book and your management careers, you had a very limited management toolbox; maybe just a hammer and a screwdriver. And without some form of intervention, you were well on your way to becoming a boss. You would have either become the boss from the outset or you would have reverted to being the boss when you realized that you had become overwhelmed and were out of control. Without the fundamental training that is so essential to managing people, how could you have done otherwise? Managing people should be intuitive and relatively straightforward; however history and my own experiences have proven it to be anything but. Without a full assortment of management tools at your disposal, you are left to rely on force (the hammer) to keep down any opposition and intimidation (the screwdriver) to control the workplace[29]. And that's what most bosses tend to do, beat people down and screw them over; and that's not a long-term winning strategy. Throughout this book I have provided you with examples of situations and circumstances that you are likely to encounter along with some techniques, strategies, tools and behaviors that will help you grow and become a much better manager over the course of your career. And while I made no attempt to fill your toolbox to capacity, I am confident that I have provided a sufficient enough assortment of tools for you to be successful in almost any situation. But if you are to succeed, you will have to be willing to change in the way you approach your work and your people, in addition, *you* will have to adapt to the nature of mankind; *mankind will not change or adapt to you*. Let's take a look back and review what we have covered so far and the tools we've collected:

---

[29] Mark Twain is quoted as saying; "to a man that only has a hammer, everything in the world looks like a nail". And if you are using force and intimidation to control the workplace, there is little wonder that your subordinates feel they are being beaten down and screwed over.

- A basic understanding of Human Nature

- Your Life, Professional, and Financial Objectives

- The need for Self-confidence, Self-worth, and Self-esteem

- The need to exercise Common Sense

- The various types of Management Training

- The difference between the Manager and the Boss

- The difference between the Manager and the Leader

- Interpersonal Skills

- The risk in hiring the wrong person

- The various Management Operating Styles and how to work with them

- Winning through Negotiation and Collaboration

- The Four Real Powers and how they are used

- Responsibility without Authority

- The Yin and Yang of Management

- Conflict Resolution

- Situational Leadership

- Root Cause Analysis and Problem Solving and Decision Making

- The Responsibilities of the Manager

- Ethics and Morality

- Communication Skills (both deliberate and inadvertent)

- Meetings, Presentations, and Writing Skills

- The 3 Tells and the 6 Cs

- Image Projection, Ego, and the Avatar

- Societal traps - pride, vanity, honor and respect causing narcissistic injury followed by narcissistic rage

- Relevant Case Studies, Scenarios, and Examples

- And others not mentioned

You should now be in a better position to take charge and manage, so let's move on to managing.

Chapter # 19:

Managing

Managing Subordinates
Flexibility; Employee Training; Employee Motivation; Communicating a Purpose – Example # 8 and Scenario # 4; Accountability, Setting Expectations, and Timelines; Ownership and Accountability; Coaching & Counseling…Ongoing Performance Updates; Managing your Managers; Performance Appraisals; Merit Increases and Promotional Opportunities – Example # 9; The Manager versus The Leader; Friendship versus Professionalism

Managing Peers
Departmental Interactions; Extra Departmental Interactions; Project Interactions

Managing your Manager
Communication; Areas of Accountability; Power and Authority; Performance Feedback; Performance Assessment; Career Development & Promotional Opportunities; Friendship verses Professionalism

In this chapter, I'd like to get more specific and talk to the four different management competencies you'll have to learn to master. When you look back at what we've covered, you'll find that we have, in a broader sense, been learning strategies, techniques and developing tools to enable us to manage ourselves, our subordinates, our peers, and our managers; and for the most part it has been a multifaceted discussion where we were juggling a collage of the different and distinct management competencies simultaneously. And while the majority of that time has been dedicated to self-management, we could really benefit from spending a bit more time working with the other three management competencies individually. Therefore, in this final section I won't spend any additional time discussing self-management, other than to say that it should be clear, from the amount of time that was devoted to it, that you should consider it to be the most important of all the management competences. As you've seen, self-management requires you to have a considerable amount of cerebral and emotional control, an unvarnished understanding of the components that make-up the human animal and the drivers of human nature; in essence, your own make-up and your own nature. You have to first learn to master *managing you* before you can ever hope to effectively manage others. If you can't manage that, you will have little success managing anything or anyone else. In order to underscore this point, I will be a bit more prescriptive and arcane... *"bis vincit qui se vincit"* or *"vincit qui se vincit"*.[30]

Moving forward, and without too much of a rehash of what has already been presented, I will walk us down through the other three management competences that are relevant to a particular environment and situation; specifically when you are managing subordinates, when you are managing peers, and when you are managing your manager. Each of these situations will be different and how and when you use a particular management skill or technique will depend upon that particular situation and environment and how you choose to approach, control, and/or resolve it. However, as I've stated at the very beginning of this book, you should not consider this or any other work on management to be sufficiently complete and comprehensive; because none are. But, I have made an attempt to be as reasonably inclusive as I thought practical and tried to include many of the challenges you're likely to encounter along your journey. It is my expectation that the tools provided will be of benefit to you in your career so long as you are able to assess the human dynamics in your environment and exercise common sense in order to recognize and avoid the traps and pitfalls that are ever present when interacting with man. If you do, you should be able to successfully navigate your way to a far brighter and rewarding career as a good effective manager.

---

[30] Latin phrases adopted by many educational institutions that roughly translates to "He who prevails over himself is twice victorious", and "He conquers who conquers himself", respectively.

Managing Subordinates:

If your job is anything like the ones that I've had and like most managers, you might have a fulltime job working in one area where you have accountability, while simultaneously having responsibility for managing a department that might be accountable for working in another. For example, when I was the Analytical Services Supervisor (aka *The College Boy*) I was a member of the facility's strategic management team, having responsibilities for supplier inspections and auditing, troubleshooting and resolving manufacturing and processing issues, regulatory compliance and corporate liaison for purchasing. In my mind, that was my real job so that was where my priorities were. That other part, where I had some responsibility for managing some 40 people over 3 different shifts, I treated it as if it was a caretaker assignment, never knowing that it was the core of my job, and the reason for my being there in the first place. I ignored the people and their work. I assumed that I was only needed if there was a problem in the work, and if there was, I would help to resolve it and the department would go back on autopilot. As you saw, it was nearly my undoing. Tell me, how many of you are as misguided as I was and are ignoring the *people management* component of your management position? How's that working out for you? I'm going to make the assumption that it hasn't been working that well, but things should be starting to look up. By now, you should be starting to understand some of the complex dynamics of human interactions. You are beginning to look beyond the projection of the aspirational Avatar in man and starting to see the basic drivers of human nature. And, you are learning to control and use those drivers to your advantage in order to step-up and successfully take charge of the agenda and your environment. You've learned to stay above the competitive fray, and be balanced and controlled in your management approach. You've learned that you have to be giving of yourself but be firm in your authority and your expectations, because you know that the Yin cannot stand without the Yang. And finally, you have to remember that *"you don't manage or lead by divine rite, but with the permission of those being managed or led"*.

Flexibility:

As was already stated, if you want to keep your work and your people moving in the desired direction, you will have to learn how to wear many different hats and learn to be flexible and adaptive to the needs of your subordinates. You'll have to become a cheerleader for your people, a multitasker to keep all your priorities moving forward, a counsellor, mentor, and career guide to help people chart and work toward their goals, a director and leader, setting the goals and pointing the path forward, a trouble-shooter and problem solver to clear the chosen path and smoothing the way, a facilitator that provides the material, documents, and/or equipment required to do the job, a confessor and a trusted confidante that is discreet and respects personal space, a disciplinarian to keep everyone on track moving in the right direction and to keep the projects under control. Lastly, a manager has to be a defender and champion of their people; they will be reluctant to follow if they believe they won't be protected in their time of need.

I'll leave it to you to decide exactly what it means to you to wear so many different hats and what each hat represents to your staff, but I will give you a hint by giving you an indication of what it might mean to be a cheerleader.

Most people, by nature or by circumstance are insecure and filled with trepidation when trying new things and/or working outside of their comfort zone, we have a fear of failure. And that fear is amplified if we are in a public setting (in the workplace or a social group). A manager needs to be aware of this fear of public failure and recognize that either on a conscious or subconscious level, no one wants to lose-face or their perceived place within the hierarchy due to a failure or an inadequacy. As part of staff training, a manager will at times, have to reassure some members of their team and provide them an added level of support and encouragement so that they can find the confidence within themselves to take the next step in their training. There will be other times when a staffer would have suffered a failure or setback, and in those instances the manager has to act as a safety net to help minimize the physical impact to the project and the public embarrassment to the employee. There will always be mistakes, failures, setbacks and miscues in a healthy dynamic work environment. You can't over react to a setback or failure, it could demoralize the staffer. Over the course of my career, I've found that it takes at least 15 *"At a Boys"* before confidence can be restored after 1 *"Oh Shit!"* Therefore, the skilled manager has to continually provide their staff the support and encouragement they need to build confidence so they will assume greater responsibility and ownership of their work and workplace. The manager has to become their cheerleader, confidante and downside protector, without which many on their staff would be reluctant to risk failure, the loss of face, and possibly even the loss of their jobs.

Employee Training:

If you are new to the position or to the department, it would be a mistake to assume that your subordinates have all been properly trained to effectively perform their duties according to the firm's expectations. People get sloppy and start taking shortcuts, never really knowing how their actions might negatively impact the company, its products and services, as well as its reputation. A manager has to spend time with their staffers in order to be assured that they have been properly trained for the particular jobs they are working, following the procedures set-out for that job, and have some knowledge of the value and importance of that job and their work to the overall success of the company. Every job is relevant and of value, if it were not, you wouldn't pay somebody to do it. But it has been my experience that an unacceptably large proportion of our workforce has been improperly trained, take shortcuts or bypass important procedures, and have absolutely no idea how what they do impacts the success of the department or the company at large. With few exceptions, there is an order and a process to how work gets done. Circle back and take another look at the widget scenario and note how chaotic and haphazard the initial process was, and the general lack of productivity. We had to re-define the process, break it apart and compartmentalize it. Then we developed standard operational procedures for each component of the process, provided training and developed quality and finished product specifications for each station. People knew what their jobs were; they were trained in the process and knew how they contributed to the success of the organization. While this was only a scenario, it is the same scenario that is playing out every day throughout many organizations. Look at the actual case study where I was the Analytical Services Supervisor, I eventually found out that next to no one was sufficiently trained to do the work that was assigned; and those that were, were taking short-cuts and even falsifying analytical results. They had no sense of how important their work was to the overall quality and safety of the products being produced for human consumption. Granted it was late in coming, but quick and decisive action to provide training and guidance to my staff was arguably the only thing that saved my job. The same can be said for the TRA 2000 case study…and while a number of other elements were at play, effective training was clearly lacking. So don't make the assumption that your staff is properly trained and are following established procedures, *verify that they are*, or expect to get blindsided in the future.

Employee Motivation:

Employees don't necessarily have to be motivated to do their jobs, but it helps when they are. Whenever you have a motivated workforce, you have people that have bought-in to the mission, the job, or the project at hand and have made a personal commitment to the success of the work; they have taken personal ownership of their work and they become aspirational and take pride in whatever they happen to be doing. People are competitive by nature and are always jockeying to be the best at whatever they do, therefore most of your employees will come to their workplace already self-motivated and ready to make a contribution. But right away and without knowing the consequences of their actions, the unskilled, top-down, insecure manager (the boss) will do everything in their power to stamp out every last vestige of their staff's motivation. The first thing they will do is ignore the basic intelligence of their staffers; the people that are closest to the actual work and the experts in the area. These are the innovators in the workspace, the creators of new ideas, procedures and methods; the people that are the first to see problems and sound the alarm when things go wrong. Also, they are likely to be the ones that would put forth the best recommendations and solutions for corrective actions. But the top-down manager is often blind to the suggestions and any recommendations from their subordinates because they, somehow, cedes some fragment of intellectual recognition (power) to them, and in their mind, puts their position of authority at risk. So they block creativity and kills innovation and motivation and sends the message to their people that *they are the know it all*, and they need only *"do what they tell them to do, that they may as well leave their intelligence and common sense at home because they are not needed at work"*. And not so surprisingly, they will, and as an added bonus, they won't even sound the alarm when things start to go south. The next thing the top-down manager does is to consolidate all the powers within their own personal control, cutting their people off from senior management, so no one can see what they're doing inside their department. This introduces stress, fear, and uncertainty among the subordinates, further destroying morale and employee motivation. And because this is a trifecta of blunders, the final thing the top-down manager does is to establish a system of cronyism, where it becomes clear to everyone that it makes no difference how hard they work or how much they contribute, it is all for not. Because of the partiality, bias, and nepotism that is apparent in their workplace, no matter their contribution, to the success of the organization, their efforts will go unrecognized and unrewarded. So, what's the point of even trying? At this point, you should expect to have an apathetic workforce, and you should also see a marked drop in productivity, an increase in absenteeism and overall departmental dysfunction. And in an effort to turn things around, the top-down manager will double down on their tyranny in a failed effort to save their own job. In effect they will be saying, *"The beatings will continue until morale improves"*.

It's my expectation that by now you know that that's a losing strategy, you know that there are only two reasons why work doesn't get done: because people are unable to do the work or they are unwilling to do it. They would be unable to do the work if they were denied access to the jobsite, the materials, the documents, and/or the equipment required to do the job. In addition, they would be unable to do the work if they lacked the training and knowhow. But you already know that it's your responsibility to facilitate their access to what they need and to provide them training. So, I'm going to assume that your people are already able to do the work. And as long as you don't stomp all over their enthusiasm and motivation, they will also be willing to do the work.

As we have discussed, insightful and secure managers recognize the competitive nature of man and his aspirational desire to be better today than yesterday, and better tomorrow than today. They also know that much of man's personal image, his self-worth, his self-esteem, and personal pride is derived from how he sees himself and his place within the greater hierarchy in conjunction with the value he attributes to what he does in order to sustain himself (his work). And because this is an important point, I want to stop here so that everyone can get caught-up. Now, this is my contention...*If we are happy and prideful doing what we do, then we are happy and prideful in being who we are.* But when we lose our motivation, we become disenchanted and apathetic about our chosen path and we begin to question who we are and our greater purpose. This sets up a conflict between the *ideal self* and the *phenomenal self* that will have to somehow be resolved. We live in a society where we identify ourselves by what we do, not by who we are. When was the last time you were introduced to someone and they asked you *who you are?* More likely than not, they asked you *what you do.* And I would bet that during your response, you lied a little, postured a little, and embellished a lot. And after you gave them time to reciprocate, you tried to strip away some of their lies and embellishments to decide which of you had the superior status within the hierarchy. Don't try to deny it; it's your nature, our nature, and the way we all operate. We are always competing for status and recognition, and that, along with our own private aspirations is what motivates us. We see ourselves through the prism of what we do, and how what we do is valued by society. Therefore, what we do in our work, to a large extent, defines who we think we are. The insightful manager uses our predilection to compete and excel to their benefit by creating a work environment that nurtures these natural tendencies. While the manager is, and should always remain, a closet dictator, they keep the trappings of their power and authority low-key and shares power and the responsibility for the work with their staffers. They cater to the aspirational needs of their employees because they recognize that they are their most valuable asset. They demonstrate an appreciation and a respect for them as individuals, and for the contributions they make to the success of the organization. And they create a fair, balanced, secure, and non-threatening work environment within which their employees can thrive.

Let's consider for a moment how motivation and a nurturing work environment would affect your new, bright-eyed, bushy-tailed employees. They would come in on their first day eager to get started learning their jobs, getting that first-weeks' pay, and settling in as a member of their new company's family. As long as Management is seen as being helpful, fair, and even-handed the new employees will feel secure and confident in their new jobs and in their future. As a consequence, many of them will become over achievers. They will begin to go beyond the general requirements of the job and begin to make observations and recommendations that might well improve both the product and the process while saving the company time and money. These employees are likely to go on to become very dedicated and fiercely loyal, as they identify themselves with the company. And while it may be a bit of an overstatement, it becomes *their personal job* in *their personal company or their personal position on the company's team,* **"their personal team"**, *and* to a large extent, a reflection of who and what they have become. All that Management has to do is create a professional atmosphere of freedom rather than fear, and democracy rather than autocracy. The boss will fail at this every time.

With respect to your older employees, those that are already well trained and motivated; they only need direction, timing expectations, and the freedom to do the work. But don't ignore them. Let them know that you recognize and appreciate their contributions to the organization, and as long as their work and procedures stay within acceptable parameters, just stay out of their way and let them do their work. You should always be current on all the activities in your area, but for the benefit of you micromanagers, *you don't have to have your fingerprints on everything.* Go back and re-read the Developmental Continuum; specifically Development Stage #1.

Communicating a Purpose:

One of the biggest mistakes managers consistently make is in how they direct their staff, they will tell them what to do, but they frequently neglect to tell them why. And the *why* is fundamental to the reason the workforce is in place, the reason you are there, and the reason that there is a business in the first place. The why is the rationale, the whole purpose for being and doing. You can have everything you need to do a job, all the materials and access, the training, and the motivation; it will still come down to the why. What purpose does it serve? Where is the benefit and justification for doing the work? Why does it even matter? Without exception, we all fall into that trap; we know what we have to do and why, but we assume that the people doing the work only need to know what has to be done. Where is the incentive for them, man is not an automaton; a stoic artificial entity with a known output. He is fickle, capricious, and mutable and reacts subject to the changes in his environment and how his situation changes within it. These are not random changes; they are purposeful and consistent with man's emotional drivers. There are no emotional drivers when you tell someone to do this thing or that. Emotion is an intangible and is imparted when the *"what"* is married to the *"why"* and a connection is made to something tangible in the real world; a purpose, a reason for an action. When we know why we're doing what we're doing, we are more likely to approach the work from a completely different prospective and have a much higher refined target as an endpoint; we know exactly what we intend to accomplish and why (why we would approach the work in one way and not another based upon the desired results).

We either forget or neglect the fact that we are dealing with man and human nature. And it would follow that, now that you have told man what to do, his immediate response would be why? Man is both inquisitive and aspirational; always looking for meaning and purpose in his life. He wants to be part of something that actually matters and is important, as opposed to having his life forces drained away on the irrelevant and the mundane. How many of you would want to go through life without a meaning or a purpose? We want to matter and we want our work to matter. I think it was Aristotle or maybe it was Socrates that said *"An unexamined life is not worth living".* Our search for a purpose in life seems to be inborn and it is evident in the earliest stages of our lives. As soon as we begin to develop language skills we start a lifetime of asking *"why"*; just spend some time with any 2 year old. Children are trying to learn the reasons and the purpose of things around them and how their world fits together. Our reasons for wanting to know why are identical to those of a child, but with an aspirational component. We are trying to find worth, merit and value in what we do. And, *"Yes"*, I am fully aware that I'm going somewhat wide-a-field. I really don't take any pleasure in these excursions away from my primary theme, and I only do so in order to flush-out, from my perspective, the essential vital nuggets of the topic at hand. And this time, I'm doing it to try to help you get a fundamental understanding and a better appreciation of the importance of communicating a purpose, a reason so your staffers will know why you have directed them to do what you've directed them to do; the incentive or motivations. No one wants to do busywork, work that doesn't make a contribution or work without merit; though sometimes it will be a requirement of the job. If you take what you already know about man, and if you can believe, that by nature, man is prideful, is always seeking higher status, is aspirational and is seeking a higher purpose and meaning for his existence, and if you can also believe that man identifies who he is, in large measure, by what he does, then you could conclude that he would want whatever he does to have meaning and purpose. Therefore, no matter what the job is; man still wants and needs to know why, what contribution is he making? This is a truism for the biggest jobs right down to the smallest. I will go as far as to say, *"It is a categorical imperative for every job and everything we do".* Let's just take a more pedestrian look at my assertion in this next scenario.

Scenario # 4:

Suppose you were sent to a penal colony. You have been sentenced to 5 years at hard labor for being a bad manager, and you were given a choice of how you want to serve out your sentence. You can break rocks (making big rocks into little ones) or you can dig holes. The choice is yours. If you choose to break rocks, the gravel that you generate will be used as the underlayment for the local roads and for the foundations for the new school that's planned. If you choose to dig holes, the holes you dig today, you'll have to fill them back in tomorrow, and you'll move to a new spot the next day and start the process all over again. At that moment of decision, you might be filled with anger, but if these are your only two choices, you would still need to choose wisely, because you are deciding your future for the next 5 years; breaking rocks or digging holes. What decision would you make? If the decision were mine, I would choose to do something that had purpose, something of value; albeit minimal.

One final example and I will stop beating this dead horse. This one goes to the benefit of having knowledge and purpose. When a person knows the purpose for something, it completes the picture and adds content and texture to their job. When taken all together, the who's, what's, when's, where's, and how's are incomplete without the why's. Take this next example:

Example # 8:

If I were Joe's manager and I directed him to take a flask of clear liquid up to the mine and give it to Sam by 4:30 PM on Tuesday, and I asked Joe to be particular and handle the flask with care, I would have given Joe everything he needed to get the job done, but nothing about the why's that would have completed the picture for him. He doesn't know why he's taking the flask to Sam at the mine, he doesn't know why it has to be done by 4:30 PM on Tuesday, and he doesn't know why he has to take particular care handling the flask. Conversely, If I were Sam's manager and I directed him to take a flask of clear liquid up to the mine and give it to Joe by 4:30 PM on Tuesday, and I asked Sam to be particular and handle the flask with care, because the flask contained nitroglycerin needed for blasting at 5:00 PM and the slightest jolt could set it off, then the job would take on a completely different complexion for Sam. Sam becomes an informed employee and is less likely to make a mistake; assuming he accepts the assignment. Joe, on the other hand, has been left in the dark and has no real sense of the danger and delicate nature of his assignment. His lack of relevant information (the why), puts him at substantially higher risk and exponentially increases the probability of accidental failure.

It's almost always possible for you to communicate a purpose for a particular directive, though many managers don't, either because they haven't been able to rationalize its importance to the work at hand, or because they perceive it as an impoverishment of their *arrogant princely authority*; that they should only have to tell you what to do...you don't have a need to know why. When you fail to provide a reason or a rationale for doing something, either benignly or callously, you forfeit any benefit that could have been available to you had your employee understood the purpose (the whys) and just used common sense. But because the employee didn't know the purpose or desired endpoint, they couldn't improvise. Additionally, man is repulsed by dominance and marginalization; when you bark directions without giving reasons, you do both. When man has had enough, he won't use common sense, or improvise, he'll do, *to the letter*, exactly what you've directed him to do. And we all know how that usually turns out. How many of you can remember some manager screaming; ***"Oh Crap...you did it exactly the way I told you to do it, but that wasn't the way I meant...I thought you would at least use common sense!!!"***

So whenever you are assigning projects or tasks remember that you are dealing with human nature and human frailties. By communicating the purpose of the work you satisfy man's inquisitive nature and gives him a sense of purpose and value in what he has been asked to do. You also increase the prospects for a successful outcome, with a known endpoint, and you avoid conflicts created by man's ego.

Accountability, Setting Expectations, and Timelines:

What is your area of responsibility and how does it connect and relate to the larger organization? What are the products and services that you are expected to deliver? What standards are your products and services expected to meet, and what is your timing? I would expect that you already have the answers to these questions from your initial orientation when you accepted the position. And I would also expect that after you've settled in for a bit, you've conducted a departmental assessment in order to assure yourself and your management that you were clear and in control of everything and everybody within your jurisdiction and you had verified the limits of your responsibilities and you are clear on the limits of your authority in each of those areas. Now you have to conduct an assessment of your department to verify that the work and the people are meeting the product and service requirements and standards within the expected timelines. And when you do, you should be prepared to find some anomalies. Whether you are new to the department or if you've just taken your eye off the ball, you should expect to find that there has been some responsibility creep and/or responsibility abdication. You should also expect to find operational glitches, conflicting priorities, and workplace redundancies. When there is responsibility creep, you have to find out why before taking any actions to curtail it. And when you find an abdication of responsibility you'll have to reestablish a presence in that area or document that resources are no longer required in that area or that those responsibilities have been transferred to a different department. Though, you should recognize that unless and until there is concurrence from your superior, you are still accountable for that area. And when you find glitches, conflicting priorities, and redundancies you'll have to clear the glitches, align the priorities and streamline the process; using the same (or a similar) process as we used back in the widget scenario.

Now you should be concentrating on the division of labor; who is accountable for what. At this point, it should be a relatively simple process, if you have already streamlined or simplified the operation and aligned the departmental priorities, it should be clear as to who is doing what. You're likely to find that the workload is not evenly distributed and that a disproportionate amount of the load is being carried by just a few individuals and it's really not a secret. Everyone in the organization knows it, with the possible exception of you. If you're new to the position, or if you've been there, and had just turned a blind eye to it, you'll have to find ways to even out the workload. I don't doubt that, if given enough time, we could all come up with reasonable explanations to justify the disparity. And while there can be any number of reasons why this happens, we all know that it's a problem and has to be fixed. Often times it occurs when managers rely too heavily on their *"go-to people"* and funnel sensitive, high visibility and special projects to them because they trust that those employees will deliver on time and to target. Other times, and with insecure and weak managers, they become intimidated by a few of their more confrontational staffers and they cowardly avoid confrontation and pushback by assigning additional work to their less vocal and more receptive staffers. There could be any number of other reasons or excuses that we could envision to try to justify the disproportionate distribution of the workload, but they all would prove to be superficial and would never stand up to objective scrutiny. You'll have to balance out the work if you intend to tap the full potential of the human resources available to you. And if you don't, you will be cultivating other problems that you really don't need. Let's just take these two examples for instance. If you are one of those managers that have your go-to people, you inadvertently setup a class structure inside your own department. There is you, your go-to people, and then everyone else. Because you rely so heavily on your go-to people, when benefits and opportunities become available, they are disproportionately provided to those few, partly because they are deserved and partly because of your personal bias, your need to keep them happy and your ongoing dependence on them. The downside is that you communicate to everyone else in your department that you are not fair and evenhanded, that you have already decided just who will be successful and rewarded and who won't. Staffers will resent you because they were never given an opportunity to prove their worth and were relegated to the margins with little hope of advancement. And in time, you will burnout your go-to people because nothing burns up a go-to person faster than you constantly going to them. They will begin to start giving you pushback. And if you are the weak manager, intimidated by a few and dumping all the extra work on the many, your problems are far more serious and if not corrected will cause you to be undone. Go back and reread the section entitled *"The Responsibilities of the Manager"*. After you're re-read, it would be a good time to be honest with yourself and decide if you're cutout to be a manager; some people are, and some people aren't. But your few bad apples are going to spoil your entire basket if they are left to ferment and fester. Just give it some thought, if you're *not* in the dominant position and in charge, you know it, and so do they. In addition, so does everyone else. You'll have to step-up and take control before others get up enough courage to challenge you as well; and they will. I have no way of knowing if this is your current situation, and if it is, I have no way of knowing how much of your position and political powers you've already squandered. But, irrespective of your possible losses of position and political powers, you'll have to deal with your personnel issues with whatever powers you have left, and you'll have to deal with them head-on. If you delay, and the entire department becomes dysfunctional, management might find it necessary to bring in new leadership in order to regain control. So you'll have to confront your personnel issues, and when you do, you'll have to be thoughtful and methodical and deal with those people calmly, fairly, firmly, and professionally. You can't let anyone push your buttons (though they will try) and you can't come roaring back as a tyrant, because you may have already loss their respect and that would only serve to garner their hatred; which would only exacerbate an already bad situation. But you'll have to assert or reestablish your position of authority so there's no ambiguity as to who is in charge. Then, you can examine the work and find ways to even out the workload so you can avoid this and similar situations in the future. As an added benefit, when the work is evenly distributed, it becomes easier to identify those individuals requiring additional training and support, those that need to be motivated, those that only need leadership and direction, and those that would prefer to be somewhere else.

People have to know what they are accountable for, and you have to be clear on exactly how that accountability translates to the job they are doing and what the expectations are for anyone doing that job. In most cases these are documented in the Job Descriptions, Standard Operation Procedures (SOPs), Key Result Areas (KRAs), or verbal instructions. You'll have to make sure that the individual in the job understands what's expected and have the resources available to them, in addition to the right training to be successful. But you're not done yet… you just assigned responsibility without any mention of authority. Everyone in your organization with the responsibility for work has to have some degree of authority to assure the satisfactory completion of the work. I'm not talking about supervisory authority over other staffers, unless they are already a supervisor, but authority over their work and workstation. They have to have the ability to make decisions on how best to complete the work within established guidelines, the ability to accept or reject work products based upon their concurrence with standards and the ability to prioritize and schedule work in accordance with the resources available and within a reasonable time frame.

The manager has ultimate accountability for assuring that their department meets the expectations of the company within the established timelines. That requires the manager to stay in contact with their people and their progress. And, the best way to do that is to *manage by walking around*[31]. Walk around your department, get to know your people, find out where things are going smoothly and areas where you can be of assistance. People are more at ease and are likely to be open and more forthcoming with you in their jobs and at their workstations than they would be sitting in a chair on the other side of your desk. So get out there and find out what's really happening.

Ownership and Accountability:

We have already talked at some length about people taking pride in their work and ownership of their jobs; and while it is desirable, it should not be a universal expectation. Because, for various reasons, some people will never take pride or ownership in the work you've assigned and they've agreed to do; but then, it was never a requirement of the job, you have only offered

---

[31] Managing by walking around is just a way to get out of your office and get out among your staff and getting involved in the work by getting your hands dirty. Starting an individual one-on-one dialog with your people, getting to know who they are and what they do, and giving them an opportunity to get to know and make a connection to you.

them a job, not a religion. So don't try to force ownership on someone that doesn't want it, it's their choice; ownership requires a commitment on a personal level that some people are unwilling to make. Your focus should be on productivity and accountability, and even though they may not take any ownership of their work, they are still fully accountable for the quality and quantity of the work assigned. You really don't have a right to ask for, or expect, anything more.

Coaching & Counseling…Ongoing Performance Updates:

Every manager has a responsibility to provide coaching and counseling to their subordinates as well as ongoing performance updates. People have a need to know how well they are performing on any given task, how their performance is being assessed, and how their performance might be effecting their status within the organization. People want to do well but they need direction and it falls to the manager to provide that direction. And that can be done through *informal coaching and counseling*. Informal coaching and counseling is nothing more than another term for mentoring. And for those of you that have associated coaching and counseling with something negative, it may be because you had been negligent in providing guidance and mentoring early on and have allowed some form of unacceptable behavior or performance to persist until a point that it required a *formal* intervention. Informal coaching and counseling should be an essential and ongoing part of any employee training and motivation program. It doesn't take much time and, in most cases, can easily be done on the floor, at the employee's workstation. It's you making a connection with the people that report to you, and it's part of what you do when you *manage by walking around*. People want your feedback; it makes no difference how successful and self-assured a person is, everybody wants to be stroked, to know that their place in the hierarchy is secure, and everybody wants to get an *at-a-boy* from their superior. For the most part, that's a lot of what informal coaching and counseling is; letting people know that you recognize their work and that they are doing what is expected and meeting their defined milestones. It also gives you a chance to see the state of the department, to see what's happening on the ground level and whether there are any issues that you should be aware of. Even when your people are well trained, you will still have occasion to provide informal instructional or correctional coaching and counseling when adjustments need to be made or have already been made to the work or the process. Informal instructional or correctional support and guidance will also be required to assist employees who are trying to get up-to-speed but are not quite there yet. On those occasions where instructive or corrective coaching and guidance is indicated, you should provide the direction and counsel from a supportive and mentoring perspective, your intention should be to support and facilitate, not to document and record, so don't write anything down. Just stay mindful that you are providing remedial training and your subordinate is likely experiencing some sense of inadequacy and vulnerability. Be clear in your instruction but avoid anything that could be construed as an affront to their competence or intelligence. Some of you consider yourselves straight talkers and you take pride in being open and frank communicators; well, this isn't the time for that. You can't inspire confidence or build self-esteem by tearing a person down with blunt and indiscreet straight talk. And lastly, whenever you're providing informal coaching and counseling that's of a personal nature, it should be done privately to avoid any risk of embarrassment or humiliation on the part of your subordinate.

When coaching and counseling is taken to the next level, where it would be considered formal guidance, it becomes *classical mentoring.* At this point your guidance and counsel is being solicited, or is required, as opposed to it being freely bestowed, as it was in an informal coaching and counseling setting. Here you're being asked, or it has become necessary for you to put on a different hat, to be an educator, a counsellor, and a career guide to help someone develop the skills and techniques that would help them reach some objective. Whether your guidance has been requested or has become necessary it should be confined to the specific topic or subject matter where guidance is requested or required. Stay on point! When someone solicits your advice and guidance in a particular area, it's because they felt they needed improvement in that area. That's the area where they are receptive to coaching and that's where you should focus your efforts. Everyone is flawed and could benefit from a thorough unbiased and objective personal assessment from time to time. But you were not asked to provide that, you were limited to a specific area, and when you go beyond what was asked; your suggestions and recommendations become an intrusion and are unwanted. The same is true when your guidance is required as part of someone's training or as an intervention. Don't let your vanity get in the way, and you undertake to reconstruct the whole person, stay focused on the problem, not on the person. Try to make your coaching and counselling as interactive as possible, where there are defined objectives, lots of dialog (specific targeted questions followed up by clearly defined answers) and, where possible, with real life examples or realistic and relevant scenarios. You should avoid lecturing, because lecturing wears thin and can be viewed as condescending, and that would only discourage the student. Mentoring is the act of giving and sharing information and knowledge to benefit someone else. But in addition to providing them a service, it strengthens individual alliances and helps build additional political power and influence for you as well; so it's important to be generous with your gifts. With respect to note-taking and documentation, when formal coaching and counselling is requested, your student should be the ones taking the notes. If you elect to keep track of your discussions using notes, that's your option. But when formal coaching and counselling is required as part of a training program or as a tool of corrective action, you are obligated to document both the process and the progress in order to protect yourself as well as the employee. In any event, coaching and counselling should be done for the purpose of benefiting the subordinate, not as a form of discipline.

When you elect to *manage by walking around* you take full advantage of an ability to get first-hand knowledge of the status of your department. You get the opportunity to make a human connection with your staff, and provide inspiration and guidance where needed. And as a consequence of your direct interactions and dialog with your staffers, they get regular updates as to how the department is performing, as a unit, and how they are performing individually.

Managing your Managers:

The frontline supervisor and the junior level manager are two of the biggest threats to the overall success of an otherwise productive and well run organization. Whether it is due to their lack of experience and maturity, a case of inflated ego and an eagerness to make a name for themselves, power intoxication, or just poor interpersonal skills accompanied by a complete lack of leadership and management acumen; many of them just don't get it. They lack your level of sophistication and though they nod their heads in the affirmative, they really don't understand your management philosophy and the culture you're trying to build within your organization. As their manager, you are far too willing to assume that they have somehow imprinted on you and have adapted your philosophy or a comparable philosophy or similar style for managing their reports...and they don't, how could they? How long did it take you to get to your current thinking with respect to leadership and management? How many books did you read, how many seminars did you attend, and how many times did you get bloodied and had to change your approach and your way of thinking? They don't have that level of seasoning, they're new to the game and it's your job to help them learn the rules. These people need to be actively managed, or at the very least, monitored. Left unattended and to their own devices your well-meaning, career oriented supervisors and managers could turn your department upside-down. Too many managers mistakenly take their eye off the ball and limit their management interactions to their reports, never bothering to look beyond to see how their directions had been communicated and rolled forward to the next level down. They make the assumption that nothing would be lost in translation and that their directions, their cultural tone, and their meanings had been communicated as they had intended. But it's not, and it's not until much later; when the quantity and quality of the work begins to suffer, when absenteeism increases, employee turnover begins to increase; morale suffers to the point of insubordination and open rebellion, do they come to realize that they have a problem in their own house.

When the manager becomes aware of the problems, they will likely schedule a crises meeting with their three direct reports; and for illustrative purposes we will give them names. Moving from right to left is Attila the Hun, Mary Poppins, and Willy Loman[32]. Attila's group is in open revolt, absenteeism is high and a few of his best people have already resigned and left the company. Productivity is down and some reference materials and documentation has been lost or misplaced. And because there has been an unusual amount of mechanical breakdowns, sabotage is a distinct possibility. Attila has made himself hated. Mary has been working longer than expected hours and the quality and quantity of work coming from her group is subpar and generally unacceptable. She continues to place the blame on last-minute scheduling from other departments and the need for her group to have more time to get the work done. However, nothing about the work has changed since the last manager was in the position, and no one on her staff appears to be overburden with work or sensitive to any time frames or deadlines. It's difficult to tell what's actually happening in Willie's group, everything is in chaos; the inmates have taken over the asylum and nothing is getting done. Attila's solution is to fire all 35 of his employees and start over from scratch. Mary has been humiliated and disappointed and feels betrayed by her staff and she doesn't want any new employees, she wants to take revenge on the ones that she has. With respect to

---

[32] These are all characterizations of failed managers we have already discussed. For example, Attila is a representation of the Tyrannical Boss; Mary is that starry-eyed and very naïve manager that caters to her staff and wants to be liked. Willie represents the Maestro, the impotent fraud, the pretender, and the out of control and overwhelmed, just as he was depicted in Miller's play (Death of a Salesman).

Willie, he has offered to step-down from his management assignment in order to take a less demanding job on staff. All three have been bad managers, and all three came up with even worse solutions to the problems. And while this is only a dramatization, it portends how your untrained and inexperienced managers could upend your entire department if you make the above mentioned assumptions and neglect to monitor your manager's activities.

Your managers tried to be successful using the tools that were available to them in order to follow your directions and to do the best job they knew how. But the tools they had were limited and their knowledge of the human animal and his nature wasn't apparent to them. So when they encountered resistance, they reverted to their defensive operating styles. For example, Attila's primary style might be the *dynamic* and his supporting style might be *animated* (animated/dynamic). Mary's primary style might be *sociable* and her supporting style might be *dynamic* (dynamic/sociable), and Willie's might be an *analytical/analytical* with the same primary and supporting styles. And because you already knew something about peoples operating styles, did it actually surprise you that your untrained and inexperience managers demonstrated domination, placation, and abdication; respectively? And, it's really not their fault...but yours.

You can select any skilled person to do a task, write a report or operate a piece of equipment and if they make mistakes, in most cases those mistakes are likely to be minimal and localized. And you often have an opportunity to try it all over again. But when you assign a person to manage other people; something that most people are wholly unprepared to do, when mistakes are made, they affect a much larger swath of the workforce, and sometimes there are no do overs. So when you promote a person to a supervisory or management position, or find one already in place, you have a responsibility to that person, to their staff, to the company and to yourself to provide that person with the training, skills, guidance, and philosophy of management that you expect and which would give them the best possible chances for success in that job. You don't play this one by ear and make assumptions; you actively manage your managers. Attila might say that that's just his management style, and I would agree, after all, what other style could you have if your only management tool was a hammer? He needs training and a set of cerebral and soft tools. Mary might say that her approach was to give people the benefit of the doubt and trust that they will do the right thing. And because her trust was misguided and people did what they chose, now she feels violated and betrayed, and is dripping with venom and wanting revenge. She needs you to restore her faith in mankind, but with the realization that man has to be managed with a carrot and a stick. Willie is out of his depth and may not have been cut out to be a manager, and if he needs to step-down, then so-be-it. But if Willie wants to give it a go, and is lacking in knowledge and confidence, then it's part of your job to help provide them; you'll just have to put on one or two of your other manager's hats. In a perfect world, none of these people should have been thrown into the maze of supervision without some basic preparation. But more often than not, they are, and it's up to you to provide their training and to manage their progress. The department and the people in it are your responsibility, and if they fail… you fail.

Performance Appraisals:

The first thing that you should know about performance appraisals is that there should *never* be any surprises. It's already a very sensitive and awkward time for both the appraiser and the person being appraised, and no one wants to have a discussion around a new emerging issue. Appraisal time is probably the most important annual calendar event in every employee's work life, and its results can lead to great satisfaction, joy, confidence and security or considerable disappointment, dejection, anger, and insecurity; the future of their job and livelihood could very well be resting on the results of the appraisal. This is a very serious time and a very serious matter, and both the appraiser and appraised are trying to put their best face forward, though both have had to revert to a substantially modified personal style in order to do so. This is not the way things should be, but it's the way they are. This unneeded and unwelcome level of stress and trepidation is a direct result of a flawed, biased, and prejudicial appraisal system. A system that is too heavily dependent on a subjective assessment of an individual's performance than of an objective measurement of it…a system that is ripe for exploitation by managers who choose to exercise powers where they should have none, and where managers use the performance appraisal process as their *ace in the hold* to keep their staffers intimidated and subservient for fear of a negative appraisal where so much could be riding. The system needs to be changed and most organizations, but not all, have recognized the problems and have moved to change how the evaluations are done; emphasizing objective criterion as opposed to capricious, biased, and subjective conclusions. And this is a very positive step forward.

In most organizations, an annual performance appraisal is a matter of policy and a require-ment of the Human Resources Department (HR). The annual appraisal serves a number of purposes, for example, it serves as a benchmark for the company and the employee to allow both to document a snapshot of how closely an employee is measuring to established stan-dards and expectations. It helps the company identify future leaders and helps to facilitate their succession planning. It helps to identify individuals with a need for additional train-ing and those that should be separated from the company due to their inability to perform to expectations. It also provides the HR and Legal Departments supporting documentation when a termination of an employee becomes warranted. And, when the appraisals are con-ducted objectively and fairly, it helps you to quantitatively define an employee's promotional, as well as their, financial merit... their true worth and value to the company[33]. None the less, in an ideal world, a performance appraisal should only be a routine formality, a documenta-tion of the facts as they exist and a discussion around future objectives. If you had done the job you were supposed to do over the past year, the employee should know how they have performed over the last appraisal period. All they should have to do is assess their own per-formance to *measurable objectives* in their job description, assess their performance against their *Key Result Areas* (KRAs) and their *Management by Objectives* (MBOs) as well as from the dialogs they've had with you over the past 12 months (informal and/or formal coaching and counseling). While their assessments for their overall rating and yours are likely to vary, they should not be so different as to make them irreconcilable. And there should never be anything new or a *"got-cha"* at appraisal time. For example, if an employee has responsibili-ties for an area and neglects it, was not aware of it, or is under performing in any area, this is not the time or place to bring it to their attention and have it included in the appraisal. The time for that was when it became apparent to you; that would have given the employee an awareness of the deficiency and given them an opportunity to correct it prior to the appraisal. No one likes to be blindsided.

Problems with the performance appraisals can be traced back to the authors of the job descriptions. In many cases, the authors would have drafted a 30,000 foot level document that is a general catch-all for the job and usually consist of one or two broad-stroked para-graphs, which really tell you nothing about the responsibilities on the ground level. In other

---

[33] One of the reasons for the high degree of anxiety associated with performance appraisals is due to their flawed design. They are far too susceptible to subjective bias and interpretation than antiseptic objectivity.

cases, the authors take a shotgun approach and try to be as thorough and as inclusive as possible, and usually end up producing a multipage document containing a litany of equally weighted responsibilities and tasks that are descriptive, but non directional. In either case, the performance appraisals that are derived from these job descriptions often force the performance appraiser to judge performance subjectively; meaning, he has to guess. And in the eyes of the ones being evaluated, when he guesses low…he guesses wrong. Let's just take a minute and take a look at some of the human dynamics that are likely playing out just beneath the surface. The competitive being, within man already resents and resists authority, and it's difficult for us to accept criticism; constructive or otherwise. We take pride in our hierarchical status but when others sit in judgment of us, it diminishes us by pointing to our lower status, relative to the judges, and strips us of any sense of power and control; we revert to our baser nature because we feel naked and vulnerable. For us, a positive performance review is an achievement. It's a recognition of our contributions to the company; an affirmation of our status, and a confirmation of our worth within the organization. And, it has a direct impact on our jobs and livelihoods. Now with so much of who and what we are hanging in the balance, do you actually believe that it should all be determined by your best guess??? Or, if you are one of those managers that has been using the performance appraisal as a weapon, then it will all be determined by your assessment of how frequently and thoroughly *I kissed your ass* over the last year. Surely there has to be a better way!!!

Every manager should review all their staffer's job descriptions and distill those 4 or 5 *key result areas* that are the most essential to the position; everything else of lesser importance, can be lumped together in a catch-all category and collectively given a reasonable weighting. Of the 4 or 5 areas that are essential to the job, find an objective way to measure performance in those areas, whether it's an objective quality or quantity measurement, timing from start to completion, percentage of complaints or rejects, anything that reflects compliance with expectations. But whatever you choose as a measure, it has to be objectively quantifiable, because, if it can't be quantified, it can't be measured. These 4 or 5 key areas of responsibility, along with the catch-all category should be used to form the bases of the performance appraisal document, and a copy of which, must be provided to the employee. In this way, you'll only have to subjectively appraise those less relevant responsibilities in the catch-all category and, as a collection; they will have a smaller impact on the ultimate rating. If you also use MBOs, to determine performance, then they have to be separate and distinct from the KRAs. KRAs are dependent variables and are determined by the overall work and the workflow within the organization, the specific responsibilities assigned, intra and inter-departmental interactions, seasonality impacts, etc. But MBO's, on the other hand, must be independent of external influences, assignments that are totally reliant on the employee's initiative and performance against them. Then, when you conduct the review, both you and your employee will be on the same page when assessing performance and comparing apples to apples.

Just a word on the performance appraisal rating scale; performance appraisals are normally scaled to 5 categories of performance (e.g. Unacceptable, Needing Improvement, Satisfactory, Superior, and Outstanding). Every employee should be counseled on what the ratings scale is and provided a written definition of how they are objectively determined and what they mean. It has been my experience that most employees know when their work needs improvement or is unacceptable. And even if they didn't know, it's your responsibility to let them know and provide them the training and counseling they need to improve. But when it comes to employees that are performing satisfactorily, they tend to envision themselves performing at a higher level, sometimes much higher, than they actually are. So when you and the employee are reading from the same objective rating scale, and if you are fair in your assessment, the final rating will be reasonable and a bit easier for the employee to come to terms with. And if they would like to try for a higher rating at the next review period, you can help them by providing the level of coaching they would need in order to work at that higher level and achieve that higher rating.

The 360 degree performance appraisal; some organizations have adopted a 360 degree approach to the performance appraisal process. This approach requires the manager to solicit input from other departments and areas where the employee has operated. I don't and cannot recommend that approach because it is fraught with bias and does nothing more than to take us back to *square-one* by reintroducing subjectivity back into the process.

And lastly, before you turn the page on this section, let's not forget about communications and the messages you send. When you conduct a performance evaluation you should be aware that the staffer is just as intelligent as you and is conducting a silent evaluation of you as well. They are assessing your character, your strengths and weaknesses, your honesty and fairness, your professional integrity, and is asking themselves whether you can be trusted or even followed. Consider this for example, if you conduct a performance appraisal and are less than objective, let's say you were too generous with the assessment. If you are too generous with an assessment you send one message to your subordinates, and if your assessment is too critical, you send another. When an underperforming employee receives a satisfactory rating for doing subpar work, it only serves to reinforce mediocrity and the work suffers. And when you assign a satisfactory rating to a high performer, it demoralizes them and they become disenchanted, and again, the work suffers. But it doesn't stop there, the inappropriate ratings do more, they provide the employee a window into your character. In their eyes, you've already failed the litmus test for integrity, honesty, and fairness. What you've done was to demonstrate *power* where you should have none, and turned what you thought were strengths (generosity and/or tyranny), into something that will ultimately prove to be among your greatest weaknesses[34]. You've inadvertently communicated a number of messages that you would like to get back. And you'll find that by deviating from professionalism and ethical conduct you've nullified all the work that went into rewriting the job descriptions, the performance appraisals, and the performance appraisal rating standards. And you'll have nothing to show for it, save a small ego boost, that in time, will come back to haunt you.

We will talk more about performance appraisals in the section on *Managing your Manager*.

Merit Increases and Promotional Opportunities:

Merit increases and promotional opportunities should be based upon job performance and not preference, subjectivity, or nepotism. But this is yet another area where some managers exercise powers and misuse authority where they shouldn't. They impose themselves into the process, and although their intentions might be noble, the consequences of their well-intended but bias actions do little more than taint the process and undermine their character and their credibility in the eyes of their subordinates. Let's start by taking a look at the merit increase process first, and with an eye towards problem solving and decision making, you'll have to come to reconcile yourself with the fact that some problems just can't be fixed.

---

[34] Generosity is self-consuming and tyranny is self-destructing.

Merit increases:

Instead of financial merit (the annual pay raise) being linked to an objective assessment of the employee's performance (their performance appraisal), some managers link the merit increase to their personal values or prejudicial systems. And for this example, I will leave aside prejudicial bias because we all know what that's about and how it disrupts an organisation. Instead, I will consider the actions of well-meaning managers, who's only offense is a desire to do good.

Example #9:

Let's suppose that it's the start of the fiscal year and the manager has just been given a copy of their salary budget that has a 4% increase over last year's budget. The 4% increase was determined by Sr. Management and is based upon the assumption that every employee received a satisfactory performance rating for the past year, and a merit raise of 4% is considered reasonable and is expected to average out across the employee base; regardless of their individual ratings. Merit guidelines have been established and they recommend no merit consideration for any employees with a rating of *unacceptable*, a 2% increase for employees with a *needing improvement* rating, 4% for employees with a *satisfactory* rating, 5% for employees rating *superior*, and 6% for employees demonstrating *outstanding* performance. The manager has 5 employees at different levels of compensation and different levels of performance. Jean has been with the company for 20 years and has always been an outstanding performer and she earned another outstanding rating again for this merit period. Phil and Tony are both superior performers but Phil is a lot more laid-back then Tony and has only been with the company for just over a year. Tony has been with the company for 12 years and has been going through some financial difficulties which are not helped by the fact that he and his wife are expecting their third child and are already having to stretch every dollar. To Phil, money doesn't mean a whole lot; he's just a young kid that really enjoys his work and the job, he just likes being here and would probably work for a lot less money just to get the experience. He still lives at home with his parents and sometimes has to be reminded to even cash his pay checks. Barbara has been with the company for 5 years and has been a consistent performer and has always earned a satisfactory rating. She is a mother of two and her husband works for one of our sister companies. And then there is Christine, Christine is going through a divorce but throughout her 10 years with the company has been another one of our outstanding employees right up to this appraisal period. But due to her divorce, she has had to take a number of days off because she couldn't find suitable childcare for her son. She has also been distracted by the unfortunate events in her personal life and the quality and quantity of her work has suffered. She was counting on a sizable merit increase this year to help her meet some of her additional expenses. But while she had been a consistent outstanding performer over time, the distractions of everything happening in her life has had a negative effect on her work and this year she was assessed as needing improvement.

There are 2 more things you should know, Jean is one of your best employees but she's thinking about taking another job in another department because she is near the top of the pay range in her current position. And while you want to keep her, she is about to max-out in her salary range and can only be given a 5% merit increase even though she has earned 6%. The second thing you need to know is that you don't have enough money in your budget to meet your merit requirements[35]. When you average the financial merits earned, including Jean's reduced award, it comes out to 4.2% when only 4% had been authorized. You can always go back and ask for special consideration; just like any other responsible manager would. But if you're not successful, what do you do? Now, this is where we begin to be betrayed by our aspirational humanity...we try to fix things, and that's when we stumble and make mistakes. We want to retain Jean and we would like to find ways to help Tony and Christine, but how can we do any of that when we are already starting out with a deficit? We could run the numbers all day and come up with all kinds of options but whatever we do that is less than fair, balanced and ethical will be a mistake. For example, we could shave off 3 percentage points from Phil and make him some grand promise for a future opportunity in order to give a percentage point 'each' to Jean, Tony, and Christine. We could shave off 2 percentage points from Phil and 1 from Barbara to accomplish the same thing. We could resign ourselves to losing Jean and shave a percentage point from both Phil and Barbara to help Tony and Christine; and on and on. However you decide, you will be engaging in overt unethical conduct; you'll be robbing Peter to pay Paul. You'll have to accept that something's are beyond your ability to fix and are beyond your control. The most you can hope for is to act professionally and unbiasedly. And

---

[35] I chose not to do any actual dollar calculation here because they will make your decisions even more complicated; using the raw percentages makes it challenging enough for this example.

it's not up to you to decide who gets what...just do the math and let it go. Take the budget you have and calculate the merit increases based upon your employee's current salaries, their rating, and do a ratio and proportion calculation of the monies available to determine your employee's new adjusted salaries. That's it, that's all you can do, and I doubt Solomon would have been able to do anything any wiser or fairer. But there are a few of you that will challenge the Wisdom of Solomon, and attempt to avoid this problem all together by just being more conservative with your assessments at the performance appraisal stage of the process. And in doing so, you reduce everyone's rating by one category and their merit levels by a percentage point. Now Jean is rated superior (5%), Phil and Tony are rated satisfactory (4% each), Barber is rated needing improvement (2%) and Christine is rated unacceptable (0%). Now your average merit pay-out is 3% when 4% had been authorized. This approach affords you 5 additional percentage points that you can lavish on your favorite people (and you will) in order to keep them subordinate, grateful, and indebted to you throughout the coming year. If you were to take the position of an outside observer, it would be clear to you that what you've done speaks directly to morality and ethics, and this approach violates them both. You have injured your staffers by reducing their performance ratings and by reducing their merit qualifications, and by doing that you've minimized the perception of their contributions to the company. Because man finds merit and worth in who he is by what he does, when you minimize his merit and worth, you minimize the person. Secondly, you took food out of the mouths of his children when you reduce or deny him financial merit. Then you expect him to grovel and pander to you and appeal to your benevolence in order to get back what was rightfully his. For those of you who were thinking that this was a reasonable solution to your original problem, it's not. You've taken a problem that was beyond your control and was not of your own making and turned it into a rat's nest of immoral and unethical manipulations so you could emerge as the good and all powerful nice guy. Well, you don't and you won't. People can see what you are doing and have done; you can't hide or disguise it. The company decides its merit budget using the *"Bell Curve"*. They've made the assumption that the majority of their employees will cluster around the centre and a few will fall either above or below the curve; but everyone will average out at a satisfactory rating. They didn't make provisions for departments where there are a large number of high achievers. But if you are an effective manager, you will always have a team of high achievers; ergo, you will always have a smaller merit budget than you need. But like in most things, *you have a choice*, you can continue to objectively assess performance and determine ratings based upon a standardized objective criterion. Then determine the merit levels and just do the math with the budget that you have...I think your people will under-stand. Or, you can get creative and violate trust by lowering everyone's performance rating. Of course when you do that, you open the door to unintended and very negative consequences. Your employee's morale will begin to fall, employee apathy will increase, and before long, your problem will resolve itself. You'll have a department of disgruntle under performers and your merit budget will likely be the least of the issues confronting you.

Promotional opportunities:

With respect to promotional opportunities, I have already stated that the selection process and requirements should be *out in the open* and available for review *by your entire work force*. The qualifications for consideration should be clear and should include: the current needs of the company, the employee's performance and length of service, attendance, current skill sets, related work experience, formal education, and the employees desire to transfer to a new work arrangement. The selection process must *never* be influenced by nepotism, race, religion, creed, color, national origin, gender, or sexual orientation. If an employee or group of employees believe that they have been unfairly treated due to bias in selections for a pro-motion or career development, it is a very serious matter and requires your immediate atten-tion. Few things can disrupt the cohesiveness of an organization as quickly and as thoroughly as partiality and bias. Every employee should have an equal opportunity to compete on a level playing field for a promotion or career development. As their manager, it is your respon-sibility to assure that it happens, and that there are no institutional, or otherwise, organized barriers preventing their fair treatment. When we look at bias, it comes in one of two guises; callous bias that is conscious and overt, and benign bias that is frequently unconscious but extremely pervasive. It is our natural preferences, "partiality", where we naturally prefer one side, or one thing, or one person over another. Our specific partialities and biases are rooted in the persona of the individual...in every individual. And yes, this then means that we are all partial and we are all bias; it's just a matter of fact, and it's an unfortunate, but very real com-ponent of our nature. If we are to grow as aspirational individuals we have to recognize that it's there and compensate for it, we can't just deny that it exist and go on with our lives. For example, when we are consciously and callously biased we modify our behavior, dependent upon where we find ourselves in the environment or social or political setting. We acquiesce to the conventions of the hierarchy and the setting so as not to call attention to our biases which could cause us to be isolated or even rejected and banished from the group. And when it comes to evaluating and assessing people for a promotion or career development, the vast majority of us (mindful of the political and social ramifications) can put aside our prejudices and do a fair assessment of the individual. But when we lose sight of our natural biases, we do more to injure *"unconsciously and benignly"* than a bigot on a soap box. When we do a promotional assessment, we hardly ever question our determinations because we know we were fair and unbiased in our assessment; but were we really? Were you too generous and accommodating to some and too hard with others; it's hard to tell isn't it? Try this; just try to imagine the faces and the voices of the people you've interviewed, that didn't get the job. I know that it will be easy for you to explain and justify your decisions for not hiring them and I'm sure you would have no difficulty in pointing out their shortcomings. Now, just look around at those that you did hire. What are the glaring differences between the two groups? I know that for many of you it's going to be hard to see; it's always difficult to see the obvious, particularly when you really don't want to look. But the majority of the people you hired tended to look, think, and act just like you; you're comfortable with them and around them. You may reject the notion that you're bias, but how diverse is your organization? I have witnessed benign bias up close, and have even been a victim of it over the course of my career. I have actually witnessed, otherwise qualified people, being discriminated against and denied an opportunity because they looked anorexic, were markedly obese, were unattractive, were too attractive, were too short, and for me personally, because I stutter. How many of these people can you count in your organization, and how many are in leadership roles or in the front of the house? When you deny and reject your own natural biases, these are some of the people you injure…benignly…but injure none the less. In order to become a better manager and a better person, you will have to learn to give people a fair and open hearing while staying mindful of your own imperfections.

People are also held back and denied promotional opportunities and career advancement because their path gets blocked by their managers for strictly punitive reasons, not professional ones. People are also held back because they become a significant component in the overall operation of the department or company. They make themselves too valuable and become unwilling captives in their manager's or company's toolbox. In either event, the individual is blocked, discriminated against and denied career advancement, and basic human rights, and that would constitute a violation of the law.

In the case of a person being held back for punitive reasons, I would suppose that if you were an unscrupulous little tyrant, you could probably see your way clear to abuse and oppress another human being just because you didn't like them, or you just wanted to abuse your position of power. After all, it's not that far out of line with some of the other things you have been doing. If that is the case with you, then, I would suggest that you look to another management training resource for alternative guidance, because it's apparent that you've learned nothing here.

And then there are the managers that hold key employees captive, preventing them from advancement or career development because they are considered invaluable to their operation and fundamental to its success. There are two main reasons for this, the first being an employee that demonstrates such a high level of skill and competence in an essential area that they become the authority and the go-to person in that area. In essence, they make themselves the company's expert, and that locks them in to that job and only that job. The danger for this employee, and for you for that matter, is when they or you get to be recognized as an expert in anything, your careers are likely to get truncated so you can continue to service that specific company need. A further downside to this is when technology advances, the company moves in a different direction, or for any reason your expertise are no longer needed...you won't be needed either. To pigeonhole an employee and hold them captive – for any reason – is a disservice to that employee and to your role as manager. And with respect to you...if you want to be a manager, you don't want to be an expert, *an expert at anything*; you'll do just fine being a generalist. If you ever need an expert...go out and hire one.

The other reason an employee can become captive is when their manager neglects their responsibilities for providing basic skills and cross training for their staff. Once an employee is trained in their specific area of responsibility, their manager considers their job done, and relegates the employee to a lifetime of monotony, doing the same work on the same job, day after day. And because the manager doesn't provide cross training to other areas or to other jobs, the employee won't have the skills that would qualify them to be considered for advancement when opportunities arise. The tragedy here is that this individual could be stuck on the bottom rung of the ladder forever. If the manager doesn't provide them an opportunity for growth and improvement they will begin to rebel, become apathetic and move on to find more rewarding work elsewhere. And we're just talking about one employee, think of how disruptive this revolving door would be if you had 20 reports. And what about backups, what will you do if one employee doesn't show up for work and no one has the training in that area to cover for them? A manager's job is to allow his employees to grow and develop, not to hold them captive or indentured. Your intent may have been to have a smoothly running efficient operation, and if that's really your intent, then this is not the way to do it. You'll have to continually provide your employees basic skills and cross training as a way to keep them motivated and productive, to provide the means to help them position themselves for that next step in their careers, and to allow you to be able to keep your operation running with fully qualified backups when and where they are needed. Training is an essential part of your job, and with the amount of turnover that you would already be confronted with, due to employee apathy, you're already doing a lot of it anyway. You just need to change the reasons for doing the training. You'll help yourself and your staff when you keep them trained and motivated, and then, you'll have to let them go so they can grow as successful individuals in their own rite.

The Manager versus the Leader:

Just to be clear, I'll walk back over this one final time. A manager is a cerebral thinker, a tactician, a director, a coordinator and a provider of oversight. They have the responsibility for planning and scheduling the work, providing the resources, and bringing the project to a satisfactory conclusion on time and on budget. A leader is someone that commands and demands respect, someone that is acutely aware of man's natural drivers, and the one that introduces risk into the equation. They are infused with both the power and the authority to incentivize people to follow their lead. And if you are to succeed in your position, you will always need to be both; *never accept responsibility without having the power and the authority required to successfully complete the assignment; if you do...you will fail.*

Friendship versus Professionalism:

As a manager, you have to decide this one for yourself, I can only advise and caution on this point. But it's no coincidence that the vast majority of organizations (both public and private) have a prohibition against having family members reporting; one to another. It's because they know, from years of experience and lawsuit after lawsuit, that it doesn't work; they know that it very often leads to nepotism and/or despotism. The manager is put in a compromising position and may become obliged to show deference to the relative over other staffers. And on other occasions, they might go out of their way to demonstrate their impartiality by being unreasonably harsh and indifferent to the family member. They will never be able to find a middle ground, and either one side or the other will see their actions (regardless of the action they take) as bias. Think about how things turned out when you were judging Grandma's rhubarb pie; it was a no-win situation, and everybody lost. Think about the managers that catered to their staffs and wanted to be accepted by them and seen in a favorable light...how did that work out for them? Having friends among your staff members would be ideal if it were not for the natural tendencies of man to try to exploit that relationship and profit from it; that's what man will do, he can't help himself, because it's his nature.

Having friends and maintaining friendships in a reporting structure is adding another unnecessary variable to a job that's already full with an excess of variables. I have no doubt that you'll be privilege to have some very fine, very interesting and wonderful people reporting to you over the course of your tenure as manager, but your purpose for being there is to manage, not to cultivate friendships, you can find friends on your own time. Throughout this book, we've talked about different environments and different hierarchical settings, and we did so to mark a clear boundary between one and the other. Friends should fall into your social hierarchy and your reports should fall into your professional arena. And there is good reason for that, friends have an expectation that your relationship will evolve on an equal footing and that you will exercise considerably more flexibility and be more accommodating in your relationship than what would be expected if your relationship was strictly professional. And in a professional reporting relationship, there is no equality of status, you are the manager. There should be no expectation of familiar flexibility or accommodation. While I would advise every manager that they should be personable, open, and even friendly towards their staffers; I would also advise them to maintain a well-defined system of professional courtesy, mutual respect and an ethical code of professional conduct. There is much more latitude in a social relationship than in a professional one, and frequently those lines can get blurred. So I would advise you to recognize and respect the people that report to you and make a human connection with them, but not a personal one. You don't need the complex baggage, the sense of obligation and entitlement, or the perception of preferential treatment that comes with having made friends among your staff.

Now, let's move to Peer Management.

Managing Peers:

"And let the games begin..." Please afford me that small indulgence, I just find that it seems so appropriate and an altogether fitting subtext for this section.

We have talked about power and the perception of power, operating styles, posturing, image projection and our little Avatars, status within the hierarchy, backbiting, sabotage and the constant competition for dominance whenever there is human interaction. Well welcome to the menagerie that is *Peer Management or Peer Interactions,* this is where most of the games originate and are being played out. This is where you'll need to rely on all your train-ing, your insight into the human animal, the drivers of human nature, and your knowledge and understanding of the environment as well as the competitive risk and potential rewards that are in play at any given time during the games. This is an arena in which every inch of turf is being contested by somebody in some way for some reason, and the questions for you will become "whether or not to compete, and if so, at what level"? But, just as importantly, "what are you competing for, and why, who are you competing against, and what is their motivation"? And lastly, "what is it going to cost you to be able to win"? However, having said that, I don't want anyone to think that they have to don all their combat gear and prepare for pitched battle when interacting with peers, because that would be sending the wrong message. But equally, I just don't want anyone to lose sight of the fact that man, though aspirational, is still a self-absorbed highly intelligent successful predator that can, and will, put you at a professional disadvantage if the rewards are lucrative enough or if they see a risk to them as being too great. So I would say, generally speaking, there's no need for panic or paranoia, the whole world is not out to get you...well, maybe just one or two of us are. But my point being, that when you're interacting with the aspirational projections of your peers, remember that there's a competitive entity standing just behind their projections, tracking your every subtlety and keeping score, just waiting for the right time to make their move to gain advantage. Actually, it's not that much different than the entity standing behind your

Avatar. They, like you, are trying to survive and thrive in whatever hostile environment you happen to find yourselves in. It's every man for himself and as a consequence, they will do whatever they deem necessary to protect and defend their turf, status and place within the hierarchy, even if it's at your expense; which, if you're not careful, could make you and your career a victim of *collateral damage.* I may have added a few dramatic overtones here…but it's about right.

I will only be able to talk peer interactions in the most general of terms; there are just too many variables and nuances associated for me to pretend to be able to put forward any reasonable comprehensive assessment or even a meaningful overview as to how any given interaction will play out. For example, peer interactions are colored by the hierarchy in which the interactions occur and are dependent on the specific culture and politics within that hierarchy. They are also influenced by the stakes of the interactions; potential for gains or possible downside loss as well as natural human frailties such as pride and vanity. Gender also plays a role in the interactions, for example; either same sex or mixed gender. In a same sex environment, women interact with women much differently than men interact with other men; and the interactions are yet different when the group is equally divided between men and women, or if it were a single female in a group of all men and vice versa. Hierarchical rank is yet another multiplier that will influence the interactions. And the complexities of peer interactions are even more complicated because we carry all our emotional and extraneous baggage and preferences and biases into every interaction. So, in a nutshell, there's no way to accurately predict the outcome of any human interaction with any degree of certainty, the human animal is just too unpredictable. The best you can hope for is to be able to rely on your knowledge of human nature, man's positive and negative drivers, their operating styles, and their desire for status and recognition to allow you to at least be able to shape the conditions of the interactions. You can't interact with peers in the same way that you interact with subordinates; they view you through a completely different set of lenses. And when you are interacting with peers, you rarely have any position power or authority over them, you might have some political influence but it's likely limited and if you tried to leverage it, it could be seen as being coercive, and that would do nothing to further your cause. So your best approach would be to build non-threatening alliances in such a way as to make your partnership a valued and a sought after commodity. And to do that, you'll have to be self-confident and giving of yourself. You'll have to stay above the daily battles for supremacy.

You'll have to remain independent and in control and above the squabbling over who's right or wrong and the constant contesting to determine who's got *the biggest dick*. Though, at some point you'll have to engage the battle, but it should only be on those occasions when you actually have a dog in the fight; when there is something of value to be gained that is consistent with your current objectives. And the things that are consistent with your objectives are those that bring you closer to your life, your professional, and your financial objectives that you decided for yourself at the beginning of this book. Anything else would be a distraction and superfluous.

Peer interactions occur at all times and can be at any level but, for the most part, peer interactions occur within a department, they can also be extra departmental, or during project assignments. In either case, you have to manage the interactions and your peers in order to facilitate a positive outcome.

Departmental Interactions:

I am going to make the assumption that the vast majority of your departmental peer interactions are, for the most part, positive and productive; although, we know that that's not always the case. There always seems to be an undercurrent of one-upmanship always going on in the background. One-upmanship is really nothing more than the *big boy* version of sibling rivalry, where each of the managers are vying for dominance over the others and competing for the favorable attention of the department's leader. This is the environment that most of us will find ourselves in, and the games that are being played would already be in progress and well underway long before we even arrived. The next move is yours, do you compete or not? Do you become another player in the game or do you find other ways to win without getting dirty? But firstly, what's the prize...what's everyone competing for and what's its value to you? If you're just competing for a few more at-a-boys, it's of low value. If you're competing for additional resources, in most cases they will be sent to where they are most needed. If you are competing for a promotion, it should be, but is not always, determined by objective measures. Don't be surprised to find that the competition isn't about any of this, that it's about dominance, superiority, and self-aggrandizement of one peer over another, and there's no value in this game for you. But regardless of their motives and the potential prize, you can put yourself in a position to win these contests or avoid the competition completely just by maintaining confidence and professionalism and by staying above the fray. You will win without ever having to go mano-a-mano with a sibling peer. But you'll need to have the right strategy and use the right tools in order to do so. You can't appear to be a combatant; you have to project an image of being a safe harbor, a neutral port that doesn't take sides or have a position. And, you'll have to maintain your independence and self-reliance to avoid being drawn in. Next, you'll have to demonstrate a willingness to be giving of yourself; generous, reliable, and a sensitive but unbiased counselor. People, particularly combatants, gravitate to safe ports and by using this strategy, that's just what you've made yourself. Peers will come to rely on your impartiality, support, and guidance to help bolster their own sense of security and success, and that should afford you enough political influence to deflect all but the most determined *'alpha-want-to-bees'* from competing with you directly[36]. Your independence is yours and is not dependent upon the generosity of your peers, and that takes away any bargaining chip they thought they may have had in their attempts to subordinate you. And you are the gatekeeper of your generosity, your reliability and dependability, and your counsel and collaboration is provided at your choosing, not theirs. The more confident and secure you are in your own position and status within the hierarchy, the more generous you can afford to be with peers. But let's be realistic, everything comes at a cost. If you are going to be as giving of your time and resources, shouldn't you have some expectation of reciprocity? I am not saying that you should be disingenuous in your giving (and you shouldn't), I'm just being practical. If your generosity cost man nothing, man will never be able to appreciate you or your added value. Man will take all that you give and use you up, cast you aside and would have learned nothing. This is not a failing in man, it's just speaks to his level of greed and his sense of entitlement; it's just his nature. Your generosity, counsel, and support should never be free, and your expectation of reciprocity should not be considered part of any game, it's a strategy, and you should have every intention of making it payoff. Let's just face reality, you want power and influence over your peers and this is a *"non-confrontational"* way to get it. You can use this approach, go nose-to-nose, or use some other tactic, but no one is just going to give you power over them; you'll have to fight for whatever you get. And by being the gatekeeper of a valued commodity, you control the amount of support they receive and have become accustom

---

[36] The alpha-want-to-bees may have to be taken on directly and unmasked so everyone can see them for what they are. They are self-centered people of dubious character and ethics. They are also the ones that will plant seeds of doubt, deceit, and discord throughout the organization. They will find ways to sabotage you, your work, and your efforts in order to make their work appear to shine. I won't provide any guidance here because I have no way of judging the size of your problem; but your problem has to be dealt with in the best and most efficient professional way you know how.

to. And when you control the valuables and incentives, you control the masses. Some of you may not fully appreciate the subtlety of this approach and how your new power is masked. If that's the case with you, just ask any married man or woman to interpret the meaning for you. When intimacy or anything else of value for that matter is lavished and given freely, the recipient often develops a sense of entitlement and becomes unappreciative, arrogant and controlling, but when their supply becomes restricted or is curtailed, they become wanting, dependent, and subordinate to their source. Yes, I'm talking about how we are controlled by sex or anything else we consider to be pleasurable, beneficial, or supportive to us; this is a similar analog.

In the final analysis, you are interacting with peers, your equals; but considering your training and insight, I really don't think that it would be unreasonable for you to expect to be considered *the first among equals* with respect to your departmental siblings. Further, and this may sound somewhat contradictory, but nonetheless a reality; equality in a hierarchy is a counterfactual, an oxymoron, and does not actually exist. There are always gradations of superior ranking, gravitas, social and political influence, and/or authority in every peer grouping. You should just want your equal standing to be just a little higher than everyone else's, which would have the effect of making them followers. In addition, you'll want your relationship with them to be one of *controlled reciprocity*. In order to survive and thrive in your environment, you'll have to get what you want and need from your peers, when you need it, and not at their convenience. Find ways to develop this, or another, effective political strategy in order to gain control so you are not just jousting about playing the customary games.

Extra departmental Interactions:

Extra departmental peer interactions are another example of a situation where you have no power or authority over a peer or colleague. I won't repeat what we have already covered, because we have already spent a considerable amount of time talking this when we walked through the various operating styles of people and how best to approach and interact with them, during our discussion on winning, conflict resolution and negotiations, the acquisition of political power and alliance building, image projection and our individual Avatars. I'll just start by reminding you that everyone is masked in these encounters and have their own hidden agendas; everyone is vying for power, status, and control, while desperately trying to avoid political missteps that could cause them to lose face. It's a lot like Kabuki Theater;

everyone is wearing an unchanging aspirational mask, behind which is a lone individual that you can never really get to see or know what they are thinking. And, there seems to always be an internal struggle going on behind the mask that manifests itself in the stylized body into-nations and overt gestures of the actors. The same is true in our world, and for our purposes, I am going to make the assumption that the struggle behind the mask (behind our Avatars) is between the baser, competitive, and aspirational components of the human being, and that the battle is being fought over ethics, morality, personal security, pride, honor, envy, hierar-chical status, respect, greed, vanity, and self-aggrandizement. You already know the games that are being played; now all you have to do is learn to become a master player. Go back and highlight those sections that you think will benefit you moving forward.

Once you're able to move beyond everyone's insecurities and defensive postures, and because there is no reporting relationship, you and most of your peers will find it very easy to form bonds and friendships that are mutually rewarding. These friendships could serve as the initial seed-stock that will enable you to start building professional and social alliances and networks within your organization and external to it. Though, not necessarily with all your departmental peers, some peers will never be a good fit for these alliances, and will never be able to get beyond their egos and their competitive mindset. The alliances and networks that you build can have many advantages, ranging from those that are completely social and recreational through those that are strictly professional, for example; mentorship programs, professional organizations, trade associations, and technical and business forums, etc. These alliances and networks can provide opportunities for training, information gathering, expand-ing your professional contact list, professional recruitment and career growth, and they can afford you greater industry exposure and visibility. Many of the people you meet can prove to be very valuable allies. They were instrumental in my being recommended as a viable candi-date to compete for a number of different jobs throughout my career. They were instrumental in my selection to chair international trade association committee meetings, and for meet-ings in which I took the lead in conveying industry suggestions and recommendations to high ranking government officials chairing United States Delegations to International Committee Meetings as well as to the Official Commission Meetings. During those meetings I was able to participate as a non-government delegate where I provided a business prospective to what were largely political proceedings. I was able to build alliances among other national delega-tions, multinational corporations, non-government organizations (NGOs), and among United

Nations representatives. And as a consequence, I was recruited by the United Nations "Food and Agriculture Organization (FAO)" to go under contract as an expert in the field of food safety and security. Professional alliances and networks will prove important to you as your career advances, and it all starts at those meetings...you know, the meetings were people from different departments and organizations come together just prior to the meeting; where everyone passes out their business cards, starts posturing while engaging in those one-on-one conversations. And as we've seen, when we've stripped away all the niceties, we found that what people were really doing was competing, and what they really wanted to know was..."are you anybody (a person of status and influence)? Are you a person I should be trying to impress, or someone I could benefit from knowing? How can you further my career or political standing, and so on?" But everyone knew the game, and everyone knew that behind all the smiling faces were the beating hearts of true competitors. This is professional networking, up close and personal. Some of you will be better at networking than others; personally, I was never very good at it because I kept struggling with the question of insincerity. That was my drawback, and it was hard for me to get around it. I am completely comfortable with my understanding of human nature (my nature), and I don't have any issues with using techniques and strategies as well as man's known drivers to get him to fulfil his obligations to the company (to do his job). But I could never get comfortable with what I considered to be shallow and pretentious prattling in pretending to have an interest in someone in an attempt to gain some benefit at their expense. To me, there just seemed to be something about professional networking that appeared to be disingenuous or dishonest. Therefore, for these and other reasons, I was never able to get comfortable with how the networking game was being played. I may be super-sensitive to dishonesty and deceit, and if so, then that's my failing. I wrote this book in order to help you become a better manager, to allow you to get an intellectual upper-hand on those that have not given sufficient importance to the study of basic human nature. I want you to win and excel, but nowhere in this book will you find me suggesting that you gain an unfair advantage by being unethical, immoral, or dishonest; even back when I would have stolen corn or when in negotiations, did I violate my own ethical or moral codes. And to some of you, I might be splitting hairs, but I have never had any issues with handling people in the workplace and seducing or manipulating them in order to get them to do what I wanted. But to me, and it might only be to me, the amount of insincerity and deception I witnessed during networking sessions was, for me, *a bridge too far*. At least, when I was seducing the staffers, it was for the benefit of the work and, in most cases, the staffer as well. There was always some truth at the root of what I would have been saying; it was not just self-serving pandering and flattery. When I networked it was because I had a genuine interest in the person or the topic, not because I thought I could pretend to have an interest in a person so I could use them as a steppingstone to a better future. Your thoughts may be contrary to mine and you could very well see the situation differently. But in the final analysis, it really doesn't matter. Networking is an essential element of the game. Therefore, if you intend to grow and develop your career, you'll have to learn to play the game, and play it well. Opportunities rarely present themselves as a consequence of *what* you know, but as a consequence of *who* you know. The challenge for you is to decide how you choose to play the game and what ethical rules you'll be using as your guide.

I apologise for getting a little preachy there toward the end.

Project Interactions:

If you are a participant on or a contributor to a project, your role is subordinate to the project leader's but is still a role in which you can demonstrate your maturity level by actively participating in a team effort to accomplish the mission at hand. Your role in the project should be clearly defined with respect to deliverables and timing and anything else the project leader requests that is project related. You're playing a supportive role and how well you play that role could have a direct effect on the success or failure of the project. Additionally, your willingness to take direction from a peer and follow through for the success of the team and the project speaks directly to your level of self-confidence and your individual character; that's how professionals operate. And from your perspective, your interactions with other peers on the team and the team's leader would be unremarkable; without all the usual jockeying for position and posturing that often accompanies a gathering of equals. But if you are the team's leader, your view might be quite different. You might see a dysfunctional group of *"Prima Donnas"* that are dissatisfied with their subordinate roles and are unwilling to take direction from someone they consider to be a peer. If that were the case, then you would have a problem.

You have to remember that you don't manage or lead by divine rite, but with the permission of those being managed or led. If you try to lead a bunch of peers and they won't follow you,

you're just out taking a walk and you are accomplishing nothing. You never accept any assignment where you have responsibility but not the power and authority to see it to a successful conclusion. Peers might like you but they really have no incentive in following you, they are far more interested in their own individualities and their own self-promoting agendas. Even though they may have been assigned to your project, they may see their being a member on your team as a courtesy to you or as an advisor to the project, and not a requirement of their jobs. And because we all have a natural aversion to *authority* they will resist you at every turn because they truly believe you don't have any real authority; at least not over them. What you have is a clearly defined project, an assemblage of very talented and capable people, and no way to move the project forward. You're like the Maestro hoping to get 80 individuals to start playing together again as a single orchestra, and they won't. Or as I've already said, you're trying to herd cats; and you can't. They just don't have any incentive to work together as a team, and they don't have any inclination to subordinate their hierarchical status to yours. They will gladly take the lead however, and each of them will tell you how they believed you should proceed with the project. And if you don't fully indorse all of their diverse approaches, their little feelings get hurt, and they just won't want to play anymore and just sit there doing nothing. Does any of this sound familiar...didn't we cover this early on? Everyone wants to manage and lead when they have no downside risk if there's a failure. But this is your project and the potential for failure is very real. And if you can't find a way to lead your team, the project is destined for failure or at best mediocrity. As the project leader, the failure of the project or the mediocre results will be yours. Everyone else will get to walk away scot-free and you get to be labeled, and rightfully so, a weak and ineffective manager.

Projects are usually assigned by an individual with enough clout, position power, and authority to expend the needed resources and to assign the necessary personnel in order to get the job done. This individual is the project's sponsor. In all likelihood everyone assigned to the project is in some way subordinate to the sponsor and reports up to them. If you are ever assigned to lead a project, this is where the power resides and this is the power you'll have to tap into if you hope to have any success. There are two different situations you're likely to experience and I want to talk to here. The first is when the sponsor defines the project and leaves it up to the team to develop the path forward. And the second, much like the first, but this time they assign you the responsibility for being the project leader but didn't overtly convey any leadership powers to you. In the first instance, the sponsor has demonstrated a very common flaw in leadership; and we have all done it. We pull together a group of competent and capable people and present them with a problem and rely on their intelligence to solve it. And when it's an analytical, mechanical or even a social conundrum they can work their way through it. And the reason they can work their way through it is because of their unrestrained competitive egos, and their personal desire to be the one to unlock the riddle or provide the most elegant solution; it's a selfish driver. Everyone in the group is competing for intellectual supremacy. There was no structure there or any attempt at teamwork. And while, from the outside, it might appear to have been a collaborative effort among equals, it was not. In reality, it was everyman for himself, and let the best man win. But when the problem that needs to be solved takes the form of a project or a precision undertaking where structure is a requirement, this approach falls apart because egos and hierarchical rank gets in the way. It's all about status and recognition and everyone wants to be the first among equals; this only leads to sibling squabbling and as a result, very little is actually accomplished. The sponsor failed to assign a leader, a single point of contact for them and for the others, and without a leader the project was rudderless and went nowhere. In the second instance, while a leader was designated, the leader appears to have been given no power to direct anyone to do anything. And this is a failing all the way around. It was a failing on the part of the sponsor for not making it clear that the leader has been authorized to use the necessary powers from them and their office that may be needed to complete the mission. The leader fails because they didn't ask for the powers and authorities that would be needed to successfully complete the mission. They believe they have to make do with their own limited powers, and that won't be enough. The individuals that have been identified to support the leader and the project failed because they have allowed vanity to distort their perception of themselves and their status and are unwilling to be led by a peer. So far, this has not been a very good start.

If you have been assigned to lead the project, you have to be open to new thinking, ideas and strategies that were not your own. You should welcome them and maintain open lines of communication between you and everyone involved in the project as well as its sponsor. You should be sensitive to the positions of your peers, realizing that some of them may be having some difficulty adjusting to your leadership role and their position of subordination; it can be a delicate issue. But you can't lose sight of the fact that you are the leader, the manager, and the project is your responsibility, all the support people report to you and are directed by you...you are the manager...so you have to manage and lead, not be managed and led. You'll have to project a level of courage and confidence from the outset even if you have them in short supply; people will exploit a weakness and will be reluctant to follow you if they see any in you. You should convene a meeting to communicate the project's objectives, time frame, important milestones and the key resources needed. Then you should solicit inputs and recommendations from the team as to what they would consider to be the best path forward. The ultimate decision on how you proceed will have to be your own, but you should take into account their recommendations and incorporate the best of them into your plan. After you've decided and communicated your approach to your team, you have to assign people to specific roles and responsibilities, including timing and important milestones and deliverables that need to be communicated to you and to the greater team. You have to setup some method whereby current project status can be provided to you on a daily or weekly update bases. And you should establish a date at this meeting so everyone will know when the group (as a unit) will reconvene to communicate their progress to date or any set-backs they may have encountered. You then have to keep the sponsor in the loop by providing them regularly scheduled project updates. All of this is just boiler-plate project management 101, but it's essential to the success of your project.

Now let's get back to the real world. During your initial meeting there may have been one or two people that were uncomfortable with you leading the project or with the path you've chosen to accomplish the mission; and that's okay and you should expect it. It's not your job to make everyone comfortable with your leadership or to argue your reasoned approach. If they express their dissatisfaction in a professional civilized manner, then they have provided you with some heads-up information and you'll know that you might have to track their progress a bit more closely and frequently then you would have normally. Sometimes, disgruntle peers will try to drag their feet and delay the project, which could be costly to the company, and would diminish your standing as the project leader. However, if their dissatisfaction was expressed overtly and belligerently, you will have to meet with them privately, after the meeting, where you'll have to decide how best to work with them or work around them to complete the project. This is a tough situation, and I won't be able to advise you here, each situation and person is different as is their level of contempt for you. But they've thrown down the gauntlet and this is a challenge that must be met. This has happened to me to varying degrees over the course of my career. And as a young manager, I might have just stood there and pissed my pants, not knowing what to do. But I'd learned from some of the older, more experienced, managers that every manager should always have a *nuclear option*. When these people look at you, they see a peer, and judging from their level of defiance and pushback, they see a powerless hierarchical subordinate. They overestimate themselves while underestimating you and see someone without power, and even if you had power, you wouldn't know how to use it. In addition, they see no immediate risk to themselves for putting you in your place, and if that's the way they want to play this game, than that's okay too. You don't want to try to use direct power with this person because you are likely evenly matched, or you might even be at a disadvantage. You need *channeled power*. So for now, just move along and sum up the notes from the initial meeting, with everyone's roles and responsibilities, the milestones, deliverables and timing, and then you meet with the sponsor to provide them their first project update. Now, this can go one of two ways, it's up to you, but whichever way you choose to proceed will leave a lasting impression on your sponsor (your boss). You can start by whining and complaining that someone on your team won't follow your directions or leadership (your poor leadership); thereby showing your sponsor that you are a weak and ineffective leader. That would certainly be one impression you could leave. Or, you could demonstrate strength and leadership by flexing your authority and thinking out loud. This is what I mean by flexing your authority and thinking out loud: toward the end of your update with your sponsor, you'll ask them if they knew of anyone that would be a suitable replacement for the person or people that were showing a reluctance to work with you on the project. There is never a replacement available, but you already knew that, you just wanted to start a different discussion; one that should trigger a discussion between the sponsor and the reluctant team member(s). This approach tells the sponsor that you are serious about the success of the project and you don't have the time or the inclination to tolerate any little chest pumping and ego mind games that one or two of your assigned reports might want to play. That lets them know that you would rather replace them (fire them from the project) and find a suitable substitute for the benefit of the project moving forward. *This is not a game, and your career is not a toy or anything you should allow people to play with*. This is a serious, no nonsense, professional approach that will leave a similar impression with the sponsor. In addition, the sponsor's discussion with the reluctant team member will usually get their attention and will likely introduce a bit of risk into the equation for them. Taking this approach shows maturity and strength, and it also helps to get the reluctant team member incentivized; and once they are incentivized, you get their permission to lead. This is a way to tap into another power base, its channeled power. But don't kid yourself, you have to realize that all is not rosy; you haven't made a friend here...but then...you didn't have one from the start either. When you use the nuclear option, you just need to be aware that there is some risk associated with it, so you need to be cautious. In using this option, it should be used carefully and only as a last resort; it could backfire, resulting in you being replaced. Before you use it, you should know something about your sponsor's management style and something about the way they think. In addition, you'll need to know something about the environmental politics and know who's buddies with who. If you're comfortable with what you find, then go ahead, but tread cautiously.

There have been other times when things were not quite this bad and I had to work with peers on projects and they proved to be deliberately difficult to manage. When that was the case, regardless of their expertise, they were omitted from any of my future projects. The message in both these cases was clear to the teams as well as to the sponsors, and it didn't do anything to further the objectives or careers of those that wanted to play games with me, my projects, and my ability to lead. However, it's important to note that in neither case did I have to result to a nose-to-nose confrontation with the challengers; nobody wins a pissing contest. However, on any of your projects, there should be no question as to where the power and authority for the project resides. Just remember that the execution of power should be subtle and discreet. In addition, you should use caution when channeling powers that are not your own; they are almost always seen as an abuse.

As a final note, when you are the project leader, particularly a successful one, there may be peers that will want to share in that success. They might want to play a larger role on the project, so as to get more visibility in the eyes of the sponsor. You can leverage your position power in order to honor their request for greater visibility while simultaneously building a stronger political alliance with them.

When you interact with peers on projects and everywhere else, you have to stay mindful of the constant game playing. But when you are the project leader, and your team is made up of peers, you'll have to establish your presents and your powers before you can get their attention. Then, once you add some risk, you will get their permission to lead. You just have to avoid vulgar displays of channeled power; people will find it, as well as you, offensive and repugnant.

Managing your Manager:

There are a host of specific situational variables that you need to come to terms with before we step off into this final section. First among them and central to your career expectations are the weighted objectives you've defined at the start of this work. You have to decide if those objectives are still valid and if the important milestones are still reasonable and achievable. You have to be honest with yourself and determine if you're on the right path, in the right job, or even in the right line of work. Is yours a transitional or a continuity position, and is it the right type of position to help you meet your objectives? What about your manager, what do you know about them, are they going to be an asset to you in your success or an obstacle to it? What's their operating style and what are their needs? Are they a great manager or just a standard run of the mill manager? Or is your situation more challenging and you report to a micromanager, a sea gull manager (someone that flies in periodically, craps allover everything and flies back out), a selfish, manipulative, deceptive and dishonest manager, a weak pusillanimous manager, an alpha dog manager that's always in your face and pushing, or some other variant of a manager. How do you plan to manage this manager, and where is your power? What do you want from your manager, and how do you plan on getting it? What does your manager want from you, and is it reasonable? What is the reality of your situation and can you live with it? If your career is on track and you report to the ideal manager, you're right where you need to be. But most of you will find yourselves in a slightly different place. Your career objectives should remain unchanged, but based upon your responses to those questions, your approach to achieving your objectives will vary dependent upon your organization, your professional competences and your reporting structure (your manager).

I would like to give everybody the opportunity to thoroughly lambaste your managers and make them the cause of any difficulty you might be having in advancing your careers, but we just don't have the time to project our own shortcomings onto someone else. Let's put a few things in perspective; the first is going from being the manager to being managed is quite a significant role reversal and your ego wants to push back. You're human, and like all humans you resent anyone and everyone having power and authority over you. And, if you are anything like the rest of us, you came to your position dragging a sack full of excess baggage, preferences, biases, and your own notions as to what you would expect to find in your manager. And when you looked at what you've got, you found that *"they weren't it"*. Think about your subordinates, this is exactly how your staff saw you; no sooner had they'd gotten the last manager trained so they stayed out of the way, the manager took a promotion and moved on in their career. Then, before the staff could turn around, a brand new hot turd hits the ground - *you*. So, now what do you do? Most of us, regardless of the type of manager we have, would like to work with them, but would also want them to see that we are already in development stage #1, and would like for them to just stay the hell out of the way and let us manage our departments without their interference. But that's not likely to happen, or at least, not right away. You'll find yourself in a position where you have to continually earn your stripes with this manager before you can be considered competent and credible in your job before your manager will give you some breathing room. But if you're unfortunate enough to report to a micromanager, they might not ever go away; so you'll have to find a way to live with it. There are however, some strategies that you can employ that could give you a bit more freedom and latitude; but more importantly, might keep them out of your way. You should study your manager's overt management style and find out where their needs are, and then you can find professional and ethical ways to service enough of those needs in order to build a professional alliance with them and/or establish yourself as an invaluable resource. If you have value, you have power, and if you have a professional alliance, you have a political alliance; this too is power. Use what little power you have to start establishing your own little independent power base, which at some point, your manager will need to tap in to. Do your job, and don't try to get cute with subtle, but overt, displays of resistance. Such displays puts you at a disadvantage, they communicate a level of resistance to your manager, and lets them know your thoughts. If they are an adversary, they know what they're thinking and you've just let them know what you're thinking too; a big mistake. Therefore, so long as what they instruct you to do is work related and is moral, ethical, honest, and legal, it falls within your contract to follow their directions. I know, I know...they might have their head up their butt and don't know what they are doing, or you might know of a better way of doing things. If that's the case, are they willing to listen to new ideas and approaches? If not, let it go and have a discussion around it at a later date. You are a technically qualified and skilled manager, and in this case you're in a subordinate position; respect that fact. You know what management is like, therefore you should be more objective and generous in your assessment of your manager, their management style, and their needs; they, like you are simply trying to survive, and if possible, thrive in the position. How can you help them so you can help yourself?

Let's take a look at the micromanager, the sea gull manager and the weak and cowardly manager. These managers' exhibit different needs based upon their various styles; for example, the micromanager demonstrates a need to be secure in their job as well as a need to be in control on every level; a need to be *RIGHT*, the Analytical base style. The sea gull manager demonstrates a need to be in charge, but more importantly they need to be seen as important and pivotal within the operation (thus the chaos they create); the need to be *IMPORTANT*, the Animated base style. The weak and cowardly manager needs to be reassured and needs an ally, a protector or a big brother (or sister) to support and advise them; the need to be *LIKED*, the Sociable base style. Clearly these managers likely have other needs but if you want to keep them out of your area and out of your hair, you'll have to communicate with them. Not just project and departmental updates but a detailed discussion of the trivia and the superfluous. You overwhelm them with information so the micromanager is always aware of everything, I mean everything. This will give them a greater sense of job security, gives them less to get their fingerprints on and try to control, and it helps them to develop more confidents in your ability to manage. Most micromanagers have an unusual fear of failure and that's what's likely driving them to try to avoid failure at all cost. Your constant dump of the minutia and the irrelevant quells that fear, and satisfies their need for hands-on control. Don't try to fight them, it's their nature. By giving them what they need, they will eventually back off, but will likely never go away. When you over communicate to the sea gull manager, they are always up to speed as to what's going on in your area and it gives them a sense of being in charge; but the greatest benefit is that they are less likely to fly in and make a mess of things in order to show their importance. Your constant updates have made them complicit and a partner to everything you're doing, and that will deprive them of their stage and a reason to perform. Your weak and pusillanimous manager needs to be able to see the world through a different set of eyes and needs to be reassured that your actions don't jeopardize their position or bring unwanted attention to them. They will stay out of your way, largely because they want to have plausible deniability if anything goes south. And though they might lack political power, they still have position power and that is reason enough to cultivate a symbiotic alliance with them, it's also an honorable and ethical thing to do. Each of these managers will be excellent candidates with which to build political alliances, you need a powerbase, so start to develop what you have.

If you report to an alpha dog, then you already know that their needs are the same as the sea gull manager, the only difference is the sea gull manager only makes periodic visits, but the alpha dog is in your face all the time. You will have to deal with their ego, their testosterone or estrogen (dependent upon gender), and their vanity; their need to project an image of superiority and dominance, and their need to be in charge, in control, and important; a need to be *IN CHARGE*, the Dynamic base style. This is exactly the kind of manager many of you are hoping to become, so don't see their actions and conduct in a negative light when they are the very same ones you're trying to aspire to. So long as they are a person of character, ethics, and integrity, I would say that you could have done worse...much worse. But again, we have a natural resistance to authority and some of your egos might get bruised working with this manager; get beyond your egos. This is their operation, and you're just a part of it. You'll have to put things in perspective; consider what you would expect from your own subordinate managers and staff... should your manager expect anything less from you? And what alternatives do you have? If you resist, your position will be professionally untenable and as an aside, where are your powers? You don't have any do you? And without any power, if you resist, you will fail. You have an obligation to the company as well as yourself, and by inference, to your manager. And the way you fulfill those obligations will communicate your value, reliability, integrity, and professionalism to the alpha dog, the sea gull, the micromanager, the ideal manager and all those in-between. You are a subordinate, not a lackey; you have to be giving of yourself and provide support to the success of the mission while holding fast to your own independent set of values.

But, if you happened to be actually unfortunate enough to be reporting to a selfish, manipulative, deceptive and dishonest manager, all bets are off. Nothing in your world will ever be what it appears and you'll have to find ways to protect yourself and you'll need to document everything. This individual is both morally and ethically deprived and they will always have a hidden agenda. Over the course of my career, the only time I was ever asked to do something that was immoral, the request came from such a manager; of course, I declined but I was made to pay for it. This is the manager that will lie and mislead and will never put anything in writing. This is the manager that will assign responsibility without giving authority. This is the manager that will have little interest in discussing ideas, projects, or events; they will be far more interested in wanting to talk people. These managers will come like Geryon, in different personas and styles, but central to all of them is their desire to deceive and control. They are opportunist, finding and taking advantage wherever they can; their intent is to acquire power and be the power behind the throne, the puppet masters, the manipulators and the sowers of discord. If this is your situation, you need to look at your career objectives and determine how best to go forward. Your professionalism, honesty, integrity, ethics and morality, even your career objectives means nothing to this person, they are self-absorbed and you can't fix them; it's the way they are, it's their nature. If you can, try to help them get promoted and out of your way, you can transfer to another department, get a new job or just grit your teeth and stick it out...I did. But you cannot cede control of your career to them, or point to them as the obstacle or the person responsible for your lack of career advancement. It's your career and your life, and it's your responsibility to control and direct it; go to your plan "B" or "C" or "D" if that's what it takes, but don't capitulate and try to blame your failure on this person or someone else.

As with all things, your window into the world and into your manager will come through visual observations and communications. Your observations allow you to see what's unfolding in the world around you and your interpretations of ongoing communications help you to question, analyze and verify what you see. And having said that, I will leave any further discussions of the immoral and unethical manager here, because there's no way for you to penetrate that world and everything you see and whatever is communicated there is more likely than not a distortion or an illusion of reality and will ultimately prove unreliable. But when working with other managers, you still need to exercise common sense and avoid the pitfalls of naiveté and political blunders. It's okay to trust...but you should also verify. It's important to maintain your integrity, your openness, and honesty, but there is no value in being transparent and predictable. Your actions should be tactical and measured, and the counsel you offer should be insightful and diplomatic. You've put together a plan for your career, so put it in to action. And lastly, you have spent years cultivating your Avatar to be your representative in this, and similar professional settings, so stay behind it and let it speak for you.

With respect to naiveté, you should always be willing to *speak truth to power*. But you have to use common sense when doing so; there is always a downside risk and very little value in speaking truth to power if power has no interest in hearing the truth. Don't voluntarily get caught-up in political dynamics that you don't understand. Provide guidance where you see a need, but only in those instances where your guidance is welcomed and will be received as being a benefit, not as an insult or a threat. And to those of you that are crusaders for this cause or that, step back from your passion and take a more pragmatic and utilitarian approach to your work; this is not your company, you are just a company employee. The company sets the priorities and the agendas, and has provided directions and expectations to their senior leaders. In turn, the senior leaders passed on those directions and expectations down to the level of your manager and to you. If you're passionate about something that didn't make the list, let it go, because you won't find an audience willing to hear your case. However, if you can develop enough support and momentum for your cause and can present a compelling enough argument, you might have a shot at getting it considered. Go back and review the section on the *Influential Presentation* to see what it will take. You'll also need to review the section on the *"6Cs"*. Short of doing that, don't martyr yourself and your career...just let it go. My last point is on ethics and honor, and it is directed at those of you that could be classified as the purist among us (the goody-two-shoes). When you make an oath, or enter into a contract with your manager or anyone else, and you find that they've failed, for one reason or another, to honor their obligations, do you feel honor-bound to honor your part of the agreement? Think it through, but when a contract, an oath, or any agreement has been violated by one party, the other party is free of any obligations to honor their commitment. Your word is your bond and it's sacred to you and your adversaries know it. In your mind, standing by your word is an ethical strength, but in the world in which we live, it can be a professional liability and a weakness. Many will use that honorable characteristic to their advantage, not yours; they will enter into an agreement with you *with no intention of honoring it.* When they violate the agreement, they will likely have an unlimited supply of actual and plausible reasons as to why they were unable to meet their commitments, and in view of their rational explanations, they will have and expectation that you will continue to honor yours. You'll have to be realistic and objective here, *the agreement has been violated...* **you owe them nothing!** You gave your word in good faith, not for the unethical to use as a tool against you. So think it through, you'll have to see the world for what it *"is"*, and not confuse it with the aspirational world that *"ought"* to be. Be flexible in your thinking and use common sense to decide if you have any ethical obligations to a violated agreement?

It's time to conclude this work, but because you are trying to manage your manager, I wanted to underscore a few of the points that I have already talked through:

Communication:

You have to insure that there is clear and open communications between you and your manager in order to reduce the possibilities for misunderstanding.

Areas of Accountability:

You need to be clear on exactly what areas you are accountable for and have a thorough understanding of the defined expectations and deliverables in each area. Whenever possible, work with your manager to establish quantifiable measurables around each area, including reasonable timelines.

Power and Authority:

You never accept responsibility without the authorization to use the power required to get the job done.

Performance Feedback:

You should make it a practice to solicit feedback on your performance from your manager as a matter of routine; particularly if either you or your manager is new to the position or if you have come to question how your performance is being perceived. You don't need any surprises or setbacks during your annual performance assessment, so open the lines of communication now. If there are any areas that need improvement, find out what they are and ask your manager to provide you some support and guidance through informal coaching and counseling; that's their job, and it should be your expectation.

Performance Assessment:

There should be no *got-chas* at your performance assessment. You should have benefitted from informal coaching and counseling so you shouldn't get blindsided by anything. However, if improvements are still needed in any area of your performance, ask your manager to give you specific examples of what they mean. If they reply with some subjective intangibles, continue your line of questioning until they give you something tangible and measurable to get your head around - this strategy will clear away all the subjectivity and ambiguity and will box them in to what they've recommended, and will give you a stationary target to shoot for[37]. The performance assessment is also the time when you get the opportunity to look deep into your manager's character and do your own professional assessment of them as well. Just leave your ego and emotions at the door.

Career Development & Promotional Opportunities:

It has been my experience that most managers are not mind readers and if you don't communicate your career objectives to them, they will be more than happy to keep you just where you are, doing just what you're doing; after all, they have their own career to think about. So if you have any career aspirations, don't keep them to yourself, communicate them. You have to work with your manager and the Human Resources Department to develop a plan that will get you to the next step in your career; it might require additional classroom training and seminars, cross training, leadership training, working with a mentor, etc.; but it will require some effort. And when you communicate your objectives, it allows the company's leadership to know that you have some expectation of career advancement. And that might have gotten you a notation or a pin on the company's succession planning chart. It's your career and you have to know what it's going to take and what the requirements are to get that next promotion. You have to stay focused on your career objectives because you'll never get to the right stop if you've taken the wrong bus. No one is going to give you that promotion, or chart your path for you, you'll have to compete for it; but before you can compete, you'll have to be qualified.

Friendship verses Professionalism:

My recommendation here is the same; a professional relationship works much better in a professional environment than one that is colored by the obligations of friendship.

---

[37] This particular strategy uses the Maieutic Method of Dialectics in order to extract the truth from someone that is being evasive or opaque. Maieutic means midwife. And using this method, you become the midwife as you continue to ask benign questions in order to help that person give birth to the truth of what they are reluctantly, but actually saying.

Postscript

I took a month off and sent this manuscript out to be edited for grammar and spelling. Editing was necessary because I don't normally read what I write, and like many people, I tend to read what I think I wrote, not what I actually wrote; I'm blind to my own errors. After editing the manuscript, and having found a boat-load of words in the wrong place, improper use of present and past tents, excessive use of the semicolon, confusing "you" and "we", and using the word "And" at the beginning of too many sentences, my editor returned the manuscript to me dripping with red ink. In addition to her corrections, she gave me her impressions, and I'd like to share them with you.

While not giving any credence to anything I had written, she said she did recognize that it was not always easy to interact with everyone in a professional or social hierarchy. But, she never gave much thought to it being caused by people having their own self-serving hidden agendas. And, while she saw firsthand, the friction at the interface between one person and the next, she never thought that it could be being caused by so many little micro-battles being fought over pride, status, vanity and the like; or at least not to the level of trivia and minute detail that I described. She came away a bit sadden and disappointed when she reflected on the many interactions that occur in her world, and was forced to accept that the Avatar was an actual, factual entity within her and everyone else. That we all project aspirational images, but nobody is actually who and what they appear. She then said the first part of the book was difficult to follow because there was a lot of information to absorb, and she didn't know where I was leading the reader. In addition, she said she learned more about managing people in the last part of the book than anything she had learned to date. However, during our conversation, I could sense (in her words) a separation between her and people; her (the manager) and them (those being managed). And to me, that was completely understandable, no one would want to own-up to being human if what I described was actually our true nature. It's only natural to want to set yourselves apart from the masses of the great unwashed and their never ending battle for dominance in the cesspool that some make of their lives. You are free to separate yourself from the species as well, if that's what you'd like. But this book was written to help you become a better manager of people, and to help you recognize and avoid some of the preprogramed traps and pitfalls that are always present when dealing with human nature; *your nature*. But at some point, you'll have to accept that if there is a single point of truth in this entire book about man, then it's a point of truth about you as well. Man is man, and he can't change his nature. If you want a better outcome, when interacting with man, it will be up to you to change the inputs of those interactions. It's your choice, you can choose to continue being a puppet in an unwinnable war or you can learn to become the puppet master, and at least have some degree of control.

In response to my editor, I explained that nothing in the world has changed from when she started editing the book till now. In fact, nothing has changed since Adam and Lilith. We all aspire to be more than we are and do good things, good works, and become higher functioning beings. But we are limited in what we can actually accomplish because we are human beings, not angelic beings. We have to live by the rules established for us by nature, and they only allow for the survival of the fittest. Our Avatars point to our better Angels and allow us to be social (communal) and civilized. But everyone should recognize that the Avatar is only a projection of our ultra-egos and not a realistic depiction of who we actually are. My use of Oscar Wilde's Jekyll and Hyde, and Dorian Gray was not serendipitous, nor was the use of Geryon to symbolize fraud and malice. And, the Tyrannical Boss and the Maestro were included because they are real, and they are both liars and deceivers who'll likely not be discovered until it's too late. But it was not my intent to have anyone think any differently about *"us"* (humans) *now*, than you had thought previously. I simply want you to accept the fact that you, like everyone else, is projecting an aspirational image of how you want to be seen, not of who you actually are. Knowledge is power, and with that knowledge, if you should find yourself lost in the woods, and you happened upon a sweet little old lady dressed in black, living in a gingerbread house, with your knowledge of the Avatar, you might exercise a little more caution then did Hansel and Gretel.

With respect to the first part of the book being difficult to follow because of the volume of information; I have to concede that she's right. In my view, it was fundamental to any learning that we dragged out and examined as many aspects of our inherent nature as possible. For example, who we are as animals, what our drivers are, the roles of hierarchical status, ego, pride, honor, fear, self-worth and esteem, our public image, personal security, and on-and-on. I thought it was important for you to learn about humans and human nature before you jumped into trying to manage an animal that you didn't understand, and one that was just as intelligent, cunning, and as dangerous as you are. In addition, I had to provide you with the necessary tools, strategies and techniques before you could have any real hope of long-term success and survival as a manager or leader of people. So, when she said she learned more about managing people from the materials in the last part of the book; that told me that all the prep work and the detailed discussions about man's nature and his interactions, that were included at the front end, actually paid off when the reader got to the back. The information that you found in the back of the book can be found in most management training courses. Although, for the most part, the information is presented as single dimensional techniques and tools, and usually comes without an explanation or a connection to why they are suggested or what they are intended to effect in the human being. My approach was to prepare you for Chapter # 19. I wanted you to see those management techniques, tools and strategies in context with the rest of the book and from the prospective of an informed manager. From my editor's account, it worked; what's your thinking? I hope my approach was successful. But for those of you looking for a shortcut, and only read Chapter # 19, you've only read words without context. While Chapter # 19 may be of some benefit to an experienced manager, I would really recommend a thorough read of the book for all others looking to learn and lead. There are no shortcuts to human management and leadership. The last point I'll make, with respect to my editor's feedback, is on my excessive use of the word "and" to start new sentences. She's right; I did use the word "and" excessively. I've removed more them half of them as a result of her feedback, but I had no intention of removing them all. It comes down to my intent. If my intent was to write a good, solid English Literature paper, most, if not all, of my "ands" would have to go. But my intent was to communicate with you. To write a document that, while not perfect, could be understood. I could have moved from one sentence to the next and had the first sentence evaporate in the ether of your mind as you moved on to the second. But, I used "and" to reinforce the fact that everything was connected, so when you got to the end of the paragraph you were dragging all the relevant ideas with you; which I thought would give you a more complete picture.

And while I won't likely be winning any literary awards, I hope I was able to communicate the connections and interrelationships between the various topics and subject matter.

A Final Word:

In order to manage man, you'll have to know man, but before you can know man, you'll have to know yourself. If you want a better working relationship with man and a better outcome, *you'll have to learn to change and adapt to man, because man will not change for you.* And you'll have to remember that *you don't lead or manage by divine rite, but with the permission of those being led or managed.*

I wish you all the very best.

Marvin Dixon

The Fox Hollow Group

Marvin Dixon

Marvin Dixon received an AA Degree in Dietetic Technology at Baltimore Community College, a BS in Food and Nutrition at Morgan State University, and a MS in Food Technology at Iowa State University. He has held leadership positions in some of the larger consumer products companies in the U.S.; has served as a non-governmental delegate on United States Delegations to international trade committee meetings hosted by governments around the world, and was recruited by the Food and Agriculture Organization of the United Nations (FAO) in a consultant capacity in Rome, Italy. Over the course of his career, he began studying the complex human interactions that were always ongoing at the interface between management and labor, competitive peers, and the manager and their manager. Through first-hand experiences and repeated observations he saw how hierarchical rank, vanity, and pride always played a role on both sides of each interaction. This book was written in an attempt to explain some of those interactions and to help *all managers*, but particularly the young and inexperienced manager avoid many of the social and political missteps that frequently occur during those interactions and which could cause them to fail. It is his hope that the material provided has been a benefit to you and will provide additional value to you as you move forward in your careers.

CPSIA information can be obtained at www.ICGtesting.com
Printed in the USA
BVOW09s0849161215

430432BV00020B/747/P

9 781484 917169